REAL MEDICINE
REAL HEALTH

by
DR. ARDEN ANDERSEN

HOLOGRAPHIC HEALTH PRESS • Waynesville, NC 28786

Published by Holographic Health Press, Waynesville, N.C.
www.holographichealth.com

Printed in the United States of America

First Printing: 2004
Second Printing: 2006
Third Printing: 2006

ISBN: 0-9752523-0-5

Cover and book design by Jennifer Sage
Cover photograph by Christopher Keiser

Truth in all its kinds is most difficult to win; and truth in medicine is the most difficult of all.

~ Peter Mare Latham (1789-1875) Noted Physician and Surgeon

Acknowledgement

I teach courses all around the world to farmers of every size, from the backyard garden to huge corporate mega farms. Regardless of the size of the operation, every farmer's family has health and medical concerns. Each one, whether urban or farm, has been affected by some illness, be it cancer, heart disease, Parkinson's, Alzheimer's, Chronic Fatigue, irritable bowel, autism, attention deficit, diabetes, migraine headaches, depression or some other malady. Concluding every course, I always take an hour or two to discuss the holistic medical options available to patients, mirroring the holistic farming options presented in the Ag courses. Repeatedly, people have asked for a book describing these medical therapies. Finally, the book is here and I dedicate it to and acknowledge every person challenged with an illness and seeking options in medical therapy. Thank you for your encouragement, patience and courage to step out and find real health solutions.

Thank you to my good friend, Dr. Theodore A. Baroody, Jr. for his unyielding encouragement, friendship, and frank advice.

Foreword

I have known Dr. Arden Andersen for many years. Throughout that time, I have watched him remain faithful to his basic premise concerning plant and animal life. This is, that all life has an almost identical physical nature. He holds that the needs of a human, animal, fish, or insect sit on a common platform with the plant kingdom - that our nutritional needs are very similar.

As we go through our busy day, we give little thought to plant life and its needs. Yet in reality we should be giving most of our attention to it. Without the plant ecosystems, higher animal life would not exist. We take plants for granted. They are like our slaves: we ignore them or treat them with chemicals for their destruction or their growth. Then we eat them or mulch them for some other part of the ecosystem to consume. But no matter how we treat these devoted servants of the earth, they continue to be the very nourishment of our existence.

Dr. Andersen has spent his life studying and experimenting with concepts of plant-animal synchronicity. By doing so, he has helped farmers worldwide to reach achievable goals of a nutritionally healthier edible plant life for our benefit. Now he goes one step further. In this book he illustrates the incredible ways our health can be improved by melding his vast understanding of sustainable agriculture with the many health problems that we face today. He shows us why unless the quality of the food we eat is improved, our health will continue on its worldwide downslide. He offers practical solutions to the plant and human dilemma. His answers are not always easy but they are achievable. Ultimately, as a race, we will either listen to his message or continue to pay a stiff price in the form of compromised health.

Good health begins with each of us. It is a personal responsibility. Reading this book will give you real health and real medicine on several levels. Dr. Andersen brings both his medical expertise and his agricultural acumen together at one time. This highly informative book needs to be in every library.

~ Theodore A. Baroody, D.C. 2004

Contents

Part 1: Introduction

*"...I believe that substances presently used in the prevention
and treatment of chronic diseases that are not orthomolecular
[natural substances that restore functional balance to cells
and biological systems] will fail. Over the long term, our
bodies will simply refuse to respond to treatment with non-
orthomolecular substances. Orthodox medicine will attempt
to compensate for its disregard of this maxim, [a disregard]
which is born of narrow-mindedness and ignorance of the
laws of nature, by spending vast sums of money, by commissioning research on a gigantic scale and by propaganda.
The attempt will fail, but not before it causes a tremendous
explosion in health costs, which, in turn, will lead to serious
social upheaval as well as economic and political crises. No
amount of money in the world will ever make it possible to
imitate the development of effective substances evolved over
hundreds of millions of years of biofunctional adaptation, to
say nothing of overtaking them.*

~ Nobel Laureate Dr. Linus Pauling (1901-1994)
From *The Curious Man: The Life and Works of Dr. Hans Nieper*

Doctor, what are my options? Real Medicine!

Good medicine is holistic medicine, combining the best of every
modality and technique available and accessible. Patients do not
come to see me, call me or e-mail me to get reams of journal
articles, loads of statistics, nor monotones of the status quo
medical protocols dictated by some HMO or socialized medicine
edict. Patients visit, call, and e-mail because they desire and
expect solutions to their problems, options to consider when I
cannot give them definitive solutions and they expect compas-
sion in either event. The intention of this book is to help people

with their quest for *medical options* and to help them understand the foundation of health vs. illness. **That foundation is diet and the nutritional integrity of the food we eat and the nutritional integrity of the soil upon which the food is grown.** To me, this is real medicine to solve the real causes of illness, resulting in real health rather than mere suppression of symptoms (with more and more drugs).

The only statistic that matters to my patients is the one that they personally experience. I wish I could provide definitive solutions 100% of the time. That is certainly my goal and my quest. I will continue my search for answers and understanding. Unfortunately, the FDA, the drug companies and many anti-free choice doctors and medical workers continue to oppress and suppress many safe, effective, and economically feasible medical therapies because these therapies do not profit the right people. Consequently, patients are compelled to travel to other countries where greater medical freedom is allowed. The saying that freedom must ever be won is as true today as it was in 1776.

I will address a number of illnesses throughout this book plus the available and effective treatments with which I am personally aware. Please know that this is not an exhaustive list nor do I suggest that I have a complete knowledge of every possible therapy available for any given illness. My intent is only to give the reader a place to start, a ray of hope, an option to consider, a feeling of control over his or her own health and treatment. You may choose to use the conventional therapy and that may, in fact, be the most appropriate therapy for your given condition. For example if a patient has *strep throat* with severe sore throat, fever and chills, rash, swollen glands, I will recommend an antibiotic preferably by injection followed by some herbs, vitamins, a Gaby-Wright (nutritional) IV, ElderZinc Lozenges, fluids, rest and a recheck if needed in a few days to a week. Modern medicine has some wonderful therapies and medicines, which I use in my practice and recommend to patients. I simply believe that we should not stop there. There are other times when the worst treatment option would be conventional drug or surgical therapy and the best recommendation could be watchful waiting and prayer.

This book will also bring together the connection between human health and agriculture. I will show how human disease is directly linked to the nutritional mismanagement of the soil upon which our food is grown.

I realize that there are hundreds, perhaps thousands of books written on health, nutrition, herbology, diets, detoxification, the connection between health and nutrition. Many of these books are true gems, and I provide a list of recommended books in the Appendix of this book. This is certainly not an exhaustive list of books I would recommend reading. For those I may have failed to mention, please do not take any offense, for none is intended.

I also recommend that one include the holy books in their health library. The Bible for example contains hundreds of entries regarding diet, nutrition, herbal medicines and lifestyle. Few people take notice of these lessons and unfortunately, even fewer clergy recognize and teach this very important aspect of spiritual education.

For those people who are familiar with my professional work, you know that I teach seminars on biological farming. Farming biologically means taking the best of conventional and organic farming practices, integrating good science and nutritional management into a soil and crop management program that maximizes yield per unit of input, quality and nutritional density, and profit while at the same time minimizing, and eventually reversing, environmental destruction. I further draw a direct connection between soil/crop nutrition and human health.

> *Leaders are visionaries with a poorly developed sense of fear and no concept of the odds against them.*
> ~ Robert Jarvik, inventor of the Jarvik-7 artificial heart

People frequently ask how I became involved in what they perceive as very different vocations: agriculture and medicine. I answer that one cannot separate the two. Health and disease are direct manifestations of one's diet and nutrition. Diet and nutrition are subsequently determined by the nutritional value of the food. The nutritional value of the food is totally determined by the nutrition of the soil upon which the food is grown. This realization was permanently imprinted upon my mind by the late Dr. Carey Reams who, like Dr. Charles Northern before him and Rudolph Steiner before him, understood the inseparable link between agriculture and medicine. It was Carey Reams who told me to study every area of health and science I could in order to gain an ever-expanding understanding of Nature, for in Nature, the answers to all questions will be found.

Every opportunity I get to speak to farmers I discuss human health because, as food producers, farmers hold in their hands the very health and well-being of their fellow human beings. Further, every farmer has either a health problem or a family member with a health problem. Consequently, I have been repeatedly asked to write a book summarizing the connection between agriculture and medicine and the overview of the various options available to people seeking good medicine/healthcare. Additionally, I find there is a great need to educate the non-farming consuming public about the connection between farming and human health. The consuming public needs to know the truth about their food quality, how it is grown and how the chemical industry works very hard to skew the truth regarding the safety of pesticides and genetically modified foods; how they have hoodwinked the public into believing that we cannot solve the problems of insect pests, diseases and weeds without poisonous chemical weapons and genetically modified "franken-foods;" how we cannot feed the world without their, the chemical industry's, bag of potions; that by merely being "high tech" it must be "good tech." These assertions by the chemical industry directly and via their academic escort services at most of the agricultural universities, are simply not true. Just follow the money!

In the Western world, especially the United States, the medical community brags that we have the best medical technology system in the world. That is true regarding trauma medicine. We certainly have the most expensive and profitable medical system in the world and if one is in need of emergency medicine the U.S. is certainly the place to be to get the best emergent care available. Unfortunately, once the person leaves the emergency room our medical care system falters greatly. In fact the 3rd leading cause of death, as reported by the JAMA, 284, 26 July 2000, in the U.S. is the medical system itself. Not a very good testament to its healing quality!

Perhaps, more importantly, is the fact that U.S. medical practice is more determined by power struggles between huge companies and the politics of the decisions that come out of their boardrooms than it is by actual science.

Patient care, health, happiness and freedom of choice, constitutionally guaranteed in this country, are considered blasphemous and necessarily DENIED to preserve the big lie. History continues to repeat itself. It took almost 150 years to get the AMA to accept the practice of hand washing as being a scientifically judicious practice. Those profiting from the status quo in medicine regardless of how many patients suffer will stop at nothing to continue the suppression of actual science and truth. Remember the same companies that perpetuate the lie that toxic chemicals/ poisons used in agriculture, termed "crop protection products" to hoodwink the public into believing these products are good, safe, and necessary in our food chain, are the same companies that produce the majority of the drugs used in medicine to treat the illnesses actually caused by the toxic, nutritionally bankrupt agricultural system in the first place. It is an ingenious business plan and the most profitable industry in the history of the world. Sadly, the quest for money and power for money's and power's sake so intoxicate many people that they are old and feeble before they realize life has passed them by.

The terrorist attacks on the World Trade Center and The Pentagon, September 11, 2001, brought the reality of life, death and what is truly important in life to light for much of America and our allies. Unfortunately, it takes times of crisis to induce most people to reevaluate their lives, inventory the truly important aspects, and actually change their actions, activities and daily routines.

As a physician, however, I observe life-changing crises almost daily in my patients. Whether the threat of incapacity or death comes from a terrorist, an invading army or a severe disease like cancer, kidney failure, heart disease, AIDS, Parkinson's, Alzheimer's, or emphysema, the crisis forces the person to take inventory of his or her life as life figuratively or literally passes in front of them. Never have I heard a person toward the end of their life say, "Gee, I wish I had spent more time at the office." Frequently, the exact opposite is uttered and people pass on, sad that they did not live as fulfilling a life as they might have lived.

It would certainly be better if we all arranged and lived our lives for the greatest happiness, fruition, and benefit of our fellow humankind. The reality is that most people do not. Such concepts are simply scarce in our culture, good or bad notwithstanding. I recognize this pattern in my own life. Great personal crises induced me to seek answers to my life's questions, to reevaluate my goals, desires, and choices in life.

Having been raised on a dairy farm by parents and grandparents who knew little other than hard work, I mastered the art of being a work-a-holic, a driven achiever. This has allowed me to become a successful public speaker, physician and consultant. Largely as a result of my driven lifestyle, commonly working 12 to 16 hours days, 7 days per week, health challenges arose demanding attention in order for me to continue any quality lifestyle. Of course over time, I had to learn the art of altering my lifestyle yet still achieve my goals. Balance, I believe this is called. It is a daily quest.

I had to learn to practice what I advise my patients to do. I had to learn that balance applies to ALL things. Though I had learned at a young age to think outside the box, I interpreted holistic lifestyle as meaning I worked the whole day, everyday and tried to be everything to everyone. Like most doctors, I thought I knew enough that I could let slip working all the time and not have it catch up to me. Ahhhhh, another lesson in the school of hard knocks! I got burned out. I dreaded going to work many days and recognized I had to change my lifestyle.

Contributing to this was the occurrence of injuries to both my wrists, a shoulder and several vertebra and spinal discs from doing manual medicine on several patients much too large for me to adjust. But I was tough, so I thought and no one else was going to help these patients. The statement of "above all do no harm" I found also applies to me, the doctor delivering the care.

Manual medicine techniques that injure the doctor must be stopped regardless of how many patients they help. Injuring myself in exchange for helping patients is an oxymoron. But I didn't want to stop. My condition progressed or deteriorated, depending upon the semantics used, to a point that I had pain in my hands and forearms every day, often severe. I worked harder in the gym lifting weights, doing pull-ups, push-ups, getting stronger to handle the bigger patients.

Two wonderful colleagues, Drs. Ted Baroody and Gary Emmerson, both recognized and understood both my physical problems (unfortunately very common among doctors doing neuromus-culoskeletal medicine) and my mental anguish in wanting to help patients with a skill at which I was very good. Every time I got together with them they would work on me and tutor me in appropriate technique, yet sporadic therapy did not correct the problem, which I continued to aggravate daily.

God has repeatedly blessed my life and has always given me nudges to get my attention, thankfully not really needing to pull out the "big" hammers. Being called to active duty for the Air Force after the 9/11 terrorist attacks on our country forced me to take a break from my civilian medical practice, my agricultural consulting and teaching business, and moved me to a military installation to focus on the duties of a full time Air Force Flight Surgeon. It gave me the opportunity to rethink my life's goals, desires and priorities. It allowed me to investigate additional options that included just dumping everything I was shouldering and continue an active duty military career; a serious consideration for someone a little burnt out professionally.

However, once word got around the base that Doc Andersen could fix one's shoulder, neck, wrist, low back, etc. (not being the typical "walking prescription pad") I was soon very busy doing structural adjustments. The problem was that I was not getting any treatment for myself. One night, while I was stationed on a small Island in the South Pacific, I awoke in severe pain and a stiff neck. Actually I had torticolis, severe stiff neck. The strength building, adjusting of heavy patients, sleeping on poor beds, and not getting my own adjustments all collided at once.

An eventual MRI showed disc and nerve involvement, several significant misalignments and some spurring. Physical exam demonstrated some thoracic outlet problem where the pulse in my right wrist disappeared whenever I raised my arm above shoulder height or merely contracted the muscles in the right side of my neck. Further the physical exam demonstrated problems with proprioception. The feedback system between brain and body was compromised.

Now, I had to stop adjusting and lifting weights and get treatment, period. Standard orthopedic practice focuses initially on symptom suppression via medications moving to more invasive means when symptoms persist. I was put on medication for pain and inflammation and referred for steroid injections in the neck. The problem with this approach was that I did not have a deficiency of narcotic painkillers and NSAIDS nor did I have a deficiency of injected steroids or surgical procedures. These therapies would not and did not correct my pain problem. What I had was a need for appropriately sequenced unloading of muscle groups, realignment and remodeling of my spinal vertebrae, proliferative repair of injured tendon and ligament attachments, removal of inflammatory triggers (particularly molds, dairy, eggs and cashew nuts in my case) and postural proprioceptive retraining.

Correction of this complex injury would minimally require 3 to 6 months of regular and consistent therapy and a 2 year rehabilitation program. If this were a case of one of my patients I would have insisted upon and written the order for such a treatment program. As is typical of doctors being poor patients, I received only sporadic short-term therapy in week long intervals. By the end of each week I would be nearly pain free only to regress back to my pretreatment state within 1 to 2 weeks after working full time without therapy. Three weeks of sporadic therapy in 6 months was just not adequate. Further, this injury complex seriously jeopardized my ability to return to civilian practice where neuromusculoskeletal medicine (manual medicine) comprised 40 to 50 percent of my practice.

Most of America returned to relatively normal life and work as usual within 9 months after 9/11. I, like all my fellow reservists called to active duty at the time of our country's need, was still living a *life on hold* away from family, friends, and profession. I was also faced with the real possibility of physically not being able to return to my civilian practice. For me, that was like telling a professional musician he could sit on the sidelines to consult and direct but no longer play the musical instrument he enjoys. Nine months of daily pain had sapped my energy. My condition was worsening and I was having more days of severe pain than moderate pain. I actually had days of depression, feelings of gloom, and total withdrawal, quite unlike what I was used to experiencing in my life. There is nothing like experiencing illness first hand to give me full appreciation of what my patients experience. In that context, this has been a blessing for me to be a better doctor.

This entire experience did bring a reevaluation of what I wanted out of life and it caused me to reflect upon an episode of the TV series "Star Trek." In this episode the starship Enterprise was in grave danger with seemingly certain demise. One lieutenant confronted the Captain with this prospect and was informed by Commander Spock that the Captain did not accept optionless circumstances and pointed out that, as a cadet at the Space Academy, Captain Kirk, then Cadet Kirk, defeated such a computer program scenario by secretly hacking into the computer and changing the scenario program. The point was that the final computer war game exam was programmed to have an unsolvable ending in order to test cadets' handling of "unsolvable" circumstances. The point was that Kirk did not believe in unsolvable circumstances, or life situations without options.

When life presents apparent certain demise, create a different option. That theme of improvisation on top of my experiences growing up on the farm learning how to improvise with farm machinery repair has stuck with me. I like options. I look for options and if they are not evident, then I figure out how to create options. Thus, the theme of this book: give patients options in healthcare.

I share this personal story to let the reader know that I do understand and appreciate chronic pain, fear, frustration and depression. I know these feelings and life's seemingly unsolvable circumstances can be overcome. In doing so they convey the "gift" of introspection and strength.

I wish to convey in this book that balance is the key to success regarding one's health. That balance applies not only to one's physical diet, but also to one's spiritual, intellectual, emotional and environmental diet. No diet of any kind in any of these categories, with the exception of prayer, is THE diet for every person. I hope to convey basic principles with which one can determine what "diet" is right for him or her to achieve the goals he or she has in mind. Health is a dynamic process. It is life, and as such it will change, cycle, throw us "curves," sometimes frustrate us, and often times conflict with society's status quo. By learning principles over memorizing arbitrary protocols we can alter our lifestyles, alter our "diets" as our lives change.

These principles include:

- Nutrition is the fuel that maintains, drives, detoxifies, and repairs the human body and every living organism on earth.
- Nutrition includes more than generic proteins, carbohydrates, and fats. It includes differentiating the source and quality of proteins, carbohydrates, and fats and their varying effects on different people.
- Human disease, illness, and performance as well as crop yield, insect infestation, and weeds are all manifestations of nutritional imbalance/deficiencies/excesses.
- Nature proves that for every cause there is an effect and for every effect there is a cause. Nutritional composition of food is directly correlated to nutritional integrity of the soil upon which the food was grown.
- Every functional aspect of the human body including psychiatric/psychological is directly correlated to nutrition just as the functional aspect of a computer is correlated to its software and hardware components.
- Drugs, chemotherapeutic poisons, radiotherapy, agricultural pesticides and genetic modification do not and will not replace nutrition in living organisms, and therefore will never repair organism damage or injury. These things will only alter the organism's functional response to damage, disease or injury.
- Nature has the capacity to detoxify, correct and regenerate every environmental disaster that humankind has inflicted upon Her if just given the opportunity to do so. Humankind has the alternative technologies that, if implemented, would stop the drive to denude

the rain forests, eliminate agriculture's polluting of the environment, agricultural soil erosion, ever increasing industrial smog and the pandemic pollution of our waters with prescription drugs.

- Patients do have more options for their healthcare than those of which they are typically made aware.
- Science is pliable, in flux, and evolves as humankind allows for the discovery and implementation of different thought.

Readers will notice as they read this book that there are many analogies and comparisons made between agriculture and human health. This is because the laws of nature apply equally throughout all living organisms and all are interconnected. Hopefully, this will give each reader a greater appreciation for the influence agriculture and the environment have on human health.

My goal is for each reader to learn something, if only one thing, that will enable him or her to improve their life or the life of a loved one. Beyond that, I hope that each reader will gain a better understanding of how all things are connected so that he or she can better contribute to the advancement of all humankind every time he or she visits the ballot box on election day or "votes with the dollar" every time he or she makes a purchase.

This book begins with discussing science. After all, medicine is supposedly a "science;" but as the reader will grow to realize, science is more "water" than "concrete." Practicing good medicine is an art. As such, it requires the doctors have a good foundation in natural science that is then applied via common sense, intuition, and experience. In conventional medicine, political science frequently takes precedence over natural science, making it nearly impossible to apply common sense and intuition to the practice of medicine. This book then focuses on the topics near and dear to life, those are energy (physics), biology and microbiology before getting into various illnesses and their treatment options.

The Mechanism of Disease

Every year more evidence is added to the already large quantity of research published in peer review journals pointing to free radical damage as being the underlying mechanism for tissue injury and demise and, subsequently, disease. Picture free radicals as sparks from a welding process flying all around. If the sparks fall into the dirt (antioxidants) they are snuffed out uneventfully. If they, however, fall into the welder's boot they cause burning of the skin (tissue damage). In our bodies, free radicals are produced every second as a natural part of our immune system to kill infective organisms, as normal by-products of detoxification in the liver and as normal by-products of cellular work. Every time we exercise, especially heavily, we produce a lot of free radicals. Our body snuffs out all these free radicals in the normal course of body functioning provided that the body has enough antioxidants and/or the building blocks for antioxidants to snuff out the free radicals.

The problem occurs when, over time, our diet does not provide adequate antioxidants nor the building blocks for antioxidants (especially trace minerals like selenium, zinc, manganese, copper, cobalt). Our body gets behind and tissue damage gradually occurs. Add to this the many poisons we are exposed to, especially agricultural pesticides and heavy metals (lead from paint, mercury from amalgam fillings and coal burning power plants, arsenic from pesticides and preservatives and some foods, cadmium from industrial wastes, aluminum from containers, immunizations and condiments), which are either directly free radicals or become free radicals in their detoxification process, and our bodies are overwhelmed with free radical damage. Depending upon the genetic susceptibility of the person, their lifestyle and environment and their diet the free radical damage shows up at different locations in different people.

Fundamentally then we look at the cause of disease as being some source of free radicals and the treatment as some means of countering those particular free radicals and repairing the injured tissue. Obviously certain tissues are much more difficult (brain) than others (colon) to repair. And since our bodies are ever complex it is more often than not our therapy approach must be multifaceted.

The next several sections will address specific health concerns/ illnesses and the options patients have regarding their treatment. I wish I had all the answers. I do not, but I do have a number of options for patients. Options give patients power, independence and hope. As patients seek options doors open and as doors open good things happen. The days of miracles are ever upon us.

This book is for information purposes only, and in no way is intended as medical advice. I recommend that the reader consult his/her healthcare professional for any specific treatment of his/ her health conditions.

Science or Political Science

There cannot be a greater mistake than that of looking superciliously upon practical applications of science. The life and soul of science is its practical application.
~ William Thomson (Lord Kelvin, 1824-1907), Famous Physicist

Science: the evasive illusion of truth, the sword of political imposition, the honest quest for enlightenment. It is the whip of hidden and monopolistic agendas. It is the "bullet" of character assassination. Science is made up of rules contrived by "men" to prove the legitimacy of a predetermined agenda. Some science is for good, some for less than good depending upon one's position in the paradigm formulated for the issue. Am I just talking double talk? Isn't "science" simply by nature organized, arbitrary, absolute, true, correct, and self evident, apolitical, and provable?

The laws of Nature certainly are but not necessarily humankind's science! Science is more a matter of opinion than most people think or believe. History is the best example and proof of this statement. Picture yourself in the time of Copernicus, the ancient astronomer who was among the first to propose that the sun, not the earth, was the center of our universe. He was speaking the "truth of science." However the "experts" of the time, the authorities of the time, had him killed. Over a century later Galileo suggested the same scientific truth and he was threatened with torture to get him to retract his statements. Today we think it absurd to suggest the earth is the center of the universe. Or think for a minute about Ignes Simmelweis, the renowned Hungarian physician who proposed that doctors should wash their hands between patients, particularly between performing post mortems and delivering babies in order to reduce the incidence of "child birth fever." He was speaking *scientific truth* yet the medical profession authorities labeled him *mad* and ran him out of his homeland. It took 150 years for the "scientific" aristocracy to accept hand washing as having scientific validity.

Nicola Tesla, who in the late 1800's invented the alternating current electrical system, proposed it to be the standard power system of the world. He was speaking *scientific truth*, yet Thomas Edison, the scientific guru of electrical power convinced the scientific world that alternating current electricity was dangerous and could not be used. Edison "owned" direct current electricity and had a vested financial interest in its perpetuation and the suppression of Tesla's alternating current system, though we know today that Tesla's alternating current system, not Edison's direct current system, supplies the world with electrical power.

It took years before Westinghouse finally believed Tesla and moved forward with the first AC power generation system at Niagra Falls. Tesla invented countless inventions including radio before Marconi; x-ray before Roentgen and most notably over unity electrical generation. Tesla demonstrated his over unity electrical generator in a 1931 Pierce Arrow automobile. Sadly, the Pierce Arrow disappeared along with its "free energy converter" shortly after Tesla publicly demonstrated the wondrous invention.

…humankind's perception of science…is in constant flux…

Shortly after the turn of the Twentieth Century, the Wright Brothers demonstrated that lighter than air flight was possible. However, Lord Kelvin, one of the most prominent physicists of the time said, *If man were meant to fly he would have been given wings.* There was no "science" for years to verify what the Wright Brothers did. Nor was there any acceptable science for years to support any of the new inventions. The science came later. Additional comments made by Lord Kelvin while in his tenure as world renowned physicist were, *X-rays will prove to be a hoax; Radio has no future; Wireless [telegraphy] is all very well but I'd rather send a message by a boy on a pony; writing to the Niagara Falls Power Company* he stated, *Trust you will avoid the gigantic mistake of alternating current.* Lord Kelvin was **the** prominent physicist at the turn of the Century and he represented the "accepted science" aristocracy of the time.

When President John F. Kennedy stated in 1961 that within the decade the United States would put men on the moon, the scientific experts in his administration and at NASA did not believe the feat could be achieved. There was no science to prove its possibility. History, as so often is the case, proved the "science experts" to be wrong.

The truth is that it is humankind's *perception* of science that is in constant flux as people learn more about Nature through new investigative technologies. Nature, the actual science, remains constant; only humankind's perception evolves. Since humans view science through their perception of science, that perception is susceptible to whatever political agenda that exists at the time and in that context.

Ah, you say we are much more educated and civilized today in the twenty-first century. Surely by now science is universally recognized and accepted. Unfortunately that is not anymore true today than at the time of Hypocrites. Human nature has not changed just because we now have supersonic passenger planes, cellular phones, artificial hearts, genetic engineering technology, fiber optic communication, virtual reality and holographic cinema. Suppression of scientific truth occurs today as much as it did in the Dark Ages. A prime example of this modern day suppression rests with Phil Callahan who proved that the primary mode of insect communication was via infrared and radio waves. He proved that insects were designed to tune to the radiations emitted by plants, their mates and their prey. He proved that the antenna found on all insects were not just artifacts, but actual very sophisticated, functional receiver/transmitters for infrared and radio waves.

The molecular fit theory espoused by entomologists for decades and to this day is, at best, a secondary modus operandi. The mechanism of scent molecule recognition lies in physics, specifically in the infrared and radio wave emission of the scent molecule that the insect detects. Dr. Callahan proved this response by demonstrating that the response can be elicited with a frequency generator and no molecules of scent present.

To this day, the entomology community denies this science though Dr. Callahan's work was sponsored and funded by the US Department of Defense, published in peer reviewed physics and optics journals (not entomology journals) and applied in the development of cloaking devices for military aircraft.

Another example of modern day science suppression rests in the work by William Albrecht at University of Missouri that proved, using scientific protocol, that crop and animal disease are directly correlated to soil nutritional balance and imbalance. Albrecht's scientific work is still adamantly opposed by every land grant agricultural college in this country. Why, one may ask, would this happen? The answer is painfully obvious, business is business is business. Drs. Callahan's and Albrecht's works in agriculture invalidate the chemical industry's *political/business science* and threaten the monopoly the pesticide industry sought after WWII and continues to seek today in agriculture. When Albrecht's and Callahan's work is fully acknowledged and applied to modern agriculture, the majority of agricultural poisons now peddled by the industry, which subsequently fund the majority of university agricultural research, would not be needed. Just follow the money!

Examples of modern day science suppression in medicine rest in the work of Bjorn Noordenstrom of Sweden which proved that all living tissue possessed electrical properties and that passing the correct current across a cancerous tumor would shrink the tumor allowing more safe and complete surgical removal of the tumor. He is considered a quack by American medicine even though he is the co-inventor of balloon catheters used for angioplasty and formerly a member of the Nobel Assembly, awarded the 2001 International Scientific and Technological Cooperation Award of the People's Republic of China. By the end of 2000, there had been two thousand three hundred and sixty Chinese doctors trained in Noordenstrom's "electrochemical therapy" for tumors and 13,000 tumor patients had been treated with a total effectiveness of 75%.

Another example of modern medical technology suppression rests with the work of Robert Becker, an orthopedic surgeon researching healing problems of bones and tissue, along with Stephen Smith and Andrew Liboff. These twentieth century medical pioneers proved that mammalian limbs could be regenerated by applying appropriate electrical stimuli to the stump of a severed limb. *Quackery* it is called by the medical thought police because it would render the multi-billion dollar prosthetic industry obsolete. When asked in 1989 what the plans were for implementing this profound technology, Steven Smith responded, "We are dropping the entire project. People are more interested in selling expensive prosthetics than regenerating limbs." (Personal recollection of magazine article.)

Perhaps the most profound and unfortunate suppression of modern technology was the deliberate and calculated suppression of the Priore device, which has French patent number 1,342,772 and U.S. patent numbers 3,280,816 and 3,368,155. This device was invented and built by Antoine Priore in Bordeaux, France in the early 1960's. It was extensively tested for the treatment of cancer and other very difficult to treat diseases with complete success. Lord Zuckerman, the scientific advisor to the British Crown, observed these treatments and found nothing negative about the device or the results. The U.S. Navy, Office of Naval Research, London Branch reported, "...the system works for the treatment of cancer." (*Revolution...* Hans Nieper, MD)

The physics department at MIT was offered and accepted a Priore device for research purposes, but the program was cancelled before the donation was received because of the adamant opposition by S.E. Luria, a prominent cancer researcher at MIT and Vincent de Vita, President of the National Cancer Institute in Bethesda, Maryland. It is interesting why cancer researchers were so adamantly opposed to the *physics* department at MIT receiving a Priore device. So much for the interest of scientific discovery. The Priore device would literally have put these cancer researchers out of business. The Priore device successfully treated cancer by restoring health to the tissues of the body via returning the cells electromagnetic homeostasis. (*Revolution...* Nieper)

We could go on and on with examples, in today's society, of good, solid science dismissed as quackery, chivalry, pseudoscience or even fraud by those, unfortunately in authoritative positions, who simply refuse to read the literature, learn their basic science and see the scientific truth. The greed for money can be very conveniently blinding, even intoxicating. Human nature remains the same. Science is not science. Rather it is *political* science.

True scientists have difficulty getting funding at universities because they are looking for truth, natural outcomes, not predetermined results that fuel profitable monopolies. I have no disagreement with free enterprise, capitalism and our American way of business as long as it allows free expression of thoughts, ideas, technologies and businesses. Unfortunately, we the people have allowed special interest groups to monopolize upon certain technologies at the exclusion of others. Many of these medicine, agriculture, industry and transportation technologies would be better for society and our world. However, because these technologies would not perpetuate the profits of the current technology monopolies, they are not allowed commercial freedom.

True science is constant in its foundation, basic sciences, causes and effects. As we learn more through research and discovery we only uncover the secrets of the how and why of nature. Nature principally remains the same throughout. It is our perspective of understanding nature that changes as we learn more. For every cause there is an effect, and every effect has a cause.

The point to convey here is that one must apply common sense to the evaluation of "science" looking at the "big" picture; always diligently asking if a new found statement or principle is plausible in the scheme of nature. It must also be evaluated to determine whose interest is best served, humankind as a whole, or some special interest looking to monopolize an industry. Looked at from this perspective, truth reveals itself, fiction fades away. Remember, truth is ever simple, fiction ever complex.

The agricultural poison and medical drug industries are great at presenting theory, elaborate statistical graphs, "warm and fuzzy" TV ads, and great plays on words like calling lethal poisons "crop protection products." I am a practical person. I have to deal with what happens on a daily basis in the trenches, on the flight line, on the job, in the field. Theories don't cut the mustard here. As such I discuss in this book life on the front line where each of us must live it daily. We may have different political viewpoints but at the end of the day, results are what pay the bills.

I will present to you a few case examples from both my agricultural experiences and my medical practice experiences. I realize that many self-proclaimed "scientists" will contend that these are simply anecdotal and of little scientific value. These nay sayers proclaim that to be legitimate bits of information one must subject them to placebo controlled, double blind studies in medicine or Latin square replicated trials in agriculture.

Current arbitrary science requires placebo-controlled, double-blind studies to legitimize any contention. In this spirit, if one were to contend that hitting one's thumb with a hammer (anyone who has done construction has done this at least once) caused significant pain, possibly bleeding, and loss of the thumbnail, the "scientists" would contend this to be only anecdotal evidence. To really be able to contend that hitting one's thumb with a hammer does such damage, we would have to set up a study whereby we hire, yes pay money, to a researcher who oversees a robot that wields the hammer striking the thumb of at least 25 volunteers who have their eyes closed. There would be an equal number, at least 25, control volunteers, randomly selected, that don't get their thumb hammered. All the thumbs have to be either left or right thumbs. All thumbs must be struck with the same force with the hammer by the robot. All thumbs have to be resting on the same surface whether concrete, wood, tile, etc. They all have to be men or women of the same age, social, ethnic, racial and religious backgrounds because any difference could change the outcome of the study. The study must be repeated several times, at several different locations, in several different countries to make the research project *scientifically legitimate*. Next, we must do statistical analyses of the data collected and submit it for peer review and journal publication. Once published, it will take several repeats of the study and analyses of the data before it will be accepted by the scientific community that striking the thumb with a hammer of the specific size used in the study will cause pain, possible bleeding and loss of the thumbnail. I am sure that every reader is absolutely riveted to his/her chair awaiting the outcome of such a study so that he/she will know for sure, with scientific certainty that striking one's thumb with a hammer is hazardous to your thumb. Ridiculous one may say. Anyone with a pinch of common sense knows that hitting the thumb with a hammer is hazardous to the thumb. No blind study needs to be done to verify that fact. Common sense in today's world seems to be very uncommon, particularly when it contradicts predetermined outcomes designed to maximize selected corporate profits.

We need scientific investigation and replicated proving studies. We need scientific curiosity and standardized research protocol. At the same time we must recognize certain common sense principles, build upon them, and keep common sense as the barometer to gauge scientific validity rather than ignoring common sense principle deliberately to in order to "prove" planned outcomes in artificial "fish bowls."

The problem with the contention that everything must be studied with double-blind, placebo controlled studies is that since living systems, humans for example, have so many variables, never could one ever control for more than just a few variables. Nature is non-linear. The current medical and agricultural research models are linear, reductionistic models introduced by Galileo (1564-1643). That model is as out of touch with reality as would be Galileo today. Alfred Pischinger, M.D., in his book *Matrix and Matrix Regulation: Basis for a Holistic Theory in Medicine*, Haug 1991 said it well.

This causal-analytical linearity thus has influence on the method theory of clinical trials and drug therapy. The individual phenomenon of being ill is subordinated to a type of disease. This is objectified in a model, and thus becomes casual-analytically instrumentally accessible. Reality is replaced by models, which have to be all the more reduced the more complex the reality. "To this extent, medical experience is not cultivated any more, since it is a question of models and not reality (Fulgraff 1985)." A model possesses neither the parameters for individual biological determinants nor for quality of life.

Since, additionally, a variety of diseases can be concealed behind the same symptoms, the randomized, double blind clinical trial can only be one way of obtaining knowledge. It is undoubtedly wrong to stylize it as the only method, since causal and experience reports can do precisely that which the "objective" controlled clinical trial cannot do: place the individual, the living, breathing person, in the foreground of medical attention, before the disease.

Each person is an individual and, as taught in most leadership training schools, once one learns the basics, he or she simply applies these principles to solving new, unseen problems.

The basics in this context necessarily are biology to include microbiology, chemistry, and physics. Further, the scientific method touted by medicine frequently gets us into trouble. The examples of Thalidomide deformed babies, DES induced cervical cancer, thyroid cancer from tonsil irradiation, Rezulin induced liver failure, Propulsid linked to sudden death and FenFen induced heart and lung disease to name a few, weren't supposed to happen but they all did happen despite the fact that the parroted scientific protocol was followed in every case. The fact that nearly 160,000 people die annually from prescription drugs is a testament to the fact that the *scientific protocol* imposed by the FDA and parroted by many people is designed more to perpetuate the drug industry and suppress viable alternative therapies than it is to ensure consumer safety.

People are not clones, though many "scientists" would like them to be clones, and therefore people must be treated as unique individuals. Ask your surgeon how many double blind, placebo controlled studies have been done on surgical procedures. Ask him or her to name just ONE.

Consider heart bi-pass surgery. It is one of the most lucrative procedures in medicine today. There is NO, NOT ONE, double blind, placebo controlled study anywhere on this therapy, yet this and all surgery is accepted in the conventional medical community as being scientific and the "standard of care."

Surgery is totally based upon outcome studies. Oh, but outcome studies in nutrition, manipulation, acupuncture, hyperbaric oxygen therapy equally reliably done, as those using surgery, are considered "unscientific." This is a double standard based totally upon to whom the money flows. We are told that the successes in holistic medicine are few and far between, no better than placebo. This is simply false. The documented successes of non-conventional therapies are extensive. Take chiropractic for example. The research proof is so overwhelming that chiropractic works in relieving suffering and gets people back to work quicker than conventional therapy that the U.S. military, despite tremendous jealously from osteopathic physicians who have dropped the ball on manual medicine, has approved the commissioning of chiropractic physicians.

The AMA states, falsely, that there is no documented need for holistic therapies. Even when there is proof that the conventional therapies are questionable or unnecessary, the AMA persists in promoting them. The long-term use of antidepressants is an example. Though the latest study done on antidepressants, reported in the July 15, 2002 issue of *Newsweek* showed their long-term benefit not to be significantly better than placebo, the medical industry continues to push these drugs carte blanche.

I have been to several medical conferences where speakers warned doctors that 80% of all antibiotic prescriptions are unnecessary yet passive dispensing of antibiotics remains commonplace and is taught in graduate medical training programs. Most doctors readily prescribe antibiotics for treating common colds and ear infections though they know most of these infections are viral. This has led to antibiotic resistant pathogens so common today that many widely used antibiotics like penicillin, erythromycin, and Metronidazol are no longer effective against many infections.

According to the AMA as many as 70% of heart bi-pass surgeries are unnecessary. Gee, that leaves only 30% being necessary and about 6000 people die each year from the surgery. Why is that OK, but let just ONE person die even remotely connected to a holistic therapy and the vultures are out in full force demanding a complete ban on such "dangerous" therapies.

Conventional medicine accounts for over 240,000 deaths per year according to the AMA while holistic medicine can hardly account for 50. But these 240,000 people were killed at the hands of "scientific" medicine not "pseudomedicine" as holistic medicine is frequently called. And since the cause of all these deaths involved "accepted science" the deaths are considered "acceptable" risk.

Tell that to the millions of patients around the world that have sought a holistic approach to their healthcare because the conventional allopathic system in all its glory failed them. Their actions of seeking "alternative approaches" to their healthcare and *paying cash for this care* attests to the fact that these people do not view "death by conventional medicine" as acceptable risk.

Even more difficult for the status quo to explain away is how and why holistic therapies repeatedly work on animals. Antagonists to good medicine contend that such results must be due to placebo effect. Indeed your cat, the neighbor's dog, that herd of dairy cows, the feedlot full of beef animals and your cousin's million dollar race horse were all cured of their ailments by herbal medicines, homeopathics and acupuncture strictly due to the placebo effect. And of course if you believe that as the "experts" want you to believe then I am sure there is a salesperson very willing to sell you vacation condominiums on Mars at bargain basement prices.

The reality of the matter is that the reason over 50% of all visits to healthcare providers is to "alternative" practitioners is because people are seeking results not rhetoric, results not party line excuses, results not accusations that it is the patients fault for the illness needing only an antidepressant to "cure." These patients want results, not the risk of being another statistic in the 240,000 dead each year from conventional medicine.

I find that patients share many of the same frustrations that doctors experience: freedom. Patients with few exceptions simply seek to be healthy, to live without pain, illness, or medical restriction. They simply want results so they can get on with living. Part of getting results is finding a doc that is compatible with the patient in personality and finesse. In other words, a patient needs to find a doc who is compatible with their physical and emotional personality. They want doctors that are open minded, empathetic and caring yet confident and aggressive in their quest for solutions. Patients want honesty but not without hope. Perhaps most importantly patients want results and doctors who can deliver results and various options how to get them.

Iatrogenic Illness

Iatrogenic illness means that the ailment is caused by the medical treatment/doctor. According to the American Medical Association and U.S. Government statistics (see Table 1) the third leading cause of death in the United States is medical treatment; prescription drugs, surgery, mistakes, or medical accidents. I think this is pathetic and a testament to the perversion of the medical system. Make no mistake about it I feel the U.S. has the best emergency medicine system in the world. However, once one leaves the emergency department to be cared for by the rest of the medical machine, it is another story. Post emergent or non-emergent medical care is industry driven rather than patient driven. This system is more interested in maintaining product and procedure flow than in human wellness. It is no wonder that over 50% of all healthcare visits in this country are to (alternative) nonparty line doctors; doctors who, at the risk of ridicule and professional character assassination, care more for their patients than the medical status quo.

> **1998 CDC, Natl. Ctr. Hlth. Stats. causes of death in US**
> Number 1: Heart / 724,859
> Number 2: Cancer / 541,532
> Number 3: Iatrogenic / 250,000 (JAMA 284, 7/26/00)
> Number 4: Cerebrovascular / 158,448
> Number 5: Lung / 112,751

There are some good technologies and medicines in conventional medicine, but this status quo does not have exclusivity on good technology. There are also equally good technologies outside of this box. There are certainly times when surgery is truly life saving; when the right medications make life livable; when therapies are just the adjunct that the immune system needed to get the upper hand. We have all heard about the surgeon that operated on the wrong leg, the patient who died from minor surgery, the person who had a seizure from a common medication. These accidents and mistakes, as in any potentially hazardous industry, do happen (steel workers fall to their death periodically, football players break their neck or die of heat stroke, etc.). It is a part of life in the fast lane so I will not dwell on these iatrogenic causes of injury and death.

The iatrogenic problems I will discuss are those that we can do something about by making different choices in our healthcare/medical care. First, we must get educated/informed of our choices.

In the Neuromusculoskeletal System section we discussed several case examples of treating severe problems that conventional therapies totally failed, even made worse. These were cases of structural injuries and pain syndromes; a category of medicine that conventional medicine grossly fails to treat appropriately and frequently actually makes the problem worse. The difficulty with this particular area of medicine is that there is so much hype associated with high technology orthopedics, professional athletic training, Hollywood workout videos, and scripted treatment protocols. Many of these therapies and programs are fine for the "average" person who accepts the assumption that scar tissue formation is normal and expected, residual pain is easily covered by pain medications, arthritis is inevitable later in life and that joint replacements are acceptable expectations. However, it does not need to be that way, there are other options for those who only seek them out.

Healing of an injury is not significantly different than healing a sinus infection. We must provide the body with the necessary nutrition to heal, remove the stressors, and allow the immune system to do its job. Once you understand that any injury carries with it a complexity of misalignments that allowed the weakening of that area and that these must be corrected along with the injured area you can then demand your treating professionals address all these areas. The most comprehensive book available for professional or patient addressing body structure is *Holographic Health Book #1* by Dr. Theodore Baroody. This book shows you an excellent way to test every joint in the body and an appropriate technique for realigning it. Dr. Baroody calls this *synchronization* because any time the body is out of alignment it is *asynchronous* in its function, physically and energetically.

One does not need to be a doctor or trainer or physical therapist to know when certain therapies make sense or seem to contradict common sense. So if your professional is telling you something that seems to contradict common sense, take time to think about it, perhaps get another opinion. The real grade comes in results.

Another area very prominent in the iatrogenic disease area is pharmacology, prescription drugs. I have had innumerable patients taking a dozen or more prescription drugs coming to see me because they feel terrible. After changing their diets, getting them off many or most of their prescription drugs, and getting some nutrition into their bodies these people feel great again, or perhaps for the first time in their lives. Make no mistake, I acknowledge that there are many wonderful medications that really do a great job with certain conditions and without them these patients would probably die. The problem is that most doctors do not look at prescription medications as adjunct therapies to nutrition and diet. They look at prescription medications as first line therapy and diet and nutrition as no therapy at all. It is not only the "walking prescription pads" to which I am referring. There are many "alternative" practitioners that have it in their minds that the therapy they practice, perhaps exquisitely, is *all* the patient needs. I have seen homeopaths say the patient needs only homeopathics and a "balanced" diet. I have heard osteopaths who practice only "cranial-sacral therapy" tell patients "cranial-sacral therapy" and a "balanced diet" are all that are necessary. These statements are no truer than saying a prescription drug and a "balanced diet" are all the patient needs to be well. No single therapy is the complete answer. It may be a significant component to a given program but not the whole program.

Regarding the "balanced diet" component, if we could actually define truly what a "balanced diet" were, that might suffice for some people. However, the fact of the matter is that the food itself today is significantly deficient in nutrient density due to the poor nutritional practices of the farmers that grow the food, including much of the "organically certified" food. Supplementation is imperative for health and healing. Diet alone in today's world is not adequate, particularly when the patient needs therapeutic doses of nutrients to achieve healing.

Getting back to the prescription medication issue, we must evaluate both the patient's health concerns and the medication side effects. I suggest that every patient first consider and have a trial with nutritional, herbal, or homeopathic therapies before moving to the prescription drugs anytime there is a possibility for this option. An excellent example of this is in the treatment of high blood pressure and irregular heart beat. Magnesium is an excellent nutrient for both conditions and should be tried before placing the patient on a drug. I have found success with many of my patients using magnesium glycinate or similar compound for blood pressure issues and magnesium chloride in liquid for irregular heart beat. I have also found with many of my patients that getting the heavy metals out of the body in conjunction with magnesium supplementation is quite effective for the more resistant cases. Exercise and stress reduction are very important therapies for high blood pressure.

Unfortunately most heart medications have significant side effects with many patients. Many patients just accept the side effect because their doctor tells them they must. This is particularly true regarding sex drive because the doctor can just prescribe Viagra for men provided they are not taking nitroglycerin. But it need not be that way. There are often, not always, other options as I mentioned above. An excellent example is a very busy professional gentleman in his early 50's came to me with complaints of angina, high blood pressure, and depression having recently gone through a complete cardiac work up. His cardiologist had him on a number of medications. He felt terrible, was feeling like he was getting worse, was told he needed heart surgery, and the medications made him feel worse than before he started the meds. He was worried that he would not be able work anymore and he was unable to have sexual relations with his wife. He was impotent from the medications. After spending 45 minutes to an hour with him on his first visit I told him that I thought we could help him. That statement alone gave him hope. I told him that over the course of his treatment I thought there was a very good possibility that we could get him off at least some of his medication and perhaps all of it depending upon how his body responded.

We put him on a higher protein diet, supplements to include 2000mg. Vitamin C, 2000IU E, 200mg CoQ10, 500mg carnitine, 400mg extra magnesium and calcium plus EDTA intravenous chelation therapy. Four months later he was off all but a reduced dose of only one blood pressure medication, was back to work full time, exercising without any angina and able to have normal sexual relations with his wife. He was ecstatic. The point here is that his problem was not a deficiency of more medications, rather a deficiency of nutrition and an overload of heavy metals. I talked to him 2 years later and he was still doing well without any additional medicines.

Another major prescription medication boon is the acid blocker industry. Acid blocking/neutralizing medication, both over the counter (OTC) and prescription are consumed like candy in this country. They are advertised as adjuncts to spicy, greasy or heavy meals without ever considering the consequences or the causes of indigestion. It could be compared to taking morphine before hitting your thumb with a hammer not to worry about the consequences or even the thought of "stop hitting your thumb with the hammer."

Again the problem is not a deficiency of medication, it is a deficiency of common sense preventive medicine, looking at cause and effect, cleaning up the diet and the food chain. Long term acid blocking medications, from my experience in practice, result in trace mineral deficiencies and problems with protein digestion because acid is needed for these functions to be normal. Improper protein digestion can result in inappropriate protein particle absorption into the blood stream resulting in IgG immune stimulation (delayed food sensitivity) resulting in systemic inflammatory responses as already mentioned previously. We will discuss the food quality issues in a later section.

Another medication problem is antibiotic use. I have read and heard at medical conferences that as many as 80% of all antibiotic prescriptions are unnecessary. This is because the infection, for which the antibiotic is written, is usually viral. Viruses are not responsive to antibiotics. By definition antibiotics treat bacterial infection, not viral or fungal infections. The practice of carte blanche dispensing of antibiotics has created numerous super bacteria, resistant or immune to the effects of the antibiotics. This practice has also increased the incidences of digestive system disorders particularly "leaky gut" because antibiotics irritate the intestinal wall thus adversely increasing its permeability to toxins, infections, incompletely digested proteins, and drugs.

I have seen a number of teenagers and young adults with significant allergy problems, digestive problems, chronic fatigue and autoimmune disorders who were loaded with antibiotics as children. Is that directly cause and effect by the scientific method? Probably not, but common sense in observing what we know antibiotics do, piecing together the histories of these people and simple patient observation tells me these problems have some correlation to chronic antibiotic use. I do not need a double blind study to tell me that hitting one's thumb with a hammer is injurious to the thumb yet there are those who contend that for a claim to be "scientific" there must be "double blind" studies promoting the claim. These same critics will argue that we cannot draw accurate scientific conclusions from common sense; only "their scientific protocol" can draw accurate conclusions from information. One simply has to remember that the people who want us to discard common sense the most are those that stand to financially profit the most by that discard.

There are numerous articles in the scientific literature warning about super infections and antibiotic resistance. *Science*, September 7, 2001 reviews the trends in both antibiotic and herbicide resistance from the 1930's to the 1980's. Every year treating common infections becomes a little more difficult because the antibiotics that once were very effective against the common infections are no longer such a panacea. I have noticed this in my own practice over time.

The points to remember regarding iatrogenic or "doctor" caused illnesses are:

1. They are common.
2. They are preventable.
3. Patients must become informed/educated about all possible options.
4. Common sense must prevail to prevent them.
5. Modern medicine is an adjunct therapy, not *the* therapy.

Part II of this book addresses particular systems of the body and the illness, symptoms and treatment options available to patients for these various body systems. The endocrine system is the first to be addressed because it is perhaps the most profound and important system of the body if only second to the nervous system. Every function in the human body is affected by the endocrine system. The minute quantities of the chemicals, called hormones, produced by the endocrine system pack a lot of power, while at the same time they are very delicate in balance and function.

Part 2: Systems, Illnesses and Treatment Options

The Endocrine System

The endocrine system is the system of the body that produces and secretes all the hormones of the body. The key players are the glands; hypothalamus, pituitary, thyroid, parathyroid, thymus, adrenals, ovaries/testes and pancreas. I find it alarming the number of chemicals, particularly, pesticides in the environment today, that are either direct or indirect hormone actors. This is, of course, how these chemicals do their dirty work to alter plant, insect, or animal function, by altering hormone balances. Many organophosphate pesticides, for example, are estrogenic, meaning they mock estrogen and can cause estrogen like consequences in the human and animal body, e.g. breast cancer. Growth hormone is used in many agricultural settings to accelerate and accentuate animal growth. Subsequently, it spills over into the human population where it causes imbalances in the normal growth hormone cycle and potential serious human consequences over time, e.g. cancer, birth defects.

Another very important and growing problem in our environment affecting human hormonal balance is the insidious supply of synthetic and supplemental hormones excreted in the urine and feces of every person taking hormone replacement therapy. These hormone products remain in the water through municipal water processing because there is no mechanism to remove them. Consequently they find their way into the waterways (lakes, streams and oceans) and eventually back into the drinking water. This is a huge Pandora's box in and of itself. Add to that all the other prescription medications additionally being excreted in the urine and feces and the potential adverse hormone and homeostatic effect on society is staggering.

It is an issue no one wants to discuss publicly, least of whom are the drug manufacturers. As usual the response by the drug lords and their prostituted scientists is that these drugs are found in such small amounts in the water that there is no need to worry. Consider an article in Science News March 21, 1998, titled, *Drugged Waters*. This article discusses the fact that every analysis done on urban wastewater effluent as early as 1991 has shown detectable to significant levels of everything from estradiol to beta-blocker heart drugs. Shane Snyder at Michigan State University studying the levels of estrogens in Las Vegas wastewater flowing into Lake Mead states that, "...estradiol in water can reach 20 ppt – a concentration that can cause some male fish to produce an egg-making protein normally seen only in reproductive females." In the March 1998 issue of Environmental Toxicology and Chemistry, Andreas Hartmann of the Swiss Federal Institute of Technology in Zurich reported finding fluoroquinolone antibiotics (ciprofloxacin) in municipal wastewater. Stuart Levy at Tufts University in Boston stated that, "Parts-per-trillion concentrations of these drugs can affect Escherichia coli and other bacteria." The 1000 times higher concentrations reported in German wastewater suggest to Levy that, "these antibiotics may be present at levels of consequence to bacteria – levels that could not only alter the ecology of the environment but also give rise to antibiotic resistance."

It may not be the single exposure to one source of drug or hormone as we are discussing in this section, but, rather the accumulated effect of having these exposures from our drinking and bathing water, our foods, plastics and the air we breath. Consider an article from *Environmental Estrogens and Other Hormones*, CBR, Tulane and Xavier Universities, New Orleans, LA titles "Where are environmental estrogens found?" This is referenced from C. DeRosa, *Journal of Toxicology and Environmental Health*, Part B. 1:3-26, 1998 and J. Zhu, Chemosphere 27:1923-36, 1993. This article notes the following sources of *estrogenic* or *estrogen mocking*/effecting chemicals found in our environment: pesticides or ag chemicals now so affectionately termed "crop protection products" such as DDT, endosulfan, dieldrin, methoxychlor, kepone, dicofol, toxaphene, chlordane, alachlor, atrazine, nitrofen, benomyl, mancozeb, tributyl tin, aldicarb and dibromochloropropane (yes many are banned in this country now but they persist in the environment and are still used in underdeveloped countries); products associated with plastics such as bisphenol A and phthalates; pharmaceuticals such as birth control pills, estrace and premarin, DES, cimetidine; breakdown products of detergents and associated surfactants including nonylphenol and octylphenol; industrial chemicals polychlorinated biphenyls (PCBs), dioxin and benzo(a)pyrene.

People wonder why female cancers are striking younger and younger women, why precocious puberty is now the norm at age 8 or 9 for young girls, why feminization is so common in animals in the wild. One could say that if these estrogens were such a problem, then why aren't men affected. They are affected. Why do you think Viagra is so popular? Prostate cancer is occurring in younger and younger men and has the same genetic correlation as breast cancer in women, which is known to be correlated to estrogen.

Obesity is a national problem and estrogen puts weight on both men and women. Common sense goes a long way in contesting the safety of these environmental pollutants especially when one considers that the normal blood levels in humans and animals of estrogens are in the parts per billion (ppb) and parts per trillion (ppt) concentrations, the same concentrations of estrogens or estrogenic compounds now found in the environment. I say wake up America. You are being drugged into oblivion.

Hormone production, like every other substance produced in our body, requires adequate and proper nutrition. Without the proper nutrition for both the production and the recycling of hormones, finely tuned hormonal balances become chaotic, body function and emotion becomes altered, even confused, and eventually illness manifests. The two most common hormonal issues I see are sex hormone problems in men and women and thyroid hormone problems more in women than men. Adrenal exhaustion will be a close third.

The following diagram is from the U.S. National Cancer Institute Surveillance, Epidemiology and Evaluation Results Program, Emory University, http://training.seer.cancer.gov.

Major Endocrine Glands

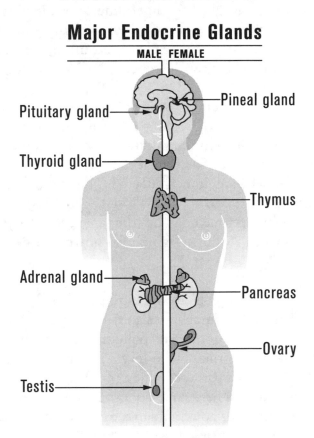

MALE FEMALE

Pituitary gland — Pineal gland

Thyroid gland — Thymus

Adrenal gland — Pancreas

Ovary

Testis

The endocrine system is made up of the endocrine glands that secrete hormones. Although there are eight major endocrine glands scattered throughout the body, they are still considered to be one system because they have similar functions, similar mechanisms of influence, and many important interrelationships.

Some glands also have non-endocrine regions that have functions other than hormone secretion. For example, the pancreas has a major exocrine portion that secretes digestive enzymes and an endocrine portion that secretes hormones. The ovaries and testes secrete hormones and also produce the ova and sperm. Some organs, such as the stomach, intestines, and heart, produce hormones, but their primary function is not hormone secretion.

Thyroid

Low thyroid is much more common than high thyroid and this appears to be more often related to auto-immune reactions. Common symptoms include fatigue, weight gain, hair loss and coarseness, dry skin, depression, among other things. The person's immune system frequently produces antibodies against its own thyroid gland or thyroid hormone, which effectively negates the functional thyroid hormone level in the body. Unfortunately for many patients, the only test the conventional doctor orders is a blood TSH level, thyroid-stimulating hormone. This is the hormone, which is the messenger from the pituitary to the thyroid gland telling the thyroid to produce more or less thyroid hormone. A high TSH means that the hypothalamus senses low thyroid hormone and is telling the pituitary via TRH (thyroid releasing hormone) to release TSH, which tells the thyroid to increase its production. A low TSH means the hypothalamus is sensing adequate or high thyroid hormone and is telling the thyroid via the pituitary to relax and not produce as much thyroid hormone.

The problem with this approach is that its limited perspective does not consider there may be adequate hormone, triggering the pituitary, from a quantitative chemical perspective but inadequate hormone from a qualitative/functional level. This may be due to antibodies against thyroid hormone or problems with the conversion of inactive thyroid hormone to active thyroid hormone. Therefore, I like to use the Comprehensive Thyroid Test from Great Smokies Diagnostic Labs that checks, not only TSH, but also T4 (inactive), T3 (active), reverse T3 (inactive yet it affects TSH), T3/T4/rT3 ratios, and 2 antibodies to thyroid/thyroid hormone. This gives me a more comprehensive evaluation of the thyroid and thyroid hormone status in the body from which to decide if thyroid medication might help the patient. If it is, I will start therapy with natural thyroid or Armour Thyroid because they contain both active and inactive thyroid hormone and are from a natural source. I find fewer side effects and better results than with Synthroid (synthetic T4 only). I know that most doctors will tell their patients that the Synthroid is better because it is standardized but so is Natural Thyroid without the synthetic side effects. Some doctors just cannot stand thinking of the human body as a natural living organism. They seethe and gnash teeth just thinking about using anything that is not synthetic.

The *patient* must be treated not just the lab values. This means we adjust the dosage more by what the patient reports than what the lab values read. We must be careful though because thyroid overdose is dangerous. Common symptoms of hyperthyroid or thyroid medication overdose include heart arrhythmias, osteoporosis, weight loss, and exophthalmoses (bulging eyes). Some people have what is termed Grave's Disease, which is hyperthyroid. Hyperthyroid presents the risk of thyroid storm occurring. This is when the thyroid produces an exorbitant amount of thyroid hormone causing elevated body temperature, rapid heartbeat, confusion, psychosis, and even coma. It is potentially a life threatening condition.

Treatment for hyperthyroid commonly includes the following: iodine to block thyroid hormone conversion, radioactive iodine to destroy part or all the thyroid or surgery to remove part or all the thyroid gland. If the doctor deems the patient is in no immediate danger, there may be time to uncover the cause of the overactive thyroid. Since it is often an autoimmune problem, I have found there to be inevitably a heavy metal and toxic chemical connection. After conventional therapy to destroy part or all the thyroid gland, the patient will be left with hypothyroidism and require thyroid medication for the rest of their life. In all fairness to the medical profession, hypothyroidism is much more easily treated than hyperthyroid and does not pose the immediate risk of death due to thyroid storm as can hyperthyroid.

The endocrine system in multifaceted and interactive. As such, one must consider several possible causes for a person's symptoms. Assuming that all the symptoms of fatigue, weight gain, low body temperature, course hair, etc. are due to low thyroid can lead one down the wrong path of treatment. One must consider that perhaps the adrenal glands need support. Hyper- or hypoadrenalism present with the same symptoms as do hyper- and hypothyroidism; therefore, these conditions must be considered in the differential diagnosis. Perhaps both the adrenals and thyroid are malfunctioning. Whether the problem is thyroid based or adrenal based, the underlying problem could be related to body toxicity.

Perhaps we need to detoxify the patient, eliminate delayed food sensitivities and heavy metals. Many people say that basal body temperature is a good gauge for thyroid hormone adequacy. I disagree because body temperature is not solely linked to thyroid hormone balance. It can be any of the above-mentioned issues or others and not the thyroid. I am familiar with Dr. Broda Barnes's work on thyroid and as with any malady or imbalance there is a group of the population that fits arbitrary standards. That does not mean that everyone who falls into these parameters has the problem and needs to be treated as if they did.

I feel that giving people thyroid medication based solely on their morning body temperature readings is shortsighted and potentially dangerous. It may be fun, quick and easy for the doctor. Patients may like the initial boost they feel from taking thyroid medication. However, giving thyroid medication to patients simply because they *want* it, but don't need it, constitutes *recreational* thyroid medication use—both medically speaking and per most state medical licensing boards. It is the same as giving the patient "speed" or any other prescription drug for recreational use.

The doctor must ask him/herself, "Why is the thyroid malfunctioning?" Certainly a dose of thyroid may make the patient feel better, however, there may be consequential costs greater than the patient can afford to bear. It is important to note that symptoms mocking thyroid imbalance (in light of) a normal thyroid evaluation are also NOT a deficiency of Prozac nor any other antidepressant. These medications may be of temporary help to some patients, but they are treating symptoms in the short term only, and putting the patient at risk for drug side effects. Antidepressant drugs have become a multibillion-dollar business and an easy cop out by doctors to prescribe whenever they cannot think of any other drug to prescribe for the patient.

The thought process seems to be as follows, "Certainly one's illness cannot be due to nutritional imbalances, environmental toxins, food sensitivities, drug side effects or heavy metals, therefore, it must be depression or anxiety necessitating an antidepressant *drug*, not a natural supplement God forbid." This is the party line drummed into doctors in training. This is what I was taught in medical school and postgraduate training and this is what the majority of doctors abide by today in their practices. Prescribing antidepressants is simple, billable, requires no detective or problem solving skills or effort and gets the patient out of the office as quickly and efficiently as possible, which is the foundation of *managed care medicine*. And of course it keeps the drug company perks flowing.

When a patient comes into my office concerned about a hormone problem or I suspect a hormone problem I approach it much like any other problem. I must get a complete history and physical evaluation regarding the problem and the person's health, their dietary and lifestyle habits and past medical history. Certainly I must rule out major illness like cancer, tumors, diabetes, drugs, etc. Then I will look at testing like the Great Smokies' Comprehensive Thyroid Test, if thyroid is in question, and address the issues as mentioned earlier.

Case example: A young lady in her early thirties came to me with a complaint of fatigue and weight gain. She was a compulsive athlete and exercised incessantly without success in abating the weight gain. She was a mother of one in a stable marriage. Her initial thyroid evaluation by her primary care doctor was unremarkable, thus, her reason for consulting me. She was certain she had a thyroid issue.

Her Comprehensive Thyroid Test from Great Smokies Diagnostic Laboratory revealed that her thyroid antibodies were significantly elevated and her TSH was in the upper range of "normal." After several months of adjusting the thyroid dosage and getting what appeared to be the appropriate dosage for her body, she continued to have problems with weight gain or the lack of weight loss and fatigue. She also told me that she felt a fullness in her throat. I determined, via palpation, that her thyroid was slightly enlarged with a possible nodule. Ultrasound of the thyroid revealed slight enlargement of the thyroid with 2 small nodules.

I referred her to an ENT (ears, nose, throat) specialist for a consultation and possible surgery. The ENT doctor concluded that the nodules were insignificant, the enlargement was inconsequential and the fullness she felt was due to gastroeso-phogeal reflux. She was completing a Master's degree about which she was a little stressed, thus, the cause of her reflux. He placed her on acid-blocking medication and scheduled her to return in one month.

My patient was very upset to say the least. She felt the ENT doctor had discredited my concern and her symptoms and treated her as an over reactive premenopausal soccer mom. I did receive an ear full. I felt it was important to heed her concerns and symptoms. Her uncle had died of thyroid cancer, so, understandably, she was frightened. I sent her for a needle biopsy of the nodules. The pathology report showed that she had thyroid cancer. She subsequently had surgery followed by radioactive iodine ablation. She recovered completely and has done well.

There are two important considerations to grasp from this case. One is that doctors must listen to the patient, heed the patient's or their own intuitive concerns, and act upon those concerns. The other consideration is that specialists are very good at what they do; but they frequently do not see the patient as a whole person connecting all the "dots" to arrive at the underlying problem. I have had similar experiences with other patients and other specialists and observed the same many times with Dr. Grant Born. Dr. Born was a master diagnostician frequently finding ailments on physical exam that other doctors missed and laboratory and radiological studies did not obviously reveal. That is not to say that specialists are not needed, they certainly are needed. It is to say the generalists make the diagnosis first and then send them to the specialists for the specialty treatment.

Sex Hormones

Once the thyroid is adequately considered, one must consider the sex hormones: most notably estrogen, progesterone, and testosterone. If the problem is a sex hormone question then I will orders tests on estradiol, progesterone, testosterone, DHEA. I have done pregenalone and some obscure hormones at times. I may check adrenal hormone levels. The most common problems are either thyroid or sex hormone issues so testing for every obscure hormone initially in neither necessary nor economically judicious.

I will ask myself why these hormones are a problem. Is it because of stress or the person's inability to handle stress due to diet, nutrition, heavy metals, exercise or lack of exercise, lifestyle issues. Is the hormone problem because we need to supplement the hormones? If I come to the latter conclusion then I do that. I prefer the natural hormones and will start with them. The options are herbal products like dong quai and black cohosh, wild yam, and soy products.

There are the "natural" progesterone creams, which help many women but not all. I frequently will use the "natural" estrogens in a capsule from a compounding pharmacy such as *biest*, which is a combination of estradiol (long acting) and estriol (short acting) or *triest*, which is a combination of estradiol, estrone, and estriol. I can also have the pharmacy compound just estriol, which seems to work well for women who need only a very little amount of estrogen but don't get satisfaction from the herbals. The last re-sort is the synthetics, Premarin being the most common. I do not like these because they are synthetics, often derived from animal sources (Premarin: pregnant mare urine) and they have more side effects. However, I have a couple patients that feel best on these so that is what they get. The compounded products can be put into any form the patient desires, cream, lotion, patch, capsule, or implantable pellet, which we insert into the abdomen for men or women that have had hysterectomies.

It is very important to keep in mind that the latest research regarding hormone replacement therapy strongly suggests that both estrogen and progesterone, ONLY address quality of life issues like hot flashes and sex drive. The belief that these hormones reduced cardiac risk factors and osteoporosis have apparently turned out to be false. In fact, the latest research suggests that these hormones actually increase the risks of cardiac disease. Certainly, as suspected, they appear to increase the risk of breast and cervical cancers. It seems that for some women, the significant quality of life improvement they receive with hormone therapy, the slight increased risk is tolerable. (Linda Smirz, MD, IOA Winter Update, 12/03)

I feel it is also worth considering that all the studies, particularly the recent ones regarding hormone therapy, have all been done with synthetics with the assumption that synthetics are equivalent to naturals. I do not believe that synthetic hormones are the same as natural hormones but, because the research studies suggest risk issues, it is prudent for the women to be informed and make common sense decisions. I think it is prudent to be cautious and give hormone therapy, natural or otherwise, after other therapies have failed and the patient makes a fully informed decision.

Hormone Therapy for Postpartum Depression

There is a group of women grossly neglected regarding hormone issues by their gynecologists and nearly 100% of the time prescribed antidepressants. These are postpartum women. Postpartum depression is fairly common and as a result of being so common it is said to be "normal." If it is severe, then the woman is given antidepressants. I find that it is necessary, only in a minority of cases, to give these women antidepressants. These few definitely do need it however. The rest of these depressed postpartum women, and also those that truly need antidepressant medication, are depressed because their hormones are out of balance.

It is frequently as simple a putting the lady on an estrogen replacement medication, starting with an herbal and working up. This may be needed for a month or as long as several months until her body comes back into balance and her ovaries settle down. I had one lady at age 27 that needed the estrogen for 8 months.

Frequently these women's blood levels of estrogen will be low or in the low range of "normal," certainly low for a woman of childbearing age. The day she starts adequate hormone replacement her postpartum blues will lift. Obviously we also need to address toxicities, diet, nutrition, etc. with these ladies but I frequently start with the estrogen because every day this lady has severe postpartum depression is another **excessively** difficult day caring for her child and family. I monitor these ladies very closely as they do themselves getting them off the supplemental estrogen as soon as possible.

A very recent study found in the journal *Prostaglandins Leukotrienes and Essential Fatty Acids* (vol 69, issue 4, pp 237-243), "DHA supplements could reduce postnatal depression," www.foodnavigator.com/news/news-NG.asp?id=39079, discusses the correlation between postpartum of postnatal depression and plasma DHA (docosahexaenoic acid) of the woman. This is a very important omega-3 fatty acid most noted for brain development of the fetus and infant. It would make sense to me that it is also correlated to depression in the mother.

Men who have low sex drive, I check the blood testosterone, estrodiol and progesterone, and DHEA levels. Often they will have relatively high estradiol and low testosterone. When these men are given testosterone they will feel better for a month or two and then regress back to before-therapy feelings. This is due the body up-regulating its conversion of testosterone to estrogen and the more testosterone given alone the worse the situation. Therefore, I prescribe a testosterone/progesterone cream applied daily. The progesterone blocks the conversion of the testosterone to estrogen and the benefits of the testosterone hold. Men with low testosterone will have low sex drive, osteoporosis, heart problems, emotional frailty, and feminization. Some of these men simply need DHEA and, when given 25 mg. to 50 mg. per day, their symptoms disappear.

Endocrinology is a very complex subject and is also a very delicate system of the body. Blood levels of hormones are usually in the parts per billion and parts per trillion concentrations. These are in very low concentrations which should tell us just how powerful hormones are in altering body function and physiology. It should also trigger our concern when "scientists" tell us that such small concentrations of hormone modulators in the form of agricultural and industrial chemicals in the environment are of no consequence. Additionally, care must always be taken when administering hormones because they can be emotionally "addictive" particularly testosterone and thyroid. In other words, people will want to take them because of the *high* or *confidence* or *strength* or *energy* they experience with the medication and not because there is an organic medical need for the hormone replacement therapy.

Diabetes Mellitus

Diabetes mellitus is a condition where the person's body has problems handling sugar. The technical classification of diabetes changes as more research is done to identify the specific malfunctions in the body that lead to diabetes. Most people think of diabetes as either type I, juvenile onset, or Type II, adult onset. Type I diabetes has been classically called "insulin dependent" diabetes and Type II as "non-insulin dependent" diabetes. These are not really correct classifications. Type I diabetes occurs when something happens to the cells in the pancreas (beta cells) that produce insulin; consequently, insulin production is compromised. Such a person definitely needs insulin injections.

Type II diabetes is typically insulin resistant diabetes because the beta cells are still producing insulin but the body is not responding adequately to the insulin. These people are usually put on American Diabetic Association diets, some given oral diabetic medication and some are put on insulin. Occasionally, a Type II diabetic may also have reduced insulin production requiring insulin injections, actually having a mixed Type I and II. In any event the academicians can work out the technical terminology for the specific kinds of diabetes.

The bottom line with diabetes mellitus is that the person has a problem with sugar, and something must be done to either correct or adequately compensate for the problem. Diabetics, especially uncontrolled or poorly controlled diabetics, develop degenerative problems of the eyes such as diabetic retinopathy, which may lead to blindness; they develop kidney failure, peripheral neuropathy (numbness, tingling/pain in the fingers and toes/feet), non-healing foot and leg ulcers and accelerated cardiovascular disease.

When I was a second year medical student I had a lecture on diabetes care from a doctor who had diabetes and was on an insulin pump. His statements stuck with me because they were so absurd. He told my class of 135 medical students that diet was unimportant in diabetes. He recommended that people eat whatever they wanted and to simply adjust their insulin according to the amount of sugar or carbohydrate they planned to eat, needing no consideration for nutritional value of the food. If a diabetic were going to have cake and ice cream he recommended they increase their insulin dose beforehand to compensate for the increased sugar load. Patients that follow this recommendation will inevitably contract all the consequences of diabetes and subsequently need expensive/profitable care for their ailments. It is a great deal for the surgeons and drug manufacturers.

Common sense goes a long way if one will simply apply it. Gee, if we are flying a multi-engine airplane and we have a fire in one engine do we continue running fuel to that engine while trying to put out the fire or do we simply cut off the fuel? Pretty easy decision I think. If your body has a problem handling sugar, reason would say reduce the amount of sugar that you put into the body, not load it with more carbohydrate and then give more drugs to compensate for the excess carbohydrate.

There are two major sources of sugar in our diets, sugar in its various forms, which includes high fructose corn sweetener, and carbohydrate, most commonly in the form of starch. However, the American Diabetic Association diet for diabetics is a high carbohydrate, low protein diet, exactly the type of diet that the diabetic person has problems metabolizing. The contention by the ADA is that diabetics must have low protein diets because the protein stresses the kidneys and diabetics frequently have problems with their kidneys. The real question to ask is "why do diabetics frequently have problems with their kidneys?" The answer? Uncontrolled blood sugar causes the kidney damage. The protein is secondary. If the sugar were controlled the protein would not be a problem.

The consistent fact, which I have observed in my practice and the practices of my clinical partners, is that diabetic patients that follow the American Diabetic Association recommended diet will always suffer from diabetes and will eventually develop all the consequences of diabetes in their eyes, cardiovascular system, extremities and kidneys and they will require increasing doses of diabetic medications/insulin over time.

There is another way to approach this condition. Change your diet to a lower carbohydrate diet, certainly eliminating all refined carbohydrates and sugars/sweeteners. This does not necessarily mean one must strictly follow the Atkins' Diet developed by Dr. Robert Atkins of New York although this is an excellent diet for many people, diabetics and non-diabetics alike. I like the approach in the book, *Sugar Busters*, which is a compromise in the Atkins Diet. I usually start my patients on this diet first. If they still are having problems controlling their sugars then I will have them move closer to the Atkins Diet. I am not suggesting that just by following the Atkins Diet a brittle, insulin dependent diabetic will be cured of diabetes and get off insulin. Not at all. I am simply saying that the low carbohydrate diet will help this person reduce, not eliminate, insulin use, maintain a reasonable weight and extend his/her quality of life. There are a lot of people, doctors and dieticians, espousing the "dangers" of high protein diets, particularly the Atkins Diet. My clinical experience indicates that about two thirds of the population does very well eating a diet that tends toward the Atkins Diet to a greater or lesser degree, particularly in America and the Westernized world.

Another book to consider is *Diabetes Solution* by Richard K.

Bernstein, MD, Little, Brown & Company, New York, 1997.

The typical Western, particularly American, diet is very heavy in refined carbohydrates and sugar, ideal for promoting hyperglycemia/ reactive dysglycemia and eventually diabetes.

Many people have a problem with the perception of the Atkins Diet that they must eat all red meat, fat and a little salad. Not true. One could be a vegetarian and model the principle of the Atkins Diet. Rather than meat, eat nuts and legumes. *Sugar Busters* suggests never eat a carbohydrate that is not a high fiber carbohydrate which means eat vegetables and fruits and whole grains, staying away from white/red potatoes, white bread, white rice, etc.

A person following the Atkins Diet could eat fish, eggs, chicken, turkey, lamb, nuts, and legumes. One must simply apply a little common sense realizing that following the Atkins Diet means eating to keep the blood sugar under control, not seeing how much high saturated fat, grain fed beef one can eat or how much fiber, omega three, and monounsaturated oils you can avoid.

You probably noticed that I did not mention dairy. That is because many people do not tolerate dairy, and the true nutritional value of dairy in my opinion, considering the way cows are fed and drugged in today's factory dairies, is very suspect. It is cooked to death and homogenized both of which adversely alter the digestibility and food value of the product. The Pottenger cat studies suggest this fact also. The work of Dr. Westin Price lends further credence to my concern about *modern* dairy products. To top it off, dairy is one of the most frequently identified allergens found in allergy and delayed sensitivity blood testing.

In any event the treatment of diabetes and the prevention of diabetes starts with diet, the kind of diet that limits carbohydrates because they directly raise blood sugar levels. Why dump fuel on a house fire when the firemen are pumping water to put the fire out?

Why add carbohydrates to the body when one must take more diabetic medications/insulin to lower the blood sugar? I realize this is really not a "science" debate. It is actually an addiction debate. Our society is addicted to carbohydrates, especially bread and potatoes. To tell an American he/she must stop eating Big Macs, Whoppers, subs and french fries is like telling an alcoholic he/she cannot drink alcohol. All sorts of complaining, moaning, whining and bargaining occur when I suggest this to many of my patients.

Bread and potatoes are an ingrained part of our culture. That does not mean they are good for us, however. In fact, the latest Swedish study suggests that cooking potatoes at high temperatures may increase the risk of cancer. The study, conducted by the World Health Organization, mentioned on the ABC nightly news 25 June 2002, showed that cooking potatoes at high temperatures (e.g. *french fries*) causes the formation of acrylamides, which are known carcinogens.

Another approach to dietary management of diabetes, particularly for what is called Syndrome X is by using "medical foods" and dietary modification. One program that my colleagues at the Born Clinic have used successfully is a program developed by Dr. Jeffery Bland and Metagenics. It is a 12-week plus program where the patient takes UltraGlycemX from Metagenics to help feed certain biochemical processes in the body coupled with a specifically prescribed diet. This program has worked very well with overweight women with sugar problems not amenable to following the Atkins' type diet. Perhaps the best book on Syndrome X is *Syndrome X: Overcoming The Silent Killer That Can Give You A Heart Attack* by Gerald Reaven, MD, Simon & Schuster, New York, 2000.

Now that we have stirred up the dust regarding diets lets move on to other therapies for diabetics who are experiencing health problems. Unfortunately diabetics, particularly those on insulin injections, have accelerated development of cardiovascular disease to include heart problems, strokes and dementia, diabetic retinopathy and macular degeneration leading to partial or total blindness, circulation problems in the hands/fingers, legs, feet, toes, and kidney degeneration/failure.

I would treat these the same as I would a nondiabetic cardiovascular problem. Diet modification is first. Then we would consider chelation therapy, which helps to remove heavy metals and damaging free radicals in the blood stream plus reduces platelet stickiness. My experience has shown that 9/10 of these patients will have significant improvement in their conditions by 20 chelation treatments. That does not mean we stop there. Ideally I would also have these patients receive 10 to 20 hyperbaric oxygen treatments to further speed the healing process.

People need maintenance levels of nutrition to survive. They need therapeutic levels of nutrition to heal.

These patients also need regular exercise and often nutritional IV support along with oral nutritional supplements to include 2000mg to 5000mg vitamin C, 1000-2000mg vitamin E, 200-600mg CoQ10, 250-1000mg carnitine, 1000mg as tolerated magnesium, 1000mg calcium, 400 to 800mcg chromium, 25-200mg vanadium. Dr. Hans Nieper had good results using calcium and magnesium arginate to help reduce blood glucose levels and increase the effectiveness of insulin in type II diabetics.

I have found that IV administration of C, B's, trace minerals, and magnesium greatly supports the heart and the kidneys and is an integral part of any recovery program. I will frequently alternate these nutritional IV's with chelation on people who have compromised kidney functions and congestive heart failure, as do most advanced diabetics. Keep in mind that all tissues and organs in the body must have nutrition to function at all and more to function normally.

The fact of the matter is that when people need to heal they need more nutrition than that needed just to survive. They need therapeutic levels of nutrition and often we can only get that additional necessary boost via IV administration. Healing any tissue whether the assault was due to an infection, injury, chemical/drug, or disease requires energy and tissue building blocks. That means nutrition; vitamins, minerals, amino acids, fatty acids, proteins, enzymes, water and oxygen. This is fundamental biochemistry and physiology. No drug provides these building blocks.

So in a nutshell, as with every illness, we treat diabetes first by changing the diet. Reduce or eliminate those foods that cause the blood sugar to rise above normal. Identifying these foods may require the IgG foods sensitivity test from ImmunoLabs in addition to food-blood sugar correlations. Then we supplement the diet with nutritional supplements. Anyone who thinks a so called "balanced diet" provides all the nutrition necessary for a person to be healthy and heal is simply ignorant of nutrition and very uninformed about food quality, the effects of food processing and the current agricultural practices employed to commercially produce food commodities.

Finally, I insist upon an exercise program. Life is movement and the body needs movement to be healthy, to clear toxins, to promote circulation. If, with diet, supplements, clean water and exercise, blood sugar levels still remain inadequately controlled, then and only then should drug therapy be continued. Using drug therapy as a substitute for exercise and diet modification, in my opinion, is ridiculous. The key to remember is that tissue healing and body recovery are *beyond* the function of daily survival. These body activities have nutritional requirements beyond basic survival requirements, thus, the need for *therapeutic levels of nutrition.*

Diabetes Summary

Issues:
- Poorly controlled blood sugars
  - Consequent multi-organ failure
- Peripheral Neuropathy (numbness/tingling)
  - Diabetic Retinopathy (blindness)
  - Kidney Failure
  - Non-healing Wounds/scrapes/cuts
  - Gangrene of toes, feet, legs, fingers
  - Accelerated arteriosclerosis
- Fatigue and "brain fog"
- Weight Gain – Obesity
- Premature Death

Treatment Considerations:
- Diet modification – reduce carbohydrates
  - No refined carbohydrates, e.g. white bread
  - Eliminate IgG reactive foods
  - Eat small meals several times per day with protein (i.e. pecans/almonds or cheese for snacks)
  - Read *Sugar Busters, Diabetes Solution* or Atkins
- Supplementation with antioxidants
- Chromium 200 to 800mcg.
- Vanadium 25 to 50mg
- Exercise 30 to 50 minutes, 3 to 4 times per week
- Consider IV EDTA chelation as appropriate
- HBOT to speed healing and fight infections
- IV Nutrition for maintenance and as needed
- Medications as needed to augment nutrition
- Regular eye and feet medical checks
- Regular blood sugar and hemoglobin AIC checks

Autoimmune Problems

Autoimmune illnesses are processes in which, for some reason, the body's immune system is triggered to react against itself. The body produces antibodies that attack self. Lupus and rheumatoid arthritis are the classical illness of this type. Multiple sclerosis is now suspected as being autoimmune due to the production of antibodies against myelin (the coating around nerve cells). Hashimoto's thyroiditis is a case of autoantibodies against the thyroid.

A very common "new" malady is *multiple chemical sensitivity*. For many people this is absolutely devastating. They are unable to tolerate the 21st Century, literally. These people react to everything from foods to food colorings, perfumes to plastics with various symptoms ranging from moderate headaches to rashes, paresthesias (numbness and tingling) wheezing and even life threatening anaphylactic shock. Some of these severe reactors subsequently develop psychological problems as a result; however, these psychological problems can be resolved relatively easily by detoxifying their body and arresting the hypersensitivities.

There are a few people who have relatively mild symptoms to environmental chemicals yet, because of psychological tendencies, become paranoid isolationists manifesting every symptom imaginable. These people respond poorly to treatment because their physical ailments are more secondary to their psychological ailments rather than the reverse as with the first group mentioned. These folks are emotionally invested in their illness. This latter group, which I feel is a minority, is the group that conventional medicine points to whenever referring to people with multiple chemical sensitivities. Consequently, all multiple chemically sensitive patients are conventionally classified as psych patients and given psych drugs. This practice is a big mistake in my opinion.

There has been a great increase in the incidence and types of autoimmune diseases over the past decade. These are very difficult illnesses to treat and often devastating to the patient. It is difficult to determine exactly what triggers the immune system to become scrambled and react against its own body. I and many other physicians feel there is a strong correlation between autoimmune disease and environment. Further complicating the environmental factors is the issue of decreased nutrition found in society today, particularly that nutrition needed for the body to be healthy enough to cope with the environment. Our bodies require extensive nutrition to detoxify foreign and domestic body toxins, rebuild body tissues, and ward off infective invasion. This need is not being met adequately by today's food.

Paralleling the increase in autoimmune diseases is the exponential increase in synthetic chemicals in our lives and environment along with a tremendous increase in exposure to toxic heavy metals like lead, arsenic, cadmium, mercury, aluminum, antimony, nickel, etc. plus extensive electromagnetic pollution. It is very difficult to get the absolute proof that the government oversight industry will accept regarding these two categories of toxins, mostly because it is politically incorrect to acknowledge these environmental problems. Almost all the public studies on the subject are funded by the very manufacturers of the products in question. Consequently, their reports will only show information the industry can tolerate.

Experience with patients dealing with autoimmune disorders has shown me that patient detoxification is first and foremost important in the treatment plan. This process must be inclusive of diet, metals, chemicals and sometimes electromagnetics.

The treatment program starts with the delayed foods testing from ImmunoLabs with elimination of the offending foods, a hair analysis and stimulated 24-hour urine for metals and saunas. Some people are so toxic however that they cannot tolerate the heavy metal stimulation test so that may be left for later. Eliminating the reactive foods reduces inflammation and immune system stress.

Saunas are important to sweat out the chemicals and metals. This may require daily saunas for months to years. Colonics are also important to keep the colon clean. Good air is also very important. Plenty of clean water is critical. A few patients will require medication intervention to suppress the significant reactions until they progress down the road of healing. Some patients will require the clearing of geopathic and electromagnetic aberrations in their homes and work places. An excellent book on this subject by Kathe Bachler is *Discoveries of a Dowser*.

During the process of detoxification, supplementation is given as much as the body will tolerate to help it detoxify and rebuild. I have found that over time, the body responds to this therapy by gradually relaxing its autoimmune reactions. This may take weeks, months, or even years for some individuals. I had a lady come to my office occasionally with her husband who was suffering from heart disease. I noticed that she was often quite restless and shied away from people, often leaving the room before his appointment was concluded. During one of our discussions, I learned that she had multiple chemical sensitivities, had been to numerous doctors only to feel worse, and was at wits end to find help. She was in her 40s, could not tolerate perfumes, colorings, cleaning chemicals, plastics, etc. She could not go to the mall for fear of severe reaction. Her reactions were anaphylactic (see appendix) in nature. Her lips would swell, her throat would close and she would pass out. It was a true emergency. She was so sensitive that she could not tolerate an IV because the solution would pick up enough plastic fumes from the IV tubing to smell the plastic and would go into anaphylactic shock. Her hair analysis suggested a heavy metal burden and her symptoms suggested great body toxicity.

Since she could not tolerate IVs, chelation of heavy metals and nutritional IVs were out of the question. I decided to start her on daily saunas to sweat out the toxins and metals. She purchased a home sauna and religiously took a sauna every day. This lady really did want her life back. I took her off her reactive foods per the ImmunoLabs blood test. After 18 months of daily saunas she returned to my office markedly improved to the point she did not have the anaphylactic type reactions (technically the allergists will say that she did not have true anaphylaxis because anaphylaxis is an IgE mediated reaction and a permanent fixture in the immune system like reactivity to bee stings; I concur with the technicality, however, the woman would have life-threatening swelling of the throat, swelling of the lips and lose consciousness, which are anaphylactic type reactions).

This lady was now able to go to the mall for brief shopping excursions, tolerated small doses of chemical fumes and perfumes and was excited about life again. I started her on IV chelation for her heavy metals and she tolerated that without incidence. She continues her saunas to this day and is living a normal life.

Unfortunately there are no drugs or magic potions that I or anyone else can give a patient to get the toxins out of the body. Some of the chemicals we find in today's environment are so odd to the body that there are no enzyme processes in the liver for the body to detoxify them. Therefore, these toxins must be eliminated via mass flow means, e.g. sweating them out.

Some people with multiple chemical sensitivity cannot tolerate heated environments very well so we must proceed very slowly. Some people, not able to tolerate hot saunas, may tolerate infrared saunas or at least baths with vinegar or baking soda or Epsom salts or clay. In these cases in either event we must seek the aid of homeopathic and energetic remedies. These are generally very benign therapies relative to intolerances and side effects; however, they can be extremely effective in helping to correct imbalances. Rarely, in extreme cases, I have used periodic injections of Kenalog, a steroid, to suppress the acute reactions, so the person can tolerate therapy to get better. This certainly is not a long term solution and I only use it as a last resort fully explaining to the patient the effects and benefits so he/she can decide if the Kenalog is for them. It must be a mutually agreed upon decision between the informed patient and the doctor.

I have found in my patient population of people with long-term autoimmune illnesses, CFIDS, MCS, etc., there is very strong victim identification. These patients seem to take on a very self-defeating attitude mirroring the very process that is taking place in their body with their immune system. There are several books on this subject of the connection between the mind and the body. I can confidently say that every physical ailment carries with it some correlated thought, word, and emotional pattern. Dr. Bernie Siegel's books are excellent for introducing one to this concept. I feel that knowledge is power and so having another angle on correcting one's illness only potentially gives one more power in helping themselves heal. God helps those who help themselves.

I have heard patients tell me that this is not Godly to think that physical ailment is correlated to our thoughts as Dr. Siegel suggests. They tell me that they will just leave it in God's hands and he will heal them if it is HIS WILL. I don't think so. I was taught that God helps those who help themselves. God does not cause illness, strife, disease, and death. These are manifestations of humankind's separations from God and denial of His laws of Nature. Pardon me for the sidetrack here, however, this issue seems to be a real roadblock for many people to get well. They will continue their *stinking thinking* and *poor me whining* while at the same time say please Lord heal me. They just wait for God to do all the work while they continue their trash diets, sedentary lifestyles and diseased thinking. And if some magic chemical potion from the drug industry fails to "cure" them, their response is that it must be God's Will for them to be sick and they will have to wait until after death to understand. I suggest reading the book *What Would Jesus Eat?* by Don Colbert, MD.

Miracles happen every day. Life itself is a miracle and God did not create illness. Humankind created illness by stepping outside of God's Will and divine plan. The laws of Nature are constant and perfect for the perpetuation of humankind as well as the earth and all its inhabitants. When we step outside of that plan with our own grand plans and schemes we reap the consequences. If you do not believe that your illness is a reflection of your thought, word, and emotional patterns then why does it matter what you read, watch on TV, listen to daily, or speak. What matter is it that you use foul language, think evil of your neighbor, and covet what you do not have? The reality is that these things do matter and do affect one's health. Therefore, pay attention to them and change them whenever the opportunity presents.

Since the big things are important, so are the little things. My point here is not to preach. My point is to take a look at the psycho-emotional victim pattern that forms with these illnesses or precipitates its happening **and** get help with that at the same time as with the physical issues. We are human beings. We require both physical and emotional nourishment/medicine for health and prevention of disease. Consider homeopathic remedies for these issues as well as counseling.

Regarding the autoimmune illnesses, a significant part of the recovery program must be psychosocial detoxification. Combined with the psychosocial detoxification will be the liver and colon cleansing for chemical toxins, saunas for chemical and heavy metal toxins. Further I recommend massage as tolerated (some people are too sensitive in the beginning to tolerate massage) and some form of body motion, if only for 5 minutes at a time, eventually leading to actual aerobic exercise. Some CFIDS sufferers may only tolerate anaerobic exercise (weight lifting), which is fine. Do something, anything.

Diet modification, as with all illness, is a must. As mentioned earlier I recommend the IgG ELISA blood test from ImmunoLabs to determine what foods to avoid. Again, whether the food is listed as a +1 or a +4 reactor, it must be avoided. The +1 to +4 does not correlate to severity of symptom/reaction/sensitivity. Additionally some patients may need IV (intravenous) nutrition to get them over the hump and on track to recovery. They may need to rotate baths of vinegar, baking soda and Epsom salts, ¼ to 1 cup. These help the removal of toxins through the skin.

Detox Baths:
>1 - 2 cups apple cider vinegar *or*
>1 - 2 cups Epsom salts *or*
>½ - 1 cup baking soda *or*
>½ - 1 cup clay such as Redmond Clay

Bathe daily and alternate additive for 20 – 30 minutes in hot water. Have one's spouse or friend assist one to get out of the tub if necessary. Some people become very weak and light headed by such baths. There are a few people that will react negatively to the Epsom salts baths because of the sulfur. These people probably have damaged sulfur biochemical pathways in their livers, which must be appropriately treated. If your urine sulfite dipstick test is positive, be very cautious with Epsom salts.

Autoimmune Illness Summary

Issues:
- Self Attacks Self: Includes but not limited to Lupus, Reynauds Syndrome, Sarcoidosis, Thyroiditis, Iritis, Rheumatoid Arthritis, and Goodpastures
- Multiple Chemical Sensitivity
- Heavy Metals
- Multiple Foods Sensitivity
- Electromagnetic/Geopathic Sensitivity
- Liver Toxicity
- Psychosocial Difficulties
- Unsympathetic Medical Community

Treatment Considerations:
- ImmunoLabs IgG Foods Testing

- Diet Modification: Eliminate Reactive Foods
- Digestive Enzymes
- Saunas and/or Detox Baths Daily
- Medical Foods for Liver Detox/Intestinal Permeability
- Colonics/Enemas as appropriate
- Clear or Shield Electromagnetic/Geopathic Energies
- Counseling for Self-Esteem Issues
- Read *Love, Medicine & Miracles* and *Detoxification and Healing* by Bernie S. Siegel
- Supplements as tolerated similar to Gastrointestinal Illnesses
- IV therapies as tolerated including EDTA Chelation and Nutrition
- Acupuncture and Massage as tolerated

Gastrointestinal System and Illnesses

One man's food is another man's poison.
~ Lucretius (c50 BC) Roman Philosopher

Gastrointestinal problems are illnesses of the stomach, small and large intestine, pancreas, liver and gall bladder. The more common manifestations of these problems are Crohn's disease, irritable bowel syndrome, ulcerative colitis, chronic reflux and/or indigestion, heartburn, chronic constipation and/or diarrhea, and cancer. The acid blocker medication business is a multibillion dollar industry. It is an unusual person that does not use some type of antacid, acid blocker or something to "settle" the stomach. It is unfortunately a common ailment in children and teenagers. Doctors quickly put them on acid blocking medication.

Since doctors do not consider nutrition an integral part of health or disease, they do not consider the consequences of reducing critical stomach acid. Our body produces this acid as an integral part of our digestive process. Without it we will not have adequate protein digestion, mineral solubilization or disinfecting of our food. Most people do not understand that the symptoms for too much acid are similar to those symptoms for not enough acid. If we have too much acid we get heartburn, reflux, etc. However, acid is the trigger for the stomach to empty into the small intestine. If acid is too low then the stomach does not empty properly and when the stomach fills there is little room for what acid is there and we get reflux. Irritation and/or poor digestive movement cause reflux.

In my practice, as many of my colleagues practicing good medicine have found, it is truly a rare patient that actually has too much acid warranting an acid neutralizing or suppressive medication. I have seen many Heidelberg Gastrogram printouts and not one in 20 shows an excess of acid. The problem is irritation of the digestive system and poor digestion. The poor digestion is commonly due to inadequate functional enzymes in the food. This deficiency is either due to food processing or due to current agricultural practices leaving the food nutritionally and enzymatically deficient.

This situation of deficient enzymes in the food forces the body to rely upon the pancreas for all the enzymes necessary to digest the food. In the short term this demand upon the pancreas is very taxing on the entire digestive system, making it difficult for the body to receive a net gain in energy from consuming the food. In the long term this causes exhaustion of the pancreas and digestive system. The digestive system gradually becomes less and less efficient and more and more susceptible to ailment and assault.

Contrary to popular belief in the medical community, the body, specifically the pancreas, was not designed to provide all the necessary enzymes for digestion of our food. The food is supposed to contain enzymes and the pancreas provides the backup or shortfall when needed. If the pancreas were the primary source of enzymes we would be able to eat 100% processed food our entire life without problems. We could be like the astronauts. However, NASA found this processed diet not to be healthful. The fact of the matter is that we can only tolerate such a diet a short period of time before becoming very ill. This is why I suggest to all my patients that they take digestive enzymes daily to supplement their food. Current agricultural practices leave our foods moderately to severely deficient in not only mineral and amino acid complexes but also enzymes.

Ideally, we would get the food production system in agriculture fixed. I am working on contributing to that goal. Until that happens we must supplement the best we can. There are many good enzyme products on the market. Don't assume that they are all the same, nor all work equally well for every person. Quality is important. I personally use HHS from Holographic Health, Waynesville, NC. These are formulated by Dr. Theodore Baroody and have homeopathic energy patterns added to help the product target the specific system for which the product is intended.

Food and GI Irritation

The most common irritation to the digestive system is food. What is food to one person may be poison to another. Most people think of anaphylactic reactions to foods like peanuts and shellfish when they think of food reactions. I am speaking of more insidious reactions, general inflammation, irritation caused by IgG reactors not by the IgE reactors, which are immediate immune reactions that can cause rapid death.

The insidious reaction to a food, to which I am referring, may be reflux initially, while later, after years of eating this reactive food, one may manifest ulcers, IBS, ulcerative colitis, constipation, diarrhea, etc. Like most other ailments however, particularly regarding the digestive system, we must consider food as the prime suspect in these ailments. The list of food in this case is not limited to only processed, genetically modified, or pesticide coated foods, though these are very important considerations.

I am speaking of immune activating foods. Foods that do or have triggered an immune response in our body as if they were invading pathogenic organisms. These foods create a defensive immune response and inflammation. This inflammation may manifest in many ways. It may be some digestive upset like reflux. It may be digestive upset plus some other local or systemic response such as eczema, sinus drainage, wheezing, abdominal cramping, depression, hyperactivity, "brain fog," fatigue, sleeplessness, etc. Without exception in my practice dealing with patients fighting Crohn's, ulcerative colitis and the like, the patients have, as their primary villain, the very food they consume the most frequently. For many of these people grain is a real problem as are dairy, eggs, and wheat. I realize the dairy, poultry and grain industries are not pleased with this suggestion, however, they don't have to pay the medical bills, deal with the illnesses nor have they taken an oath to "first do no harm." Some people can learn what foods are problematic by simply following an elimination diet but many people cannot.

Elaine Gotchaw's book *Breaking The Vicious Cycle* is an excellent treatise on such an elimination diet. However, I like being specific as quickly as possible with the treatment plan. The IgG foods blood test from ImmunoLabs is the recommended test to learn what foods specifically are the culprits. This is different than what the allergist doctors look for in their bank of tests, either blood or skin.

The allergist doctors, with a few exceptions of course as usual, have a very difficult time with the IgG blood test for delayed food sensitivities. It is simply a matter of semantics. The word allergy according to the allergist means something that involves the IgE antibody and is an immediate reaction in the body to some allergen. If the skin or Rast test is negative, then the person is said NOT to be allergic to the substance or food.

Allergists will acknowledge the IgG antibodies are the mainstay of the immune system, pass through the placenta and breast milk to transfer immunity to certain diseases from mother to infant.

Yet they ignore that this antibody can also be involved in food and environmental inflammatory reactions particularly on a delayed basis. The proof is in the pudding. Patients get results by eliminating the identified foods on the ImmunoLabs IgG foods test and results are the goal, pure and simple.

It only goes to reason that if this antibody will be produced by the body in reaction to invading organisms, generally the protein component of the organism, that it can also be involved in the same response to food and environmental proteins. It is! However, in a delayed manner. This is the concept of "delayed reactivity." The body sees these proteins as foreign and reacts accordingly. Once these antibodies attach to the foreign protein a cascade of inflammatory responses occur in the attempt to rid the body of the invader.

The initiator of these reactions is some stressor of the intestine such as the flu, food poisoning, medications, antibiotics, parasites, and chemotherapeutic drugs, trauma such as an auto accident or even intense stress. This causes an increase in intestinal permeability so that foods are absorbed only partially digested. These partially digested proteins are unrecognized as appropriate for the body and, thus, seen as invasive foreign proteins triggering the immune response.

The major differences between IgE immediate reactions and IgG delayed reactions are: IgE reactions once experienced are lifelong while IgG reactions are potentially correctable, IgE are immediate, IgG delayed, IgG are passed from mother to baby via placenta and breast milk, IgE are not.

The key point to understand regarding IgG delayed food sensitivity is that the net result is inflammation. Since we eat daily, every meal that we consume foods to which we are reactive, we trigger more inflammation. This daily inflammatory stimulus may manifest as sinus congestion, joint achiness, headaches, skin rashes, indigestion, behavioral alterations, heart palpitations and serum cholesterol/triglyceride elevation. Not only does this inflammation cause a variety of symptoms, it daily irritates the immune system and consumes valuable nutrients, enzymes, immune products, and energy.

Further, this continuous immune stimulation up regulates our immune system, consequently with some individuals, making it hyperactive. This subsequently may contribute to the development of autoimmune reactions and hypersensitivity to environmental chemicals/materials. I frequently observe patients who later in life developed significant allergies to environmental materials receive significant reduction in these allergic reactions once the culprit foods were eliminated from the diet. Further, when dealing with a patient that is environmentally sensitive, the sensitive foods must be eliminated from the diet first.

The most common symptoms for some people with IgG reactive foods in their daily diet are chronic constipation, diarrhea or loose stools, and bowel gas. For some people, these are life long symptoms, which their doctors tell them are "normal" for them. This is not correct. These symptoms may be common for some people but that should not be confused with normal. People should have a bowel movement at least 2 to 3 times per day; preferably each time they eat a full meal. This is normal even though it is uncommon for many people. Is colon cancer "normal" just because it is "common?" I think not.

People do not necessarily like to discuss their bowel habits, however, whatever goes in the mouth, will in part, eventually come out in the stool. This is the primary means for the body to eliminate waste. If the waste products are not eliminated in a timely manner through the colon, they accumulate inside of the body. This accumulation of toxins stresses the colon, the liver, and the rest of the body and places demands upon valuable antioxidants that would otherwise be used for better purposes.

These toxins contribute to fatigue, skin problems such as acne, brain "fog," foul breath and body odor, stress on the immune system and contribute to premature aging. The body will attempt to detoxify and/or eliminate these toxins via the liver, kidneys, lungs and skin. In turn, these organs are unnecessarily stressed.

Eliminating the IgG reactive foods from the diet is the first step in returning the bowel habits to normal and in improving the elimination of toxins from the body. Sometimes it is helpful to get colonics (gentle water flushing of the colon) or regular enemas to aid in the expeditious elimination of toxins and take the toxic pressure off the liver, kidneys, lungs and skin. In turn the constipation, diarrhea and/or bowel gas are improved, sometimes eliminated.

Another very significant consequence of this daily inflammatory reaction from stressing foods is infection. Inevitably infecting organisms must have an environment conducive to their invasion, survival and proliferation. Constant inflammation of the mucous membranes provides the perfect campground for infecting organisms. People that have frequent and recurrent upper respiratory and urinary tract infections inevitably are eating foods that are creating significant inflammation of these mucous membranes. Treatment of the infections does not correct the cause of the inflammation. One must eliminate the causal foods so the infections fail to occur at the outset. This process I have learned personally for myself and in observing many patients with chronic infections. Inflammation, in these types of infections, most always precedes infection.

Consider the following analogy to help explain the above paragraph. If one lives in the city where there is a rat problem, the typical response is to either poison the rats or shoot them. This becomes a never-ending task. The rats become smarter and the poisons cause collateral damage by threatening pets and children. The real issue is not the rats but rather, what is providing the rats their sustaining home. The answer is garbage. The rats are present because they are after the garbage. When the community eliminates the garbage, the rats leave on their own. So it is as explained in the previous paragraph regarding infections. The inflammation is providing the comfortable environment for the infections to reside. Treating the infections with poisons (antibiotics, although sometimes necessary) does nothing to correct the inflammation that supports the infections. Thus, like eliminating the garbage to rid the area of rats, eliminating the inflammation due to reactive foods will prevent recurrent infections.

Once the offending foods have been eliminated and digestive enzymes added to the diet, most people will need no further therapy. Their symptoms will remain silent as long as they follow their diet of non-reactive foods.

Helicobacter Pylori Infection and Gastric Ulcers

One issue that must be considered and treated if present is H. pylori infection. Helicobacter pylori bacteria is a common infection, discovered by an Australian physician in the early 1990's, that causes about 90% of all gastric ulcers. Usually when a person has an endoscopy (scoping of the stomach) and an ulcer is identified, a biopsy is taken and evaluated for H. pylori. If it is positive, the patient is treated with a combination of antibiotics and acid-blocking medication. Prevpac is the common prescription given for 10 days to two weeks. Sometimes this is repeated another 10 days to two weeks to get resolution of the infection. Zinc Carnosine at 150mg per day is also beneficial as an adjunct therapy especially for ulcer healing.

Another method of testing for H. pylori is by breath testing for chemical residue produced in the stomach when there is an H. pylori infection. I have not used this testing method extensively so I cannot comment upon its value. Another method is by blood test for IgG and IgM antibodies. If they are positive, then I treat, provided of course the patient is experiencing gastrointestinal symptoms that warrant treatment. I have found this to be a reasonably reliable test and retest though some doctors contend that though it is a good initial test for infection, it is not a reliable retesting method. Clinically, I have found it to be reliable for both initial and retest provided I correlate the results with patient symptoms.

Despite every effort to treat noninvasively, some people will continue to have mild to severe symptoms. These people may need endoscopies or colonoscopies to rule out organic disease. Once ruled out, I will consider comprehensive digestive stool analyses from Great Smokies' labs and possibly include evaluation for ovum and parasites. I may also suggest a Detox I test from Great Smokies' labs that evaluates phase I and II liver detoxification pathways and intestinal permeability.

People with inflamed intestines have alteration of their intestinal permeability. Consequently, I will treat the patient based upon clinical symptoms whether I have the Detox I test or not. Tests are only tools to confirm diagnoses and they may not be absolute for a given patient. I prefer to treat the patient, not the lab test.

I will also recommend daily intake of cold processed, whole leaf aloe vera juice. This must be kept refrigerated or it will spoil. If the label says it doesn't need refrigeration, it is probably not the quality I prefer nor that needed to do the job in the intestine. The aloe vera is excellent for promoting healing. The only caution is that for people with actual elevated stomach acid, they should not use aloe until the acid issue is corrected.

The treatment plan for these difficult to correct intestinal problems will include a *medical food* powder. This is a product specifically designed to provide the nutrients necessary for healing the digestive system. I have mostly used the Metametrics products, but, because they insist upon continuing with including canola oil in their formulations, I am seeking other sources. I have found many patients with positive IgG reactions to canola oil and thus adverse reactions to the Metametrics products.

When used, I will use the UltraClear Plus first, starting at a low dose until one or two containers is consumed. The Plus helps bring phase II of the liver up to optimum functioning so toxins can be eliminated. Next, the UltraClear Sustain is used if there are intestinal problems like Crohn's, Irritable Bowel, or Ulcerative Colitis. These patients may be on Sustain for life at low dose. The final product, UltraClear, is used to feed the phase I and II detoxification pathways of the liver to achieve optimum detoxification and elimination. When patients do not tolerate the rice base or the canola, individual supplements of various amino acids must be given or an alternate powder mix found.

I also recommend plenty of fiber, beneficial GI bacteria such as acidophilus and bifidus and for some people I recommend colonics and/or enemas for colon health and detoxification. Regarding the beneficial bacteria, be sure the product used is free of any components that are listed on the ImmunoLabs IgG foods sensitivity test such as dairy. Some people, like myself, are sensitive to FOS, fructooligosachharide, added to many lactobacillus products as the carrier food for the beneficial bacteria. Also, make sure the product is refrigerated to ensure freshness.

When I have patients, and I have had a few, that still have some lingering symptoms after all of the above, I will call upon the testing system developed by Dr. Ted Baroody. This system consists of over one hundred eighty biochemical tests, using specific muscle groups, for everything from organ systems to infections, hormones to minerals. It is not the same as getting blood, tissue and fluid chemistry testing, but rather it is testing for the energetic functioning of the body. When chemical testing is exhausted and the patient persists with the illness, I feel I am obliged to seek answers where they may rest and I have never been disappointed with the consequent results and subsequent treatment plan. This entire testing program is available in Dr. Baroody's book *Holographic Health Volume II*, 800-566-1522.

Intestinal Permeability

This refers to the state of the intestine related to foods, fluids, chemicals and toxins passing through the intestine into the bloodstream. In healthy people, toxins and foreign materials are prevented from passing into the bloodstream. Due to some type of stressing factor(s), the permeability of the intestine can become compromised, thus allowing the free passage of partially digested foods, toxins, chemicals, organisms, etc. directly into the bloodstream. This condition is termed *leaky gut*. This can occur because of antibiotics, infective agents like the flu virus, chemicals such as chemotherapeutic agents for cancer, reactive foods (IgG list), alcohol, certain medications and social stress. As can be imagined, if this condition persists, the person can become very ill, the liver significantly overloaded, and the digestive system very irritated and inflamed.

Gastrointestinal Illnesses Summary

Issues:
- Indigestion/Acid Reflux/Intestinal Inflammation
- Poor Food Quality: Enzymatically & Nutritionally
- IgG Reactive Foods
- Toxicity: Liver and Colon
- Leaky Gut
- Crohn's
- Ulcerative Colitis
- Irritable Bowel Syndrome
- Ulcers
- Chronic Constipation and/or Diarrhea

Treatment Considerations:
- ImmunoLabs Blood Test for IgG Foods Sensitivities
- Digestive Enzymes
- Colonics, Enemas, Saunas and Detox Baths

- Liver Detoxification Test
- Intestinal Permeability Test
- Medical Food Powders
- Whole Leaf – Cold Processed Aloe Vera Juice
- Nutritional Supplementation:
  - Milk Thistle
  - Glutamine
  - Glutathione
  - Glycine
  - MSM
  - Antioxidants
- Medications as appropriate
- Endoscopy, Colonscopy and Surgery as appropriate Stress Relief
- Exercise 30 to 50 minutes, 3 to 4 times per week

Childhood Illnesses: Colds, Ear Infections, Asthma, Bronchitis, Tonsillitis, Acne, Colic, and Immunizations

In a selenium-deficient state, the coxsackie virus may be transformed from a benign virus into a far more virulent form that can attack the heart of infected individuals and even cause death.

> ~ From *The Curious Man: The Life and Works of Dr. Hans Nieper* discussing work done by Dr. Orville Levander at USDA and Dr. Melinda Beck at the University of North Carolina showing that selenium and vitamin E deficiencies can cause permanent genetic alterations in the coxsackie virus which over 20 million American children contract annually.

Children are our future. They are both a joy and a worry to parents. They are particularly a worry regarding their health and safety. Most parents want only the best for their children and will do any and everything to get the best for their kids. Unfortunately in today's Western world this desire by parents has created a serious dilemma for many parents. This dilemma is in regard to immunizations.

Our public health reporters and professors tell us that immunizations are the most profound advancement of modern medicine in extending life expectancy, reducing disease and reducing loss of parent's workdays. In medical school we are vehemently instructed in the virtues of immunizations and the need for doctors to enforce childhood immunization schedules. Further, many states use patient immunization compliance as a significant factor in rating the competency of physicians practicing in that state. Michigan is one such state. My rating regarding this is therefore quite low. I wish to be very clear at the start of this discussion that I am NOT anti-vaccination nor am I pro-vaccination. My professors would of course cringe at that statement thinking they failed in brainwashing me to be a good comrade in medicine. I am pro-health. I feel that in areas where children are not cared for appropriately, be it the ghetto or Beverly Hills, meaning appropriate diet, nutrition, lifestyle, etc. there is a place for vaccinations.

On the other hand in homes where parents are well informed about diet, nutrition, lifestyle, homeopathy, natural medicines, etc. and practice it, there is reasonable argument not to vaccinate or at least minimally vaccinate.

Vaccinations are not benign injections that only stimulate the immune system to create protection against disease. They are mixes of foreign materials that also stress the immune and nervous system of the receiver. Depending upon the other stressors present when the vaccination(s) is/are given there may be no significant adverse consequence or there may be a devastating consequence and anything in between. I do not hold the communistic belief or philosophy that the good of the masses is worth the sacrificing of a few, particularly a few children. Additionally, countering the "mass population benefit" argument is new epidemiological research showing that mass immunization of our children doubles the incidence of both Type I and II diabetes. (ACAM lecture, May 2001, Nashville)

Wonderful, your kid doesn't get measles, mumps, or whooping cough but contracts diabetes for the rest of his/her life and eventually loses both feet, eyesight, both kidneys, the ability to heal minor cuts and scrapes, sexual function and has heart failure all due to the diabetes. Or your child is one of an increasing number of susceptible children developing autism or similar neurological syndromes as a result of vaccinations.

There is great debate today regarding the consequences of vaccines on child development. (Autism is just one of these glaring conditions that in some, not all children, was the direct result of vaccines given to the child.) I have seen many such cases in my own practice and, contrary to the party line mouthed by the public health service and "comrade doctors", good clinical medicine points to vaccines as the culprit, the trigger, in some children, of autism.

I suggest one read *Silent Spring* by Rachel Carson. In the late 50's early 60's she predicted an environmental disaster from the organophosphate pesticide DDT. The "experts" vehemently denied any such substantiation of her claims. We know today she was correct. The "experts" were either paid puppets or ignorant sheep following the herd mentality. So it is today with immunizations and drugs like Ritalin. Ritalin is the same type of drug as cocaine and can result in the same type of small vessel damage to the heart as cocaine resulting in sudden death of the child.

My recommendation as a physician and parent is to become as informed as possible about immunizations, homeopathic antidotes, nutrition, heavy metals, protocols and options. As a physician I demand it from my parents of patients and then fully respect whatever decision they make. If the parents' decision is to give vaccinations to their children then I recommend giving only 1 or 2 vaccines in the same week combined with nutritional and homeopathic support.

The MMR combination vaccine is unacceptable in my opinion. More information on MMR can be obtained from the published works of Dr. Andrew Wakefield, a pediatric gastroenterologist from England. If the decision by the parents is to abstain from vaccinations, then I respect that decision. I will do my best to consult on nutrition, homeopathics, options, etc. I am comfortable that with good nutrition and hygiene, appropriate diet, fluids, etc. that those informed parents who chose not to get their children immunized will be able to handle most childhood illnesses. I have to admit that I am on the fence regarding polio. This would be the exception only because of the limited availability of means to deal with that virus.

To or not to immunize is a difficult decision for parents and many agonize over the decision, either way. Become informed. You are allowed to change you mind at any point. If your child does contract the many childhood illnesses such as chicken pox, measles, mumps, rubella, croup and whooping cough, be sure to get an accurate diagnosis from a competent physician. Follow this with good hygiene, fluids, nutritional supplementations, homeopathics, herbal remedies for children and good diet. Most of these children will be just fine. Keep their immune system supported and their digestive systems healthy. If their temperatures get above 102 degrees and they are lethargic get them to a doctor. As long as they are playing and active, a temperature of 102 degrees is acceptable. I have seen children with temperatures of 104 degrees and still the children were happy and active. Fever is a natural process to fight the infection. Be aware and proactive. Keep them hydrated. Be ready with a plan of action should the child encounter problems and get them to the hospital emergency department.

Childhood illnesses such as colds, ear infections, asthma, bronchitis, tonsillitis, acne, colic are commonplace. Most people think of these as normal expectations with children. They certainly are commonplace but they are not normal. Health is normal, illness occurs as a divergence from normal due to some trigger or inducing agent. Most people believe that infections are due to exposure to infecting agents (viruses, bacteria, fungus) from other people, children in this case. Granted, exposure to these infecting agents plays a role in infection, however, it is not the determining factor whether or not a child becomes ill. Children are exposed to infecting agents daily yet some children rarely become ill while other children seem to be chronically ill. The child's immune system plays the key and determining role whether or not the child becomes ill.

My experience in medical practice caring for many children has revealed to me that there are two key components affecting the child's immune system and consequently common infections particularly upper respiratory and ear infections. These two are nutrition and diet. Inevitably illness upon infection occurs when "housekeeping" has been set up for the infecting agent(s) to thrive. This condition is inflammation of the mucous membranes and exhaustion of antioxidants.

Children that experience chronic upper respiratory and ear infections are consuming foods that keep the mucous membranes inflamed and irritated. Some of these children can overcome this situation with the addition of a good children's multiple vitamin/mineral. Some require a little more supplementation to include essential fatty acids (for membrane health and balancing body oils with omega 3's for anti-inflammatory metabolites) and citrus bioflavonoids (help assimilate vitamin C).

In the case of an acute upper respiratory illness I will also add vitamin A drops (15,000 IU per drop) at four drops per day for four days "on," four days "off," four days "on," and stop. Do not give this dosage more than a few times per year when the child is ill, because the vitamin A can build up and become toxic to the liver. I had a mother decide upon her own that since a little was good, more would be better so she put her child on vitamin A daily and after a few months wondered why the child was getting lethargic. We got her off the vitamin A and the child was fine. No damage had occurred.

I find this protocol, multivitamin, essential fatty acid drops, citrus bioflavonoids and vitamin A drops, works very well for upper respiratory and ear infections. Eight out of ten are viral so an antibiotic is contraindicated anyway. I find it also helps speed recovery the two out of ten times the infection is bacterial and warrants an antibiotic. Additionally I will recommend chewable vitamin C and ElderZinc Lozenges for children that will take them and certainly for adults with URI's (upper respiratory infections). I have also had good results with an essential oil ear drop *Disinfect* from Holographic Health (800-566-1522) for mild and viral ear infections. Another great product form Holographic Health is *Eye-C*, which I have found to be helpful with minor eye irritations, antibiotic resistant eye infections like pinkeye and also for mild elevated eye pressure.

When the URI's become chronic there is an underlying trigger. That underlying trigger is, 95/100 times, food. I will get a blood test for IgG food sensitivities from ImmunoLabs and recommend elimination of these foods from the child's diet. The most common offending foods seem to be dairy, eggs, wheat, sugar and corn. Depending upon how interested the parent is in helping the child I will get responses from the mother ranging from "this will be difficult but if it will help Johnny or Jenny not get all these ear infections we will do it" to "no way, he/she won't eat anything else." About half the mothers in the latter group will come back in 6 months to a year, and several more URI's later, admitting that once they decided to follow the diet the URI's stopped. The other half of the mothers will continue the antibiotics and ear tubes.

This same process seems to hold true for childhood, and adult to a lesser degree, asthma. Food sensitivities are the primary triggers for these children. It is well founded in the scientific literature that asthma is an inflammatory disorder. The point here is that we must find the inflammatory trigger(s) and curb them. There are probably some IgE offenders (true allergies per the allergists) but my experience has shown that the IgG food sensitivities are the greater inflammation inducers. Therefore, I recommend we get these children off the offending foods. Again, dairy, eggs, wheat, sugar and corn are the most common offending foods. I am also finding canola oil and citrus showing up more frequently. In fact I am finding canola so often now that I recommend people avoid it as a matter of habit. Perhaps it is because of the genetic modification of canola.

The citrus reaction, when it shows up, means that we cannot use citrus bioflavonoids for these children. Asthmatic children also need the essential fatty acids particularly getting the omega 3 essential oils, which are anti-inflammatory. They also need plenty of water (stay away from the diet drinks) to keep the secretions thin.

I had a mother (very conscientious) come in to my office with 4 young children, all of which had chronic sinus and upper respiratory infections. One of the girls, age 7, had severe asthma to the point that mother was taking her to the emergency room 4 to 5 times per week with acute asthma attacks. She had taken this child to several doctors including a pediatric pulmonologist, all of who simply kept loading this child with more and more medication. The mother was in fear of the child's life. Within two months of getting this child off the offending foods her ER visits were down to 1 to 2 per month. Dairy was a significant trigger and her parents were dairy farmers.

The 4-year-old son of my colleague Dr. TB was having recurring ear infections. Blood tests revealed eggs as one of his offending foods. Removing eggs and egg components from his diet resolved the ear infections. After 6 months of abstinence from eggs Dr. TB decided to let her son eat an egg, since it was one of his favorite foods. Within 72 hours this child had a flaming ear infection. Dr.

TB, subsequently, kept eggs away from her son for a year and he did not incur a single ear infection. She figured that certainly he had been away from them long enough that he would no longer be so reactive and consented to letting him have an egg. Again, within 72 hours this child had a flaming ear infection. Now that her son is nearly a teenager he can have eggs occasionally without getting an ear infection. However, if he gets them too frequently he becomes very "cranky" and "whiney" and usually develops a cold.

I had a mother bring to my office an 11-month-old baby covered over 90% of its body with eczema. This infant had been suffering with this condition since shortly after birth and the mother was nearly in a panic searching for some relief for her baby. She had been to pediatricians and dermatologists without success. She was nursing the baby so I ordered the IgG foods test from Immuno-Labs for her and within 2 weeks of her eliminating the identified foods from her diet, the baby's eczema was 90% cleared. As can be imagined, mother and baby were pleased.

As discussed earlier in this book regarding autism and ADHD, food sensitivities play a key role in child behavior. Most parents note that when they get their child off the foods triggering upper respiratory and ear infections they notice an improvement in attention and behavior. Certainly there are no "magic bullets" or "miracle cures." The first step in establishing health and harmony in a child's young life is to take the child off of their offending foods.

Unfortunately the school breakfast and lunch programs include the foods that top the list of offending foods: dairy, wheat, eggs, and sugar. This can present a real battle for parents working to keep their children on clean diets. Then there are the cupcake, ice cream and cookie parties in elementary school that fuel the reactivities in the children. Parents have to send alternative snacks to school with their children for these occasions so their children are not left out of the fun. It would be great if we could educate elementary school teachers. However, we must start with doctors and public health workers.

Colic

As for colic in babies I have found that there are two most common triggers for this problem. The first is compression of the cranial nerves, particularly 9, 10, and 11 coming out of the base of the skull as a result of the birthing process, even with cesarean births. When these nerves get irritated the child's throat and digestive system become irritated leading to colic. If this is the trigger for the child, one or two cranial-sacral treatments will correct the problem. This is a very gentle manual medicine technique, used primarily by osteopathic physicians, which takes about 15 to 30 minutes. There are also some chiropractors and non-physician therapists that offer this therapy with great skill and success.

Offending foods in the diet are the other most common trigger for colic and even if the child benefits from cranial-sacral therapy I suggest identifying and eliminating offending foods from the diet. I had an infant in my practice that, from day one, had se-vere colic and projectile vomiting. There were no anatomical deformities. The parents tried numerous baby formulas per their pediatrician without success. They were exhausted emotionally and physically by the time they consulted me.

The child was too young to blood test for IgG foods (I recommend 18 to 24 months minimum age) so I started him on Metametrics UltraCare for Kids. This is a rice-based product. Starting with the first meal his colic stopped and he settled down. This product is not sold as a complete formula, rather as a supplement but it worked and was the only thing that this child would keep down for his entire first year of age. He grew and developed normally.

I have recommended UltraCare For Kids™ as a supplement for

a number of children. They either love it or hate it and that has been the biggest problem with it. Those children that hate it are very difficult to get to drink it. The more sweet drinks and treats the parents have gotten the child used to the more difficult it is to get the child to drink this product. Other than severe colic I recommend it as a supplement for children failing to thrive or children with frequent infections who also I feel need extra nutrition. As a side-note, my main complaint with Metametrics is that the company continues to add canola oil to many of its products, a practice which greatly limits the patient population to whom I can recommend the product. There is now a choice in this matter. Biogenesis Nutraceuticals BioFocus for Kids™ in either rice or whey base is a comparable product with a more pleasant taste.

Acne

Acne is another common complaint of children and young adults. There seems to be no easy absolutes in dealing with acne. Diet is an important component and I recommend eliminating the offending foods, frequently, dairy, eggs, and wheat. Since this is the foundation of pizza, few teens are willing to eliminate these foods. That is their choice of course. Additionally, these patients are toxic in that the body is trying to eliminate waste products via the skin. I recommend daily skin brushing and saunas with lots of fresh, clean water. They should stop the soft drinks especially the diet drinks. I recommend essential fatty acids particularly EPA and GLA, flax and borage oil respectively at 1 to 2 grams each per day. A good multivitamin, 1 to 5 grams of vitamin C daily, extra magnesium and calcium at 500mg to 1000mg of each per day, digestive enzymes with each meal are all recommended. Some acne sufferers will benefit from dilute weekly injections of Staph Phage Lysate, which is a vaccine against staph.

A complete history and physical, as with all patients, must be completed to identify any specific clues to why this young person is having the acne. Some young people will want the standard therapy of tetracycline and Accutane. These are not panaceas, however. Accutane is very toxic and can cause depression, psychosis, and suicidal ideation (already concerns in teenagers).

Children are really quite resilient regarding illness provided they are given appropriate nutrition, fluids and rest. With these well in hand even when children do contract illnesses, the illnesses will be short-lived and much milder than what is normally expected. Diet is the foundation of health or disease.

Childhood Illnesses Summary

Issues:
- Recurrent Infections
- Eczema
- Colic
- Acne
- Health
- Immunizations

Treatment Considerations:
- ImmunoLabs IgG Foods Testing
- Diet Modification
- Medical Foods
- Vitamin A Drops 4/4/4
- Bioflavonoids
- Vitamin C
- Essential Oils: Disinfect for the Ears
- Cranial-Sacral Therapy

Behavioral Illnesses: Autism, ADD/ADHD, Schizophrenia, Bipolar Disorder, OCD, and Aggressive-Defiant Disorder...

These disorders are complex and yet at times they are very simple and straightforward to correct. This is the true epitome of the statement that everyone is a unique person. There are a number of components to each of these illnesses, which may vary between individuals. There are also some consistent commonalities with these illnesses across all people. One is nutrition. In his book, *Nutrition and Your Mind*, 1972, Dr. George Watson discusses his findings that each and every psychological illness had some significant dietary issue that either directly triggered the illness or was closely linked to the illness. Dr. Carl Pfeiffer in his book *Nutrition and Mental Illness: An Orthomolecular Approach to Balancing Body Chemistry* further iterated the correlation between mental illness and nutrition.

Today we know that nutrition plays a significant role in all mental illnesses, some to the point that correcting the nutritional imbalance/diet effectively eliminates the illness. We address this a number of ways. First we start with the IgG food sensitivity test from ImmunoLabs. There may be other obvious things to address like indigestion, constipation, skin rashes, sinus problems, heart palpitations, headaches, etc. yet many of these will be corrected or at least improved by just eliminating the foods identified by this test. I always give digestive enzymes because a) most people are not digesting as well as they should and b) the food itself does not contain adequate enzymes for good digestion as evidenced by its quality, e.g. low refractometer reading. If there are still problems after a second to third month trial off the identified foods then I will look at heavy metals, perhaps liver and colon issues and eventually the Pfeiffer Treatment Center protocol.

This protocol calls for measuring blood manganese, copper, zinc, histamine and urine ketopyrroles. This gives us a picture of the biochemistry and allows us to formulate a custom supplement program for the patient. The Pfeiffer Treatment Center in Naperville, Illinois has the largest data bank in the world on biochemistry numbers correlated to mental illness. They have long done the profiling for the FBI on murders and violent criminals. The current lead biochemist there is Dr. Bill Walsh. A wonderful man, very adept at biochemistry and behavior, Dr. Walsh has helped me understand this link much better.

At one point in 1999 with the impetus of Mrs. Sharon Heath, the Wellness Foundation in Battle Creek, Michigan formulated a study of 100 junior high delinquent youth correlating their delinquency with their brain/body biochemistry. The project moved forward with support by State Representative Mark Showers, key Michigan State employees, the Pfeiffer Treatment Center, and myself. The project-funding proposal passed the State House but partisan politics in the State Senate killed the project. Sad indeed that petty politics both in the government and private industry stopped a wonderful project that would have proved, in a public setting, a real rehabilitation solution for a high percentage of delinquent youth.

Independently from this project, I have sent the test results of several youth to the PTC and Dr. Walsh for evaluation and subsequent customized supplement compounding. The results have been wonderful, successful, and at the same time very disappointing. The patients have responded well to the initial customized supplementation, but the logistics of appropriate follow-up for this patient population have been cumbersome and difficult. Many of these children are in foster homes, are wards of the state, and have supervisory complications including problematic parents. It is frustrating to me to have a legitimate, proven therapy for behaviorally problematic young people only to get bogged down with administrative and political gobbledygook.

In any event, we have found that with any of the behavioral

illnesses we must look at diet, heavy metals, digestion, detoxification, infections, and structural integrity (cranial-sacral issues). Once these have been addressed satisfactorily, yet functional behavioral problems remain unresolved, I will look to the PTC protocol, psychological/psychiatric considerations which may include the use of homeopathics, Bach Flower remedies or anything else that may help the patient. Certainly one must combine any of these therapies with appropriate professional counseling and psychiatric treatment/oversight.

I had one young man brought to me by his mother because this boy was failing 7th grade for the second time. Teachers, counselors, school administrators, doctors and parents were at a loss what to do. Returning him for yet a third retake of 7th grade seemed futile. After just three months of dietary change per the ImmunoLabs IgG foods test, this young man was getting all B's and approaching all A's in his classes. Most impressive was the fact that he needed no parental supervision to avoid the offending foods. He was also off all medications.

There are a couple other systems of therapy that can be investigated for behavioral illness. Reichian Therapy, developed by Wilhelm Reich, M.D., available through the American College of Orgonomy in Princeton, New Jersey by licensed psychiatrists may be appropriate www.orgonomy.org This therapy is a bit aggressive for some people and very effective for others. If nothing else the College offers a great orgone physics lab class that I recommend every teenager and adult attend. A modification of the Reichian therapy is Lowen Therapy, developed by Alexander Lowen, M.D. His books are available in libraries and bookstores and through the books a therapist can be found.

I also recommend the book *Delayed Post-Traumatic Stress Disorders From Infancy: The Two Trauma Mechanism* by Dr. Clancy McKenzie, coauthored with Dr. Lance Wright.

One other possible evaluation and therapy for these young

people, actually anyone with learning challenges/disabilities, is "behavioral optometry." This is a subspecialty of optometry that evaluates how the brain is seeing what the eyes are taking in. The therapy program seeks to then bring the two together. I initially learned of this from Dr. Beth Ballinger, a gifted behavioral optometrist in Southern California. Also this therapy is available from Dr. Wayne Pharr in Florida. One may learn more at www.vision.cc/visuopathy/drpharr.html or at www.pavevision.org/behavioraloptometrist.html.

The message to get regarding behavioral problems, particularly in our children, is that environment is truly the key trigger for aberrant behavior. Yes, there are some genetic quirks and susceptibilities. These genetic quirks and susceptibilities, however, only manifest when the environment triggers them. The diet and environmental pollution determine which of these genetic behavioral traits express. It is not some drug deficiency, certainly not Ritalin. In our medical system today it is so much easier to just write a script to drug these kids into oblivion. The teachers are happy, the parents are happy, the doctor gets off without having to think and the drug companies prosper. Happy Days! That is until you learn that these drugs are classified similar to cocaine and cause the same small vessel heart damage, as does cocaine.

So what do you do when your child suddenly drops dead of heart failure? Oh, gee, that is just a rare possible side effect. Sure it is, and not every person that takes cocaine recreationally will suddenly die of heart failure either. Nonetheless, the side effect is there and if your child has a susceptibility to small vessel heart disease he/she is at greater risk.

Heart disease is pandemic in this country. It accounts for the second leading cause of death which means Americans are already at high risk of heart disease and now we drug the children with a drug that accelerates heart disease just because nine out of ten times the parents, teachers, and doctors are too lazy to address the underlying cause of the problem: diet and environment. It is real easy to say that diet and environment have nothing to do with ADHD when you know nothing about it, refuse to get educated and simply read the peer reviewed medical literature, when you are little more that a walking prescription pad. Doctors notoriously present themselves as experts about things they know less than nothing about, most often nutrition and environment.

In May 2000 I attended the Michigan Osteopathic Conference in Dearborn, Michigan. The Wayne County Coroner attended as a guest luncheon speaker and opened Pandora's box regarding the heart implications of Ritalin. He had recently been involved in a case of a 14-year-old child suddenly dropping dead of heart failure. There was no involvement of illicit drugs or history of heart problems. The child had been on Ritalin for 6 or 8 years. When the autopsy was done the child was found to have small vessel disease like that found in cocaine users. The Coroner noted that this was not surprising since Ritalin is a similar class drug and he and his profession felt it was only a matter of time before such side effects were seen in the population of Ritalin kids. His office checked with FDA and learned the FDA had received many reports of similar deaths.

My dismay came when several doctors in the room whiningly inquired of the Coroner what in the world were they going to do if they could not use Ritalin. What was the medical profession to do? Wake up and become physicians is my response to that question. Look for the **reasons** these children are ADHD. The first place to start is with the diet and a blood test sent to ImmunoLabs to evaluate delayed food sensitivities.

Another childhood disorder, originally (absurdly so) classified by the medical community as being caused by neglectful mothers is exploding in the US. Autism or autism-spectrum disorder is an epidemic. In 1970, 1 in 2000 children were diagnosed with autism. In 1996 the incidence had grown to 1 in 500 and by 2000 the incidence of autism was 1 in 150 children. There is a four to one ratio of boys to girls. In some areas the chance of a boy developing autism is 1 in 85. There are a number of causes to autism all of which appear to be linked to the child having a predisposed genetic susceptibility triggered by some environmental factor. Without the environmental trigger these children DO NOT become autistic. This environmental trigger can occur during gestation or any time after birth up to the age of about 5. Once the child passes age five it appears that the brain is sufficiently matured to negate the genetic susceptibility even if exposed to certain environmental triggers.

Contentions are made that the increased incidence is simply a reflection of better diagnosis. This is a false premise and an insult to the thousands of fine pediatricians practicing across this country. Further, a recent California study disproved this contention. The epidemic is real and growing. There have been significant occurrences in our society/environment since the 1970's when the incidences of autism began to increase exponentially. Our country had a significant increase and accumulation of pesticides in the environment and food chain, multiple immunizations at one time and particularly MMR were introduced into pediatric medical practice and Thimerosal, a mercury compound, was introduced as a preservative in many immunizations.

Mercury is the most assaultive environmental trigger for aberrant behavioral problems followed by measles virus from the MMR vaccine, gluten and casein, pesticides and environmental chemicals. These children have a hypersensitivity to mercury with an impaired ability to detoxify from it. Fetuses are exposed to mercury inutero from several sources including Rhogam residue infections the mother received if her blood rH factor was different from her previous child, from mother's diet or environment in which she lives. Air pollution is a major source of mercury. After birth the most potent mercury insult susceptible children receive is via immunizations containing Thimerosal, though they also receive mercury from silver amalgam fillings, air pollution and contaminated fish. The regression of the susceptible child to autism happens within a few hours to days and may happen with the first MMR and/or Thimerosal containing vaccine or subsequent vaccinations. I had one little girl that became autistic after 5-year-old preschool booster shots. Thankfully, she is normal today after extensive treatment.

Dr. Andrew Wakefield, a pediatric gastroenterologist from the UK, discovered and has rigorously proven that there is a group of children that become autistic secondary to the MMR vaccine. This appears to be due to a genetic susceptibility combined with the combination of the measles vaccine with the mumps vaccine. Dr. Wakefield's recommendation is to give only single vaccinations, wait until the child is at least 2 or 3 years of age, and test for genetic susceptibilities.

Autism starts with the genetic susceptibility to assaults on the brain and central nervous system and immune system. These susceptibilities combined with environmental triggers precipitate the disorder. There seems to be problems with the metallothionein system which regulates metal transport and detoxification; sulfoxidation which processes sulfur containing molecules for detoxification of toxins, alteration of amino acids and manufacture of important compounds such as mucin which is part of the protective intestinal lining; digestion of gluten (grains) and casein (dairy) which, in these children, forms gliadomorphine and casomorphine, potent morphine-like compounds. These children will behave toward wheat and dairy as a drug addict will act toward his/her drug of choice.

In any event, mercury seems to be the dominant environmental trigger and nemesis for these children. It seems to be the most pervasive and potent poison for their central nervous system, intestinal tract and immune system. Despite the blatant false rhetoric expressed by the American Dental Association regarding the use of mercury, the medical, dental and toxicology literature abound with peer reviewed published articles on the poisonous effects of mercury. Humans are exposed to mercury from "silver" amalgam fillings, eating fish, especially swordfish, shark, tuna, salmon and fish from the Great Lakes, from air pollution due to coal burning power plants and vaccinations containing Thimerosal. Dr. Boyd Haley, Professor and Chair of the Department of Chemistry, University of Kentucky, who has perhaps studied the biological effects of mercury more than any other scientist, has also correlated mercury exposure to Alzheimer's disease.

The good news regarding autism-spectrum disorder is that it is treatable. For many children, the disorder is reversible at least to the point where these children can enter regular classroom programs and carry on normal lives. The treatment protocol for this to happen is well thought out and trialed, yet evolving as more is learned about the causes of ASD. The Autism Research Institute, 4182 Adams Avenue, San Diego, California 92116, (619) 281-7165 has compiled a treatment protocol, *Biomedical Assessment Options for Children with Autism and Related Problems*, October 2002 edition. This report was written for clinicians to help them formulate treatment protocols for ASD children. It is an excellent publication. For specific references and details regarding autism-spectrum disorders mentioned in this section I refer the reader to proceedings of the Fall DAN! (Defeat Autism Now) 2002 Conference held in San Diego, California, October 25 – 27, (609) 921-3717.

Child-Pesticide Study

The link between agricultural pesticides and child health is well researched:

Sonora, Mexico, Yaqui Indian preschoolers in farmed valley where groundwater was contaminated with pesticides compared to children in foothills with "clean" groundwater. Valley 4- and 5-year-olds showed difficulties with simple tasks, had poorer memories & showed more aggression and angry outbursts.

~ Dr. Warren Porter, University of Wisconsin, Mid-March 1999
Toxicology and Industrial Health.

Demand and buy pesticide-free foods. Demand pesticide-free lawns, gardens, athletic fields, golf courses, landscapes, and public parks. These areas are potential sources of pesticides that our children, who are at the greatest risk for adverse health effects, frequent the most.

Behavioral Illness Summary

Issues:

- Diet and Food Sensitivities
- Heavy Metals
- Immunization Protocols
- Nutritional Imbalances
- Digestive System Problems
- Eye or Vision – Brain Coordination
- Daily Activities/Schooling

Treatment Considerations:

- ImmunoLabs IgG Foods Test
- Diet modification to remove IgG stressor foods, eliminate refined carbohydrates and sugars
- Eliminate diet drinks
- Reduce or eliminate soft drinks and sweetened juices
- Chelation to remove heavy metals
- Consider Pfeiffer Treatment Center testing protocol with appropriate customized nutrient supplementation
- Medicinal foods/enzymes to address remaining Digestive system problems
- Pure water - half the body poundage weight in Ounces or 30 ml per kilogram body weight daily

- Testing/treatment with Behavioral Optometrist for eye/vision – brain coordination
- Consider FGF-2 therapy
- DAN! (Defeat Autism Now!) Protocol
- Limit TV and video game time to 2 hours daily
- Place child in challenging learning environment
- Stop using lawn and garden pesticides/herbicides

Cardiovascular System and Illnesses

Cardiovascular illnesses are epidemic in the developed Western society. It is the second leading cause of death in the US. It is without question a reflection of the American lifestyle, which includes diet, environment, physical activity, and social stresses. It is very interesting to me to notice that many patients and doctors alike will deny any connection between diet/lifestyle and heart disease until after the patient has some heart disease event, most commonly a heart attack. Then both doctor and patient miraculously recognize that a change in diet/lifestyle is necessary and beneficial to the patient's health. This includes a cardiac rehabilitation program that integrates exercise and diet programs. I suggest these programs start before the disease event occurs. That is called preventive medicine.

Most commonly also the patient is put on a regimen of medications that include blood pressure medications, a beta blocker or calcium channel blocker and frequently including an ACE inhibitor, aspirin, perhaps another platelet aggregation inhibitor like Plavix, nitroglycerin if and as needed, and a lipid lowering drug such as Zocor, Pravachol, Bacol, Lopid, Lipitor, Niaspan, etc. These medications all have side effects, liver damage being the most common.

Finland Heart Study

An even more troubling revelation regarding conventional cardiology therapy came in 1991 when the Journal of the American Medical Association (JAMA) published an article by Finnish doctor Strandberg, et al. This article discussed a long term Helsinki study of 1200 heart patients, 55% of whom received conventional medical therapy of diuretics, lipid lowering medicines, nitrates, antihypertensive drugs and calcium channel blockers. The other 45% of the patients received no medical therapy.

The initial phase of the study ran seven years and as one would expect based upon the pharmaceutical industries propaganda, the therapy group fared slightly better regarding survival rate and recurrence of heart attacks than did the control (no therapy) group. All American studies would have been terminated at this point because the desired pharmaceutical outcome was accomplished. However, the Finns, concerned about long-term public health, continued the study another ten years.

Shocking to the investigators was the fact that during this subsequent ten-year period the **therapy group had twice as many patients die** as did the control (no therapy) group.

The take-home message from this study is that heart disease is not due to a deficiency of pharmaceutical drugs and that these drugs short term compensatory benefits in no way address the cause of the disease. They only address the symptoms of the disease. In fact, their short-term benefit may actually be outweighed by their long-term detriment.

I acknowledge that elevated cholesterol and triglycerides are a significant risk and cause of "heart disease," but so are elevated homocysteine, lipoprotein (a), fibrinogen, platelet aggregation, C-reactive protein, possible infections, and stress, none of which are routinely addressed by family practice or cardiology physicians.

Common sense would tell us that if this diet/lifestyle change makes any difference, is of any value in increasing life-span or improving quality of life, it is certainly just as recommended BEFORE the cardiac event occurs. Many doctors want to believe that genetics is the primary factor affecting heart disease. Genetics certainly do affect one's susceptibility to heart disease or any disease for that matter, however, and this is a big however, **genetic expression is determined by environment**, e.g. diet/lifestyle.

Diet and lifestyle must be altered before the disease progresses to a heart attack and/or death. Diet and nutrition are the key things for us to change for they will help our body deal with life's stresses, but there comes a point where we must change our lifestyle if the stresses become pathologic. A good place to start with diet is getting a blood test sent to ImmunoLabs in Florida to test for delayed food sensitivities and then eliminate these foods from the diet. These identified foods cause inflammation in the body and contribute to the progression of cardiovascular disease either directly or indirectly due to elevated cholesterol and triglycerides. One friend and patient of mine had triglycerides in the 700's due to his reaction to rice and eggs. Once these were eliminated from his diet his triglycerides remained below 200, provided he also practiced moderation with carbohydrates. No medications were effective for him regarding this problem.

Regarding stressors, there are factors in our environment that we as individuals cannot alter easily such as radioactive fallout, heavy metals like lead, mercury, cadmium, arsenic, aluminum; pesticides in the air, water, and food. Stress also plays a very important part in the manifestation of heart disease. Stress is either physical/environmental, which includes all the items previously mentioned, or it can be emotional/psychosocial, which most people consider as stress factors. Actually more important is how the person handles or reacts to stress, which determines the net effect of the stress.

The common heart conditions include heart attack (myocardial infarction), congestive heart failure, cardiomyopathy (diseased heart muscle), cardiomegally (enlarged heart), cardiac arrhythmia (irregular heart beating), angina (pain with or without exertion). There are four basic issues with the heart: a) blood flow to the heart muscle b) electrical signal to and through the heart c) heart muscle integrity d) pericardial sac integrity. A patient can have a heart problem due not to the heart itself per se, but rather due to the fibrous sack in which the heart sits called the pericardial sack. This can become infected, inflamed or filled with fluid/blood and inhibit the function of the heart, even to the point of death.

A brief overview of the heart is necessary before proceeding.

The heart is divided into 4 chambers; left and right atriums, left and right ventricles. Blood from the body enters the heart through the inferior vena cava into the right atrium. The right atrium then moves the blood into the right ventricle. Little force is needed so the musculature of the right atrium is minimal. If the right atrium is enlarged it means that higher than normal force has been required to move blood into the right ventricle. This may be due to right ventricular compromise or failure so it does not move blood out or there is a problem with the right atria-ventricular valve allowing blood to leak back from the right ventricle into the right atrium thus overloading the right atrium or the valve may be calcified with reduced opening.

The net result is blood back-up in the right side of the heart. This may be seen with jugular venous distension in the neck, peripheral edema (fluid retention in the extremities), angina, dizziness, etc.

The right ventricle pushes the blood out through the pulmonary artery to the lungs. This takes a little force so the right ventricle is mildly muscular. If the right ventricle is enlarged it means that the force required to push blood to or through the lungs is increased. This may be a compromise in the pulmonary valve, due either to calcification or having a diminished opening. This may be because the pulmonary valve is leaking, thus allowing blood to flow back into the ventricle. This extra blood increases ventricular load. Another possibility is that there is a problem, perhaps a restriction, in getting blood through the lungs (pulmonary hypertension) thus requiring greater force by the ventricle to move the blood. The same symptoms as with atrial enlargement can be noticed.

The blood passes through the lungs picking up oxygen and getting rid of carbon dioxide and back to the heart into the left atrium. The left atrium moves the blood into the left ventricle. This requires little force, normally, so the left atrium is small. If the left atrium is enlarged there is usually a problem with the left atria-ventricular valve (leaking or calcified) or there is compromise/failure of the left ventricle. Either way the left atrium has to pump blood against pressure, which is not normal for it, thus it becomes enlarged. Symptoms can include congestive heart failure, edema, shortness of breath, etc.

The left ventricle pushes the blood out through the aorta to the body. This last push of blood into the body requires considerable force, thus, the large musculature of the left ventricle. People with high blood pressure have even larger, perhaps muscle bound left ventricles, due to the tremendous force required to push the blood out through the aorta to the body. The left ventricle can also be enlarged when the aorto-ventricular valve is leaking or calcified or the aorta is constricted.

For a pictorial view of the blood circulation, go to The Franklin Institute, http://sln.fi.edu.index which shows the venous blood flow in blue and the arteriolar blood in red. HEART ATTACK (myocardial infarction)

Heart Attack (myocardial infarction)

Most people have experienced a heart attack either personally or with a loved one. Unfortunately many heart attacks are fatal and the person never makes it to the emergency department at the hospital. Everyone has heard of the person who was never sick a day in his life and suddenly at age 33, 45, 50 or 65 dropped dead of a heart attack. Actually heart attacks don't suddenly happen without cause or warning. It takes years of gradual change in the heart for the conditions to line up in such a fashion that "suddenly" the heart attack strikes. These are the diet/lifestyle factors coupled with genetic susceptibility/response to these diet/lifestyle factors.

A heart attack occurs when the blood flow through the coronary arteries is sufficiently reduced (or perhaps completely stopped) that the heart muscle "cramps." Without sufficient blood flow there is not enough oxygen and nutrient flowing to the heart muscle and waste products flowing away from the heart muscle. If the "cramp" lasts long enough, then blood pumping to the rest of the body also stops and the person dies. Most people have experienced a leg cramp or "Charlie horse." They hurt and make it very difficult to walk, run, or even move one's leg. Picture the same thing happening to your heart muscle. That is a heart attack for all practical purposes. Most people when they think of something causing problems with blood flow to the heart they think of cholesterol and plaque in the arteries.

An entire industry has grown out of this thought, selling cholesterol lowering drugs and surgical equipment to address it. It is a very profitable business.

Further there are hundreds of "food" products also riding on this band wagon; low fat, no saturated fat, no cholesterol, "heart safe," etc. The problem however is that they all merely address symptoms or seek to suppress symptoms rather than actually addressing the causes of the problem or supporting the heart to function more efficiently. This may be fine for part of the treatment plan in the emergent crisis, but not as the sole approach for the problem.

Consider for a moment when the blood flow is impeded to the heart muscle. This is called ischemia. The heart muscle cramps causing pain (some people, particularly diabetics, may not feel this pain because the sense of pain is inhibited, thus a silent heart attack), waste products of muscle work accumulate causing congestion in the tissue and if the problem lasts long enough (many minutes) the tissue affected begins to die. If the damage is in a very small area then there may be little or no net decrease in the efficiency of the heart. If the damage encompasses a large area then the damage can be extensive and significantly compromise the function of the heart, which can usually be seen on an echocardiogram. The doctor interpreting the echo will note heart wall motion normality or abnormality and calculate "ejection fraction." This is the percent of blood pushed out of the heart each time the heart beats.

The normal range is typically 50% to 70%. If the heart attack was mild the person may notice no change in his or her ability to function daily but if the heart attack is severe and the person survives he/she may notice great difficulty in ability to perform daily activities. Typical or conventional medical therapy here simply applies drugs to alter the body's reaction to this damage and tells the patient to live with it. This may be after heart catherization ballooning, stinting, or bypass grafting which are only procedures/stop loss measures to prevent further immediate damage/infarction.

At no time does the conventional cardiologist recognize that the process of myocardial infarction (heart attack) is a biochemical process alterable by nutrition and that a heart experiencing ischemia or infarct needs greater quantities of nutrition to survive and repair. This is where conventional and "good" medicine really need to integrate. The peer-reviewed literature proves this but few internists/cardiologists choose to read it. See *Clinical Pearls* at www.clinicalpearls.com for an excellent cataloging of medical literature supporting nutritional therapies for various diseases. For most doctors, recommending an aspirin is their only action outside of prescription drugs.

What should actually be done is much more. Upon arrival to the ER the person experiencing the heart attack should, more often than not, be started on a magnesium IV along with the nitroglycerine and medication IV. Further the patient should receive high doses of coenzyme Q10 600mg – 1000mg along with vitamin C, E, A, carnitine and ideally once the patient is stabilized relative to the attack gotten to the hyperbaric oxygen chamber for HBOT.

HBOT, as trialed by Richmond Medical Center, Columbia, SC given ASAP after the heart attack will prevent any heart muscle damage from the heart attack by getting oxygen to the damaged/ ischemic area of the heart. I learned this while attending the HBOT physician-training course at Richmond Medical Center in 1997. Not only is this HBOT proven, it follows common sense which is, unfortunately, quite uncommon these days in medicine. We are not speaking prevention here, simply holistic emergent care for the distressed patient. Once the patient is over the immediate crisis, out of the emergency room, we can consider ongoing supportive care and prevention of future events. Again, supportive care and prevention are not at all considered in conventional medicine beyond standard cardiac rehab protocol and low cholesterol diets. It is amazing how many doctors, especially surgeons, are down on what they are not up on.

Congestive Heart Failure

Congestive Heart Failure (CHF) is a condition where the heart is not keeping up with the demand. In other words there is more fluid in the body circulatory system than the "pump" can handle so the fluid/blood gets backed up primarily in the heart and lungs. This gives the patient the symptoms of shortness of breath, wheezing, fluid retention especially in the extremities. If the CHF progresses beyond the point where the pumping demand is greater than the heart's capacity to pump, considering current blood supply and oxygenation, that heart experiences ischemia (oxygen deprivation) and the person may experience cardiac arrest: the heart stops pumping altogether.

Frequently people experience CHF after a heart attack because there has been some damage to the heart, it is not as efficient as it should be, and thus the "pump" gets behind. The standard protocol for treating CHF is initially giving a water pill/diuretic like Lasix or Bumex. These drugs trigger the kidneys to get rid of more fluid than they would normally.

As the heart begins to fail the kidneys sense that blood flow is decreasing. The kidneys interpret this reduced blood flow as blood loss and thus begin retaining more fluid to replace or increase the blood volume. This then puts more load on the heart which causes it to fail a little more which reduces blood flow to the kidneys even further, which triggers the kidneys to retain more fluid, etc.

For many people with only mild heart failure the addition of a simple diuretic does the job and no further therapy is needed, at least at first. In full blown CHF there is frequently a three drug plan which includes a diuretic to dump fluid, an ACE inhibitor to help the function of the kidney, dump fluid, and stabilize pressure plus some type of heart muscle support frequently digoxin (Lanoxin) which increases the strength of the heart contractions.

Depending upon the cardiologist, his/her schooling, and additional complications, the patient may also be given a beta blocker or calcium channel blocker to regulate rhythm, pressure and heart dynamics. The patient will also be put on fluid restriction and low sodium diet so the water pills can work the "magic" they are designed to do.

The entire issue in CHF is heart function, its ability to pump the blood around the body. The conventional mindset is that this is a given function that eventually wears out and can only be directly or indirectly altered with drugs. However, like every other living tissue/organism the heart's function is dependent not upon the drugs given but rather the nutritional fuel supplied it especially when under heavy work.

When and if the heart is supplied the necessary nutrition, the pump failure will decrease and possibly cease depending upon the degree of heart muscle damage and the amount of nutrition that is successfully supplied to the heart. To the degree that we are able to supply these nutrients, so will be the degree of resolution of the congestive failure.

I find that IV (intravenous) combined with oral medicinal nutrition go a long way in addressing this problem. This would include 500mg to 1000mg of magnesium chloride, 2000mg to 5000mg vitamin C, one ml of trace mineral mix to include zinc, copper, manganese and selenium, one ml each of B-complex and B6 and possibly one to two cc of procaine. Patients in severe CHF would benefit from this IV mix three times per week until the CHF improves and then on a maintenance schedule at once per week until the CHF resolves and then once per month as a preventive for life. I will also supplement orally with 200mg to 600mg of coenzyme Q10, 500mg to 1000mg of carnitine, 1000mg to 2000mg of taurine, 1000mg each of calcium and magnesium and/or potassium-magnesium aspartate and 1000mg to 2000mg of creatine.

I had a gentleman, still working at age ninety-two, come to me, originally for low back pain, which we solved. He developed CHF, not unusual for elderly people. He was tired of all the drugs and felt they were helping him less and less. He was a wealthy man and it seemed that his wife and children were more interested in their inheritance than this man's health and quality of life. His wife did everything in her power to prevent him from coming to my office and prevented him from taking his supplements in the home. He soon became wheelchair bound and a friend, his employer, brought him to me one day in severe CHF. I gave him the nutritional IV over ten minutes and within twenty minutes he could think and talk clearly and stand without shortness of breath. I got him started on supplements and suggested he return for the IV three times per week. After a couple weeks he was up and working again in sales. He wasn't driving so his wife put a stop to his visits to my office once she learned the friend had been bringing him to the clinic. Within a month he was again at death's door and the friend literally snuck him to my office for therapy. He again improved and went back to work. This cycle occurred three times before he died. His wife caught on to the process and prevented him from coming in for therapy. She took him to the local hospital when he worsened. Prior to his coming in to see me for the CHF, he had been taking heart medications without adequate relief for the CHF, but at age ninety-two, his family doctor thought there was nothing more that could be done, told the family so, and waited for him to die, which he did.

I had another gentleman in his mid-sixties come to me with severe CHF, obesity, and uncontrolled diabetes on insulin with compromising kidneys. We affectionately call these people *train wrecks*. Medications were maxed out and inadequate. He was almost wheelchair bound as a result. I immediately started him on the nutritional IV's, supplements and a high-protein diet. He responded very well and is still alive, doing well and working five years later.

Cardiomyopathy

Cardiomyopathy is a condition where the heart muscle becomes diseased, thins out and becomes less functional or even non-functional and death occurs. Frequently, these people are in their thirties or forties when they begin to experience excess fatigue, exhaustion and/or shortness of breath with exertion. They may or may not experience angina but ultimately if not treated, they develop CHF. These are the patients that usually are recommended for heart transplant. There are a number of possible causes to this disorder including heavy metal toxicity, viral and bacterial infections, autoimmune reactions, and genetics. Many cardiomyopathy cases are labeled as idiopathic, meaning no known cause is identified. I have found that many of these idiopathic cases are actually cardiomyopathy caused by toxic metals, especially mercury. An article in the Journal of the American College of Cardiology May 1999, 33(6) p1578-83 stated that the heart muscle of patients with IDCM (idiopathic dilated cardiomyopathy) had 22,000 times the amount of mercury and 12,000 times the amount of antimony as did normal heart muscle. I have known a number of people who were diagnosed IDCM in their 40's, rapidly deteriorated and died in their early 50's. Unfortunately, they sought conventional treatment, which is very weak for cardiomyopathy short of heart transplant. My experience in practice dictates that if these people are treated appropriately and early after the initial diagnosis, they do extremely well and many return to their normal life activities.

My first experience with this was regarding Dr. Grant Born at the Born Clinic in Grand Rapids, Michigan. Dr. Born was my mentor and friend for the first fourteen months of my medical practice. At age forty-four he suffered a heart attack and went to Mayo Clinic in Rochester, Minnesota for bi-pass surgery. After surgery he felt worse and the doctors diagnosed him with IDCM, told him he would have only a few months to a maximum of a couple years to live and sent him home. He confirmed the diagnosis at Cleveland Clinic and went home to contemplate his future. Through his own voracious quest for answers and with the help of his patients he learned about and started chelation therapy. He discovered that his body burden of mercury was extremely high especially in the liver and heart. He chelated for several years and as long as he could keep his mercury level at bay he was able to practice full time and enjoy life. He lived fully another sixteen years before succumbing to heart failure.

Dr. Born was so toxic with mercury that during his last couple years of life if he took any product including a homeopathic that would stimulate mercury movement in his body, it would immediately throw him into congestive heart failure.

His nemesis was that he loved to in fish Lake Michigan and subsequently ate Lake Michigan fish several days per week much of his adult life. Lake Michigan fish are notorious for their problematic mercury levels.

Another gentleman came into my office in his early fifties having recently been diagnosed with cardiomyopathy and severe congestive heart failure. He too was an avid Lake Michigan fisherman, was exposed to numerous toxic chemicals in Viet Nam and poisoned with PPB during the Farm Bureau feed scandal in the 1970's. He had advanced disease and passed on in just a few months. He was a good friend of fifteen years. Based upon the few tests we were able to run on him I feel that a combination of heavy metal and toxic chemicals led to the development of his cardiomyopathy. If only I could have treated him a couple years earlier.

The next patient was a young farmer in his late thirties who went to his doctor complaining of fatigue and shortness of breath. He was diagnosed with IDCM and congestive heart failure and told he would soon need a heart transplant. His heart's ejection fraction (amount of blood pumped each beat) was less than 40%, normal is 50% to 70%, he was unable to farm, play basketball and many of his daily activities frequently taken for granted. After four months of treatment his congestive heart failure had disappeared without using drugs, his ejection fraction had improved into the normal range and his stress test was normal. His cardiologist was amazed. He was able to return to his normal life activities, which included playing organized basketball.

Not only did he change his diet and health habits, he and his brother also changed their farming practices to a more balanced nutritional management practice and a trend away from so many farm poisons which he and his brother continue to this day.

Cardiomyopathy is a difficult illness but because heavy metals (I feel chemicals are also involved) are so often associated with its development, chelation must be seriously considered in the treatment plan. The heart is a muscle and requires a lot of energy, a lot of nutrition. CoQ10 at 400mg or more, Carnitine at 1000mg, Taurine at 2000mg, magnesium at 1000mg, vitamin E at 1200 IU to 2000 IU and 1000mg to 2000mg creatine are a minimum plus alternating the chelation treatments with Gaby nutritional IV's are a must. These patients need energy for the heart and the 25 to 30cc nutritional IV's once or twice weekly are critical to renewing the sick heart. I also make sure that these men (I have never had a female patient with cardiomyopathy) have normal testosterone and DHEA function. These are important hormones regarding heart function and energy. Too much testosterone, though, puts too much stress on the heart so appropriate function is important. Level of testosterone is not as important as function.

Cardiomegally

Cardiomegally is enlargement of the heart frequently due to hypertension. People who are more athletic will generally have larger hearts. This is not necessarily classified as cardiomegally, at least not pathological cardiomegally, meaning the enlargement of the heart is compromising heart function or a result of compromised heart/valve function. There are times where athletes may develop pathological cardiomegally particularly if muscle enhancement drugs are involved. The problem arises when the heart becomes too large and muscle-bound to the point that it cannot pump blood with adequate efficiency. I am sure you have seen some body builders or weight lifters that have become so muscle-bound that they can hardly move. They waddle. This is the same restriction the heart may experience. This frequently occurs with hypertension, heart valve leakage and blood outlet restrictions (aortic stenosis) leading to CHF. We must, ultimately, treat the hypertension, heart valve problem or outlet stenosis to correct the cardiomegally. Supportive heart nutrition is a given, CoQ10, Vitamins E and C, magnesium, calcium, carnitine and taurine. Be careful with the creatine, however, because increased heart size is not desired.

Cardiac Arrhythmia

Cardiac arrhythmia occurs when the electrical signals to, from, or within the heart get interrupted, scrambled, or altered in some way so that the normal electrical signal to the heart is disrupted or altered. This is a very common occurrence during heart attacks, after open-heart surgery, or unknown disturbances in the heart.

The heart beat that one hears and the pulse one typically feels is the result of the left ventricle contracting, pushing blood out through the aorta to the body. There is a much "quieter" pre-pulse in the heart, that of the atriums moving blood into the ventricles. Though this pre-pulse is relatively weak compared to the ventricle pulse it is nonetheless a pulse and is necessary to get blood moved. When a person experiences atrial fibrillation, the distinct, single electrical signals going to the atriums triggering them to contract becomes a blur of signals which cause the atriums to twitch or tremble. As a result the atriums cannot completely contract/ collapse, pushing blood into the ventricles. This results in excessive blood remaining in the atriums and an inadequate amount of blood making it into the ventricles. Blood gets backed up in the lungs causing fluid buildup in the lungs, and, subsequently, blood gets backed up in the body causing fluid accumulation in the extremities. This is congestive heart failure. Also since the blood is stagnating in the ventricles it tends to thicken and form clots. These clots gradually slough off and get out into the body where they plug small vessels in what is called a stroke.

Unfortunately, a stroke is often the first indication of atrial fibrillation in many people. Typically, the cardiologist will put the person on some antiarrhythmic drug like Rythmal or Lanoxin. When drugs do not work he may opt for cardioversion, which is shocking the heart back into normal rhythm. The latest treatment is ablation where the cardiologist places a probe via the veins into the heart, identifies the area where too many electrical signals are passing and "fries" the area hopefully stopping the stray signals and, thus, the fibrillation.

Another arrhythmia that people frequently experience is SVT or PSVT where the electrical signals are getting just enough disruption or scattering that the person drops a heart beat. Some people live for years dropping a heartbeat without any noticeable consequences while others develop more severe complications. Typically the cardiologist will give the patient a calcium channel blocker or beta-blocker hoping to control the arrhythmia or at least help prevent further degradation of the arrhythmia.

As is all conventional medical theory, heart disease is seen as simply a deficiency of some drug, mechanical device, surgical alteration, genetic splicing, or simply bad "luck of the draw." Despite thousands of articles in reputable, peer reviewed medical journals correlating nutrition to heart function, conventional family practitioners, internists, cardiologist pay no attention to such information, in fact they generally discredit it. See *Clinical*

Pearls at www.clinicalpearls.com.

The fact of the matter is that many arrhythmias can be prevented, treated or at least assisted with the addition of nutritional therapy. Magnesium is a key nutrient in this therapy. I have had many patients that with the addition of 400 to 800mg of magnesium chloride liquid (from Cardiovascular Research Ltd., Concord, California) per day orally stopped or significantly reduced their cardiac arrhythmias generally better than any drug therapy. Unfortunately, some people get loose stools easily with magnesium so that must be countered with fiber. I have not found that other forms of magnesium work quite as well as magnesium chloride liquid for this specific application.

A wonderful cardiothoracic surgeon, Dr. Gerald Lamole in Delaware gives all his patients nutritional supplements prior to surgery and during heart surgery he gives them several grams of magnesium directly into the blood. He found that his patients' post surgery arrhythmia rate went from the typical 35% down to 11% with that addition only. His colleagues are unmovable and simply think it an interesting observation.

Angina

Angina is heart/chest pain due to an inadequate amount of blood oxygen reaching the heart muscle. This can occur with exercise or just sitting still. It can happen solely from emotional stress. Typically, people will take nitroglycerin tablets that cause dilation of the coronary arteries so more blood can flow to the heart muscle. This same pain/discomfort can affect any muscle in the body any time that muscle does not get adequate blood flow. This is called *ischemia*. It frequently occurs in the legs of people with blood flow problems to the legs. This is called *intermittent claudication*.

Once the angina gets so bad that the patient cannot function without nitroglycerin then the conventional medical system looks at angioplasty (putting in a balloon to open the artery), stinting (putting a wire sleeve into the artery to keep it open) or bypass surgery (sewing vessels taken from other parts of the body around the blockage so blood can flow around the blockage). No nutritional therapy is considered; usually it is shunned.

There are very good studies in the conventional literature demonstrating that carnitine and Co enzyme Q10 combined are as or more effective in relieving angina as is nitroglycerine, however, without the headache side effect. I recommend 200 to 600mg CoQ10 and 500 to 1000mg carnitine for this therapy and have observed many of my patients get good relief of their angina symptoms with this therapy. See *Clinical Pearls*.

A promising conventional therapy gaining popularity for angina, not responsive to medical therapy, is EECP, Enhanced External Counterpulsation. This is a therapy where pressure cuffs are put on the legs from the ankle to the groin and these cuffs are inflated during the resting phase of the heart beat. This pushes blood into the coronary arteries and stimulates angiogenesis, blood vessel growth, of collateral vessels in the heart muscle. It is an excellent therapy with great success. Like all successful non-invasive therapies, EECP carries with it much political baggage.

Approval of this therapy was given by the FDA and paid for by Medicare with the stipulation that a cardiologist must recommend the therapy. The problem with this is that EECP is in direct competition with much more profitable invasive cardiology procedures such as angioplasty and bypass surgery. Therefore, one must find a non-invasive cardiologist who is also informed about EECP and open minded enough to recommend it. The list of such cardiologists is growing and many now have these machines in their practices.

I feel this is an excellent option for many patients with angina and coronary artery disease. I would also recommend HBOT because of its angiogenesis stimulating effect plus its hyperoxygenation benefit. Additionally, I would consider every other appropriate therapy from diet and nutrition to IV EDTA chelation.

Thousands of doctors, including myself, and patients have also found that chelation therapy with IV EDTA is very effective in relieving angina on a longer-term basis. There are some people that feel oral EDTA can do some of the same things as IV. I cannot say either way for I have not seen it in my patients or personal experience. You will have to judge that for yourself.

In my practice I have observed over 5000 patients at the Born Clinic receive IV EDTA chelation therapy. Between 90 and 95 out of 100 patients get reduction or resolution of their angina and improved vascular flow in the extremities proven by ultrasound Doppler vascular flow studies. By personal observation I have also seen non-healing diabetic foot ulcers subsequently heal, the feeling return to their feet and ankles and the foot edema markedly improve all after IV EDTA chelation therapy.

There is a significant debate in the medical community regarding IV EDTA therapy, commonly referred to simply as "chelation therapy." It is acknowledged and accepted that IV EDTA is effective at removing certain metals such as lead from the body. However, thousands of doctors have observed that most patients who receive EDTA chelation therapy show significant and noteworthy improvement in their cardiovascular conditions. This latter observation enrages the "diehard status quo" clique of the medical profession. This clique claims these beneficial observations by doctors administering IV EDTA are only anecdotal at best, certainly unscientific bordering on quackery. This clique also said the same thing about Simmelweis regarding hand washing, Still and Palmer regarding manipulation, Jenner regarding vaccinations, etc.

The most vehement antagonists of chelation therapy are the same doctors that religiously promote invasive cardiology and surgery ALL of which fail the same "scientific proofs" they claim chelation therapy fails, placebo-controlled, double-blind studies. They use comparative outcome studies, as do chelation researchers, to justify and validate therapy.

The truth is that there have been successful double-blind studies with chelation but since they were not done in a university medical center setting, they are considered invalid. The catch 22 with university based studies is that the cardiology department heads, always named to oversee the studies, are cardiologists trained in invasive cardiology and chelation therapy would severely cut into their lucrative practices; so they "sabotage" any study using chelation therapy. From my perspective as a physician treating many of these patients, it appears that their greed seems to outweigh what is in the patient's best interest.

There are several other heart conditions that exist in our society. Regardless of the fancy diagnosis given, one must remember that nutrition is the cornerstone to reestablishing normal function whether alone or in combination with conventional therapies.

We must look at the nutritional demands of the heart when planning the minimum cardiac program to follow. The heart uses a lot of energy. It cannot just take a break from the action for an hour or two every day to catch up. It must work all the time. As such, we must provide it with nutrition at greater levels than other muscles of the body. Minimally one must consider supplementing with CoQ10, Carnitine, vitamins E and C, Taurine, Potassium-Magnesium, Calcium, zinc, selenium and perhaps arginine and DMG. The minerals (calcium, magnesium, potassium) should be in the 2-AEP, oratate, aspartate, and/or arginate forms for best results.

For patients with significant congestive heart failure I have found that one to three 25cc nutritional IV's per week significantly improve heart function and patient energy. These IV's include vitamins C and B, magnesium, trace minerals and perhaps a couple other items as patient condition dictates. Dr. Alan Gaby developed this formula and we call it a "Gaby IV" for short.

Congenital Defects

There are a number of people walking around, seemingly healthy, with heart defects with which they were born. These can include defective heart valves, holes in certain parts of the heart such as in the septum between the left and right side of the heart, or constrictions of the aorta. Very serious defects are usually detected at, or shortly after birth and surgically corrected. Unfortunately, some are not detected until after the person dies suddenly of heart failure. The untimely sudden deaths of notable athletes such as Pete Maravich are examples of such cases. A majority of people with congenital heart defects gradually develop angina and/or congestive heart failure, which subsequently leads to the diagnosis of a congenital heart defect. These defects are then surgically repaired and the person recovers full cardiac function.

People with congenital heart defects can and do develop chronic heart disease on top of their congenital heart defect. Arteriosclerosis occurs whether there is a congenital defect or not. Consequently, the nutritional and dietary therapies mentioned in the previous heart sections apply equally to congenital heart defects.

Cardiovascular Summary

Conditions:
- Heart Attack (myocardial infarction)
- Congestive Heart Failure
- Cardiomyopathy
- Cardiomegaly
- Cardiac Arrhythmia

- Angina
- Congenital Defects

Treatment Considerations:
- Diet modification eliminating hydrogenated oils and IgG stressing foods, refined carbs and sugars
- Supplementation:
  - Magnesium 1000mg
  - Calcium 1000mg
  - Carnitine 500 to 1000mg
  - Taurine 2000mg
  - Potassium-Magnesium Aspartate 1 - 2 daily
  - Trace minerals as needed
  - Vitamin E 1000 to 2000 IU
  - Vitamin C 1000 to 5000mg
  - CoQ10 200 to 600mg
- Arginine, DMG, Asparagus and other antioxidants as needed
- Nutritional IV's as needed
- EDTA IV Chelation therapy as tolerated and appropriate
- Hyperbaric Oxygen Therapy ASAP after heart attack
- ERCP to stimulate collateral heart circulation
- Exercise 30 to 50 minutes, 3 to 4 times per week
- Life: reduce stress, increase enjoyment
- Daily laughter
- Stop smoking, reduce alcohol consumption
- Aspirin, medications and surgery as needed

Neurological Illnesses: Alzheimer's, Stroke, MS, ALS, Parkinson's, Dementia...

Neurological illnesses seem to be on the rise. As our population ages (the experts tell us aging is the "cause") we are seeing more of these diseases. The real alarm to me, however, is that we are seeing these illnesses in younger and younger people. If these are just "common" illnesses of the aging, why are we seeing them in young people? I do not buy the excuse that more people are just getting older.

The wonderful work and research of Dr. David Perlmutter annotated in his book *BrainRecovery.com* points out that the above named diseases have many characteristics in common. They all seem to be "free radical" induced. In other words they are caused by "little sparks" damaging the nerve tissue (picture the sparks of burning metal (free radicals) flying around when one is welding metal. If these sparks fall into the dirt (antioxidants) they are snuffed out harmlessly; if they fall into the welder's boot they burn his foot).

The most concerning free radicals in our body are caused by environmental toxins such as pesticides and heavy metals. Over the past five decades we have been dumping millions of tons of pesticides and heavy metals (lead, arsenic, cadmium, aluminum, mercury) into our environment, our food, our water and our air.

Unfortunately, brain tissue is very difficult to repair or replace. In fact it was only recently that medical scientists discovered that brain tissue could be repaired/replaced. The human body is truly remarkable. The truth of the matter is that, given the correct conditions and the appropriate nutrition, the body can repair/replace any and every tissue in the body. Keep in mind that there are no magic potions, drugs or devices that miraculously achieve this goal.

Regeneration of any tissue requires a complexity of inputs, perhaps the most important being nutrition. Brain tissue is one of the most difficult to regenerate under the best of circumstances. So it only stands to reason that if one has a chronic disease he/she will never reverse this disease by continuing the same things that have allowed the disease to manifest in the first place.

Reversal of disease will generally include the following. We must eliminate the delayed food sensitivities identified via the ImmunoLabs (I realize there are many labs offering this test. This is the lab whose results I find correlate to patient results. I have no financial connection to them.) IgG foods test, chelate out the heavy metals and improve the blood circulation, customize the nutritional supplementation program, maximize oxygen concentrations without creating oxygen toxicity and finally apply energetic stimuli which key the brain cells to regenerate.

For many people all we can feasibly do is arrest the disease to prevent further degeneration. For other people we can arrest the disease progression and make minor to major improvement in their functions. For a few patients we can get regeneration. Part of the answer lies with the patient, what changes this person makes in all areas of their life and diet and part of it lies with God and the patient's relationship with God. A person's attitude about life significantly influences the program outcome. Miracles happen every day.

The work done by Dr. Hans A. Nieper in Hannover, Germany on neurological illnesses especially multiple sclerosis is noteworthy. I first learned of Dr. Nieper in 1986 through his book *Revolution In Medicine, Technology and Society* and further via a visit to Germany in 1987. Dr. Nieper's orthomolecular (a term coined by Linus Pauling) approach to disease led him to the discovery that the 2-aminoethylphosphates (calcium, magnesium, potassium 2-AEP) administered both orally and IV are very effective in treating MS. Dr. Nieper treated over 3100 MS patients with a greater than 80% positive response. I feel this therapy should be incorporated in any MS treatment program. It probably has validity in all neurological illness programs.

Regarding Parkinson's disease in my practice while at the Born Clinic in Grand Rapids, Michigan we added the "Cochran protocol" after Dr. Tim Cochran of the Cochran Foundation in California. The reason for this addition was that after two years of giving IV glutathione and oral Brain Sustain (a great supplement powder) we observed some patients' progress plateauing with the return of symptoms (tremors, stiffness, memory lapse…). These patients had a couple seemingly good years on this therapy, but, like what happens in drug therapy, the benefits began to fade. It is noteworthy to mention that **unlike** what happens with drug therapy, these patients had no adverse side effects from the nutritional therapy. This did not occur with all the patients we were treating this way. Several patients have continued on the original therapy and continue to do well living fairly normal lives for people in their age groups.

Cochran Protocol

The Cochran protocol requires a complete blood test, history and symptoms. Dr. Cochran takes this information and formulates a customized therapy program that includes a daily powder and additional medicinal supplements. Follow up blood tests and physical exams are obtained and the program adjusted accordingly.

Dr. Cochran explained his program philosophy as follows: "The brain uses a lot of glutathione but it is not the only amino acid/ antioxidant needed for the brain and liver. As people age their blood levels of glutathione and other nutrients drops. When we elevate the level of glutathione in the blood, initially it will greatly help the brain function and reduce tremors and stiffness in Parkinson's patients. However, over time the liver sees this new level of glutathione as too high compared to the other hormones, amino acids, antioxidants and proceeds to break it down and eliminate it. Essentially, we have a seventy year old (if the patient is seventy) liver seeing a level of glutathione consistent with a twenty-five year old."

"What we must do is bring everything up to the level of a twenty-five year old so the liver will think it is also twenty-five years old relative to the levels of nutrients in the blood. This requires a customized nutrition mix for each patient, which is further altered according to patient response." This is the theory. The proof is seen in the results. We have found that many patients have responded wonderfully, exactly as anticipated. The problem with this program is that it is too complex and too expensive for long term patient compliance. Many patients also have significant digestive upset with the supplements used. Alternatively, we have found that a program designed by Dr. Marty Hinz of Duluth, Minnesota using a custom set of amino acid mixes is a better option. This program is less costly and follows patient progress with afternoon urine tests to adjust supplements and dosages. Most patients can tolerate the supplements and long term compliance is much easier especially as the Parkinson's symptoms lessen and in many cases disappear. It is not a cure for the disease, but it does seem to decrease the symptoms, including the tremors, as long as the amino acids are taken regularly. This is an excellent program for all neurological illnesses including chronic depression, anxiety, panic attack, Parkinson's as well as weight loss. Regardless of what option works best for the patient, we see these patients better off than if they follow only the typical party line of drug therapy.

All the drugs have side effects. Some patients tolerate them well while others do not. Unfortunately Sinemet, the most commonly prescribed drug for Parkinson's, generally only works for about five years and it accelerates the disease process meaning that the person will be worse off after five years of taking the drug than if they took nothing for that same five years. The entire goal behind drug therapy is to suppress symptoms. In the case of Parkinson's this means suppressing the tremor and the stiffness. That is fine but does not address the reason for the tremor and stiffness, which is free radical damage to the part of the brain that regulates nerve connection to the muscles, the substantia nigra, locus ceruleus and brainstem dopaminergic cells. Now if this damage is in the myelin then the illness is called multiple sclerosis. If it is in other areas of the brain it causes dementia, ALS or some other malady.

The key issue to note in these illnesses is that they are all caused by free radical damage to the nerve tissue. This occurs because the body's and specifically the brain's antioxidant protective system is either inadequate or simply overwhelmed. When we consider the amount of toxicity in our environment and then the high free radical/low antioxidant diet of most Americans it is simply a logical consequence to have the growing incidence of neurological illness in this country. Since this book is intended for the patient, the bottom line is what am I going to do to help prevent the illness and what am I going to do to treat it.

We need to reduce the exposure to heavy metals meaning aluminum, cadmium, lead, mercury, arsenic, nickel, and antimony by getting them out of our environment and by eating cleaner foods not grown with high acid fertilizer inputs. Highly acid fertilizers such as sulfuric and nitric acid used commonly in conventional agriculture make these heavy metals more soluble and easily transported into the plant.

Further, we must stop using hydrogenated oils such as margarine and heated vegetable oils because these contain trans fatty acids, which are foreign fats in our body. Any "part" of our body that requires fats or fatty acids as a component (every cell membrane) will be defective when built with a trans fatty acid. Next, we need to eat foods that are high in antioxidants and nutrient density, which means we need to change the way farmers grow crops so that the quality of the food needed will be available to consumers. This is why I teach seminars in soil and crop nutrition.

Gulf War Syndrome

The last topic I wish to mention in this section is *Gulf War Syndrome*. Like most post war ailments with which U.S. military personnel have been struck, Gulf War Syndrome is most often said to have no conclusive links to experience or exposure during the Gulf War. It took over twenty-five years before the DOD admitted that Viet Nam War veterans exposed to Agent Orange had a 50% risk of developing diabetes among other illnesses.

Recent work by doctors at the University of Texas, showing that Gulf War Syndrome's ALS-like symptoms are linked to the chemical cocktails to which these veterans were exposed, is very indicting. (*Archives of Neurology*, 9/2000) According to Alison Johnson, author of *Gulf War Syndrome: Legacy of a Perfect War*, Gulf War vets have twice the incidence of ALS documented by the DOD. Gulf War Syndrome is an illness suffered by a variety of people with common experiences, exposure to chemicals. One such sufferer, Captain Julie Dyckman, USN Retired, was a hospital commander in the Gulf and reported being dowsed with pink mist after two SCUD missile attacks. Shortly after she began experiencing skin lesions, fatigue, blood pressure changes and multiple chemical sensitivity. She was eventually diagnosed and medically disabled with autonomic nervous system damage. (Alison Johnson Speech, Gulf War Syndrome, C-SPAN, 6/3/2002)

The point here is that these vets are suffering from toxic chemical exposure that has injured their nervous systems and overwhelmed their body's capacity to detoxify. They, like their Viet Nam counterparts, need comprehensive medical care to include the nutritional programs previously mentioned, IV nutritional supplementation, saunas, detox baths, time, and patience. Some may also need to be treated for mycobacteria infections, which take months to control.

Unfortunately, the Afghan and Iraq wars bring the next wave of ill vets and the latest small pox vaccination program by the military, since stopped by the FDA because of too many adverse reactions, is just another assault on their already stressed bodies. The U.S. Supreme Court recently ruled that the military cannot force military personnel to receive the anthrax vaccination because it remains an experimental program. My concern regarding the anthrax vaccine is that each shot of the six-shot series plus annual boosters contains 0.89 mg of aluminum injected directly into the bloodstream. Aluminum is known to be toxic to nerve tissue and immune cells and has been associated along with mercury in Parkinson's. Parkinsonian symptoms are what many Gulf War vets exhibit. I don't believe it is worth the risk and strongly suggest that anyone vaccinated with aluminum should receive EDTA chelation to remove the aluminum.

Another serious consequence of the wars in the Balkans and the Middle East is the thousands of tons of DU (deactivated uranium) spread all over from the bunker busting bombs. This radioactivity can contribute significantly to all types of illnesses and is a significant stressor on top of all the other factors in these regions for ill health of both civilians and military personnel.

Neurological Illnesses Summary

Issues:
- Free Radicals – metals, chemicals, toxins
- Heavy Metals – lead, arsenic, cadmium, aluminum, mercury, nickel, antimony, uranium
- Environmental, Agricultural or Military Chemicals
- Diet and Nutrition including hydrogenated oils
- Electromagnetic and Geopathic Energies

Treatment Considerations:
- Antioxidants – vitamins B's, C, D, E, Beta carotene,
- Trace minerals, CoQ10, etc.
- Chelation to remove heavy metal
- ImmunoLabs IgG foods testing
- Diet modification to include removal of IgG stressful foods
- Medical foods to feed the liver, digestive system, and nervous system
- Nutritional IV's to achieve therapeutic level of nutrients
- Additional oral nutritional supplementation as needed
- Detoxifying baths with vinegar, Epsom salts, soda or clay

- Saunas to sweat out chemicals and toxins
- Pure water: minimum of 3 to 4 quarts/liters/day
- Consider HBOT to assist healing, increase oxygenation
- Stop diet drinks due to neurotoxicity/sugar craving
- Eliminate all hydrogenated oils
- Replace corn/canola with olive or butter for cooking
- Daily ingest beneficial oils – flax, borage, fish, etc.
- 15 to 30 minutes of sunshine or full spectrum light daily
- Exercise 30 to 50 minutes 3 to 5 times per week

Neuromusculoskeletal Medicine

The Rule of the Artery is Supreme
~ A.T. Still, M.D., Founder of Osteopathic Medicine

Neuromusculoskeletal medicine is the restoration of appropriate motion and function of the body. This may be purely via the touch, through soft tissue balancing or synchronization as my good friend Dr. Ted Baroody describes it, through fluid drainage and flow, through bony tissue realignment and remodeling, through electromagnetic therapies or a combination of all these therapies. Regardless of the modality, restoration of appropriate neurovascular and neuromusculoskeletal function in the restricted, painful or injured body area in question is the goal.

Patient personality, body type, injury or malady character, and practitioner characteristics/skill personality all play into which modality or modalities will be most successful.

No technique is necessarily appropriate for every patient nor will every patient respond to every technique. Thank God for individuality. At the same time we must consider the whole person in order to really get healing over just suppression of symptoms. This means we must consider diet, nutrition, environment, detoxification, toxic metals, genetics and psychosocial issues in their relation and interaction to the physical body, body mechanics, pain, injury, and healing. Further, every modality employed must have definite indication for its use and be applied at the proper time in the healing sequence.

For example, the ice modality would be appropriately used and timed at injury occurrence to stop bleeding but would not be appropriate when healing of the same injury is desired. In other words, ice during the healing process causes ischemia, weakened and increased scarring. Healing requires blood circulation and controlled inflammation. The same goes for anti-inflammatory drugs. Another example is using aloe vera topically on puncture wounds to accelerate healing. Aloe is an excellent product for speeding healing of open wounds and burns but its application to puncture wounds could lead to closure of the puncture wound prematurely and consequent abscess formation and/or cellulitis. Finally another example would be timing mobilization of tissue after injury is ideally 10 days post injury. Too soon and the healing is disrupted. Too late and the scar will be weak and enlarged.

It is true that when two or more persons come together, much more can be accomplished than any of the individuals alone. It is exciting to employ multidisciplinary approaches to therapy where chiropractors, orthodontists, oral surgeons, medical practitioners, biochemists and pharmacists combine their skills in a joint effort to solve otherwise unsolvable medical cases.

As a result we have helped some people who after years of suffering, uncountable visits to specialists, tests upon tests, drugs upon drugs, are now either completely well or well on their way to wellness. We have treated everything from long term RSD and TMJ problems to chronic pain syndromes after injury/surgery; unexplainable abdominal pains to auto and athletic injuries.

Keep in mind that structure and function go hand in hand. The network of our nervous system is literally networked throughout our body to every tissue, organ and structure. That nervous system originates in the brain and disperses from the brain and through the spinal column. Running along with all the nerves are the vein and artery, combined called the vascular bundle. Anytime there is any impingement or stress upon the vascular bundle it is felt both above and below the stress point to whatever degree the stress imposes. As a result manipulation can be a key therapy in relieving these stress points and the consequent results of the stressors. Technique is unimportant because a technique that works for one person may not for another. The consequent relief of stress is the goal. Complete uninhibited functioning of the body is the ideal. The following are several case histories from patients who came to me for help. Some were not obvious manual medicine candidates upon first thought.

Case Histories

Case #1 - A young man in his 30's came to see me with a complaint of ankle pain lasting for several months. He had been to several doctors, had x-rays and MRI all negative, given pain pills and told nothing was wrong. I listened to his story, figured that he must have some misalignment in the foot/ankle and proceeded to evaluate his ankle. My hunch was correct. I found that his tibial-talo joint was jammed together inhibiting proper motion of the joint to the point of causing significant pain and a noticeable limp. I adjusted his tibial-talo joint with a quick decompression move and his pain instantly disappeared never to return again. He was elated and walked out of my office free of pain and without a limp.

Case #2 - A very pleasant lady in her 30's came to me with a complaint of ankle pain and significant limp for over 2 weeks. She had been to her family doctor, had x-rays which were negative, saw an orthopedic surgeon who found nothing wrong and was about to the end of her rope dealing with the pain and limp. She heard about the Born Clinic and decided to give us a try as a last resort. She had no recent trauma to the foot or ankle and had never had a problem with the ankle. She was otherwise in reasonable health.

After listening to her for about 45 minutes taking her history I thought to myself that I had little idea what was wrong with her either. For some reason in the last 5 minutes of our discussion of her history she mentioned that she had a root canal the day the ankle pain started. The root canal was in a tooth on her right and the ankle pain was in her left ankle. I remembered my good friend Dr. George Schuchard III, a wonderful holistic dentist from Beverly Hills, teaching me about the tooth-body reflexes/correlations while I was in medical school.

The problem was that there was supposed to be direct correlation between right teeth and right side of the body and left teeth and left side of the body. This lady did not have that correlation. I called another friend, Dr. Chris Hussar, a physician and dentist who was one of my clinical professors in medical school. He suggested that I inject the gum over the root canal and see what happens to the ankle pain. He said that there is occasionally a cross over effect between the teeth and the body. If the pain disappeared in a few seconds then the root canal was the culprit and he expected the pain would return once the anesthetic wore off.

I did the dental injection with local anesthetic and, sure enough, the ankle pain disappeared within a few seconds. I was amazed and she was too. More astonishing was the fact that the pain never returned after the anesthetic wore off. She walked out of my office pain free, delighted and limp free. Sometimes it is better to be lucky than good.

The answer to the long-term correction of this particular problem lies with a therapy called *neural* therapy. Neural therapy was popularized by the Germans and entails injecting a local anesthetic into nerve ganglions (picture a train station where many tracks come in from and exit to many directions) or specific nerves associated with an acute or chronic irritation or due to over stimulation of the nerves. This therapy gives the nerve network a brief rest allowing it to return to normal functioning after the anesthesia wears off.

Injecting a local anesthetic into a triggering area like the gum line around a tooth relaxes the autonomic nervous system. Cranial nerves V and VII stream through the jaw and were apparently irritated in this lady by the root canal. This irritation apparently triggered a referral irritation of pain fibers in the brain associated with the ankle. Relaxing the irritated nerves in the jaw allowed the nervous system to reset and the pain, subsequently, stopped. Every thing is connected to everything so it seems.

Case #3 - One day a twenty year old female with her parents and stepfather came to my office to see me regarding her chronic abdominal pain lasting for about three years. This wonderful young lady was currently a junior in college but was contemplating quitting because the abdominal pain was getting so unbearable. When the abdominal pain began, her mother, as one would expect, took her to their family doctor. He put her on birth control pills thinking (as is commonly thought in conventional medicine) that the pain was due to menstrual problems. This did not help so he referred her to a gynecologist who changed the birth control pills. She still had no relief of the pain. He consequently decided that her problem warranted invasive measures so he did exploratory laparoscopic surgery, found minor scar tissue but no endometriosis (becoming more common with young women these days due, in my experience, to toxicity) or other abnormality. He then decided to experiment with injections called *cervical blocks* to numb the nerves around the uterus/cervix *hoping* these would stop her pain.

The first injections made her abdominal pain worse, the second set gave insignificant temporary reduction in pain and the third set did nothing. Since the second set of injections altered the pattern of pain the gynecologist decided that further surgery (the surgeons motto: a chance to cut is chance to cure) was warranted. (he perhaps needed the practice, had a boat payment, or had too big an ego to say he could not help). He performed what is termed a sympathectomy, cutting the nerves to the uterus/cervix. There are many nerves in this area. Not only did the surgeon cut the nerves to the uterus/cervix, he also cut the nerves to the bladder and the vagina.

Keep in mind ladies and gentlemen that at this juncture in time and treatment, this patient is an eighteen or nineteen year old female who is extremely bright, attractive, and very athletic. As a result of the treatment for abdominal pain this young woman *now has no feeling in her vagina, no bladder control* AND STILL HAS ABDOMINAL PAIN!!! She can no longer run and play field hockey, must now go to the bathroom on a set schedule by the clock so as not to wet herself. Her parents subsequently took her to Mayo Clinic in Rochester, Minnesota. After extensive evaluation they concluded she had irritable bowel and had no clue why she had the abdominal pain and could do nothing for her severed pelvic nerves.

Her parents searched everywhere they knew for answers, praying for any possible help for their daughter. The specialists had no clues, no answers, no further treatments. They had done more than enough already.

It was at this point that they came to see me. When I asked them why they came to see me they said that they had heard I was the miracle worker. Wow!!! I acknowledge that miracles happen everyday. God however has full credit for all of them. I simply pray that He may use me as a channel for His blessings.

This young lady presented some very important principles of health and healing. First, everything is connected to everything. Second, pain in a given area does not necessarily mean there is disease in that area. This is particularly true in the case of young women who periodically present with abdominal pain. The typical medical response is to drug them first with birth control pills. Once that trial is exhausted then do exploratory surgery to look for something, anything, and if nothing is found, create something if possible. If the initial pain symptom remains then put her on antidepressants because she must be somatosizing. She must be depressed and causing her own pain. It must be "her" fault. And society thinks that the abuse of women in medicine is past tense. Even if the woman is having pain because of endometriosis or ovarian cysts, it does not mean she has a deficiency of surgery and synthetic hormonal therapy. I understand that many women are very conventionally minded and are not willing to change their diet and lifestyle necessary to heal their body. They prefer the suppression options of conventional medicine, which is their free choice to do so. However, there are also many women that are willing to do whatever necessary to actually correct their problem.

Back to our patient at hand. I knew from all the testing and experimentation performed on this lady what she did **not** have and what was **not** wrong. I knew she did not have any tumor or terrible disease. I knew she did not have a need for surgery. The diagnosis from Mayo Clinic of irritable bowel was helpful regarding her overall state of health and it indicated her body's propensity for developing inflammation. I knew by this that diet was an issue regarding her general health. I needed to address the various aspects of inflammation so she could heal. Since all the previous studies did not find anything organically wrong with her to cause the pain I knew I had to look elsewhere for answers and proceeded with a treatment plan to address these issues.

I evaluated her for delayed food sensitivities, heavy metals, liver detoxification effectiveness, altered her diet accordingly, put her on specific supplements, and treated her with acupuncture and manipulation. The nutritional and dietary program was both to correct developing/impending chronic problems and provide the foundation for her body to heal. I (at that point in my limited knowledge) did not know exactly what was causing her abdominal pain, physically. I am better able to solve that issue today. I did know however, that there was certainly a disruption in her body's electromagnetic system. There was pain, cut nerves, and bowel problems.

It took several months of therapy to get her pain and bowel problems resolved. She graduated from college and actually began getting minor sensations/control back in her pelvic area. She was able to start jogging again and is now able to live a fairly normal life as long as she follows her diet and takes her supplements. Will she ever get all feeling and control back? What will happen when she gets pregnant? Miracles do happen everyday. I think she will be just fine. If she has problems, we can help her at that point in time. What was the cause of her abdominal pain? I feel it was directly due to referral patterns from her lumbar spine being misaligned plus a disruption in function of her acupuncture meridians associated with liver, large intestine, and female organs. Add to those irritations the inflammation induced by her diet and the stresses of graduating from high school at age sixteen and about to enter college, the normal stresses of being a teenager and finally, add to all these stressors, an early childhood trauma.

Case #4 - A gentleman in his fifties came to me with complaint of shoulder pain that he had for years. He remembered injuring it playing football. It did not prevent him from his job but he was not able to throw a ball. He was frustrated by the nagging problem. He had been evaluated by his family doctor and an orthopedic doctor, put on anti-inflammatory drugs and told he just had arthritis and would have to live with it. That is a common response from doctors; you will have to live with it.

He actually did not come in to our office with the intention of getting me to look at his shoulder. He came in with his wife for a structural problem she had which we solved. My good friend Dr. Baroody was in the office with me that day and he assisted me in the evaluation. We found that this man had misalignment of the various bones forming the shoulder joint, particularly an anterior-inferior humerus. After adjustment he claimed that his shoulder was over ninety percent better. He came back one other time for me to adjust his shoulder and proclaimed it was completely well. He had no more pain and had full range of motion. He was very happy.

Headaches

Case #5 - I will address headaches in general because they are so frequent and I myself have experienced this problem. The amount of aspirin, acetaminophen (Tylenol), ibuprofen (Motrin) and other pain drugs consumed annually is mind-boggling. And certainly there are perhaps times when one must take one of these to relieve a headache to complete a task and then work on the cause of the headache.

There are many possible causes of headaches. I have found from the teaching of my good friend Dr. Baroody that many headaches can be relieved within just a few seconds with an intraoral manipulation technique. I muscle test key points in the roof of the mouth. Any point that tests weak I apply pressure to that point for a few seconds feeling the resistance change in the cranial bones under my finger. Nine out of ten times I find that the headache disappears, occasionally only for a short while but most often long term.

I have used this technique many times in my civilian practice and as a flight surgeon in the Air Force to relieve headaches of the troops under my care. I always check structural issues when people complain of headaches. As with myself the headaches can be caused by TMJ misalignment and/or occipital-atlantal compression (base of the back of the head is jammed down on the first vertebra best corrected by the Krane Condylar Lift technique), misalignments of the cervical, thoracic or lumbosacral vertebrae, muscle tension, or altered cerebral spinal fluid dynamics corrected by cranial-sacral therapy.

Headaches are also often caused by constipation and retained body toxicity, immediate and delayed food sensitivities, drug side effects, drug withdrawals, dehydration (frequently part of the alcohol hangover effect), low blood sugar, eye or vision problems and post spinal tap. Certainly headaches can be caused by trauma, some blow to the head, and aneurysm or tumor. These latter three causes are the first causes that must be ruled out with any patient that seeks treatment. Once those are ruled out we can proceed to get at the cause and treatment of the headache.

There are times when either we do not know the cause (tumor and aneurysm have been ruled out) or we cannot find a physical cause. We must consider the energetic possibilities, thus, we use acupuncture. At the Born Clinic we have found acupuncture to be extremely effective for treating both chronic headaches and raging migraines. Nine of ten migraines will relieve a minimum of 50% on the first treatment, over half the headaches by 90%, and 100% by the third treatment. Sometimes with chronic headaches it takes longer than three treatments.

One of our receptionists at the Born Clinic was in her second trimester of pregnancy and still having daily morning sickness and headaches all day long, everyday. One day was particularly bad for her and I convinced her to have an acupuncture treatment. She was initially very skeptical having never before received an acupuncture treatment. She felt so ill this day that she required little convincing to have the treatment. The numerous acupuncture needles were left in place for about 2 hours primarily around the ear. Not only did her headache completely disappear by the end of the treatment never to return, so did her morning sickness disappear never to occur again during the pregnancy.

Headaches are a very common problem in our society. Certainly one can take aspirin, Tylenol, naproxen, or some other headache medication and not think about it again until the next headache.

That works for many people. The problem arises when these headaches become chronic and debilitating causing people to lose sleep, lose work and have their life adversely disrupted as a result of the headache. In these cases one must realize that the headaches are not due to a deficiency of some drug. Find the cause, correct it and the headaches will cease. Ice may also be appropriate in rare cases of acute occipital migraine headaches until one gets to the appropriate physician who will seek out, identify and correct the underlying cause of the migraine headache so that it does not recur.

Case #6 - A delightful lady in her sixties came to see me with a complaint of bilateral foot pain with which she had suffered for months. The bottoms of both feet hurt her everyday, all day long to the point that she was unable to perform her duties as the township treasurer, a position she enjoyed immensely. She had been to her family doctor and subsequently to a podiatrist. Neither doctor offered her any help for this problem. They could find nothing wrong either by examination or by x-ray films. I suspected a chronic misalignment of the bones in her feet. I called my friend Dr. Emmerson for an immediate consult on his technique for evaluation. She was found to have bilateral cuboid and navicular misalignments (foot bones). I adjusted these bones twice that week with immediate pain relief after each adjustment and weekly for a couple months. I also had her purchase custom shoe inserts and she became completely pain free and stable after three months of therapy.

Many people suffer foot pain. Inevitably there is a problem with the alignment of the foot bones. With many people as they age or if they have had an injury to the foot, the ligaments of the foot are stretched or torn allowing the structure of the foot to break down. Their feet become flatter and flatter. Frequently they develop heel spurs, large bunions, tender calluses and neuromas. I have found through practice and seminars that most of these foot problems can be corrected without surgery. Restoring bone alignment is an important part of the treatment as is obtaining custom orthotics (shoe inserts) and prolotherapy to reconstruct the ligaments that hold the foot together. I have found that "CalMatrix" from Metametrics taken twice daily helps many people with heel spurs. This latter note impresses the point that even with foot problems, nutrition is a component of the corrective treatment. Some patients' foot problems actually reside in their ankle, leg, knee, hip, back or elsewhere in their musculoskeletal system and not in the foot. This must be traced out and corrected. When it is corrected the foot pain ends.

Case #7 - A very stout man in his forties came to me with a complaint of shoulder pain and difficulty with range of motion after falling off a pile of materials in a warehouse. His job required that he do heavy physical labor, which now he was unable to do. This was a simple, stoic, hard-working man of few words. As with many men I had to get the real story from his wife both initially and after treatment. The injury had occurred several weeks before coming into my office. He had initially seen his family doctor who ordered x-rays which showed no fracture or dislocation. He was subsequently given the typical injury protocol of anti-inflammatory and pain medication plus ice without relief. This was a man who did not complain unless he was in severe discomfort and only came to see me after great effort on the part of his wife.

Upon exam, I found this man to have a significant misalignment of his clavical medically, his acromial-clavicular joint, his humerus bone moved anterior-inferiorly plus misalignment of his cervical and thoracic spines. He had never had manipulation and was very vocal with expletives when I adjusted him. He was a little frightened to say the least. After the first treatment he was over 80% better and by the third treatment in as many weeks he was 100% and working daily without discomfort or restriction. After each treatment I injected his shoulder ligaments with a sclerotherapy/prolotherapy solution to strengthen his ligaments. Additionally, he had some digestive problems, which we addressed with diet modification after delayed food sensitivity testing and digestive enzymes with each meal. His wife was elated and he was stoically appreciative.

I could go on and on with cases where manual medicine was the key modality in helping the patient. Not a day goes by that I do not adjust several people. Even during my time as an active duty flight surgeon in the Air Force for operation "Enduring Freedom" I became the doc of choice because I would look for causes to people's ailments rather than just give them a drug. I kept many pilots flying with simple adjustments for their significant aches and pains when they otherwise could have been taken off flying status. It was very important to flying crews to have alternatives to drugs because the Air Force is quite strict about what flyers may and may not take while on flying status. Even when I moved to different bases, the word would soon get around and people from other units came to me for manipulation.

It is sad that there are so few doctors that do manipulation anywhere but particularly in the military. I had to go outside the military and pay out of my own pocket to get my treatments. There are very few practitioners whom I will allow to adjust me. Most are not quick enough or don't have enough finesse or just don't have the appropriate techniques for my body personality. If I were not persistent in my quest for relief of my own structural problems, I would probably do as many people do, assume that manual medicine is of little value. Even more frustrating is that there are very few practitioners that know how to and will do extremity manipulation. Very few chiropractors know how and few state licenses will allow them to manipulate extremities. Very few DO/MD's do extremity manipulation. So if your problem resides in an extremity, it is difficult to find a doctor that can correct it.

Manual medicine is a wonderful therapy and a very integral part of any complete/holistic medical practice. Billions of dollars are unnecessarily spent every year on pain management drugs when manipulation employed appropriately would solve the problem naturally. Anyone interested in learning about manipulation either as a patient receiving manipulation or as a doctor seeking to further his/her skills, I recommend that you read Dr. Ted Baroody's wonderfully illustrated book *Holographic Health Book #1*.

Injury Medicine

This brings us to a very common and important topic regarding our musculoskeletal system: injuries. Injuries are daily occurrences in most families. Whether the injurious activity is as benign as peculiarly stepping off a curb, hurriedly picking up a heavy box, rearranging furniture in the house, playing that once a year pickup basketball game or whether it is the normal daily lives of children and the consequent injuries they produce, injuries seem inevitable, even expected for some.

I have personally experienced and observed as a doctor that most injuries are inadequately and even inappropriately treated. I say this after seeing the short-term and most importantly the long-term consequences of these injuries. Inevitably injuries that occur in childhood sporting events become, at best, arthritic torments as the person ages and often, years later, joint replacement surgeries.

The majority of amateur and professional athletic/work injuries become chronic problems that restrict, to some degree, the activity of the patient. This should not be the case. The human body has the capacity, the design to repair itself fully from these injuries if just given the chance. One would think, actually expect, that with all the publicity and popularity given to *sports medicine* today, injury treatment and rehabilitation would produce better results. So why doesn't it especially with all these "sports medicine" specialists and high tech orthopedic surgeons practicing? The answer, in my opinion, is because these people do not apply common sense and holistic thought to treating injuries. *Sports medicine* has become a "gimmick" in or catch phrase in the care of injured patients. The thousands of certified amateurs obscure the few true sports medicine professionals.

This point can be seen if one considers a young person who has injured their ankle dancing. This young person may have a strain or even a partial ligament tear. The standard treatment protocol would call for ice, nonsteroidal anti-inflammatory drugs (NSAIDS), and rest. If this protocol did not resolve the pain and weakness, a shot of steroid and continued icing with any swelling would be recommended.

The problem is that at this stage, after twenty-four to seventy-two hours from the injury, the ice will only reduce circulation, thus, inducing ischemia, which reduces healing and precipitates more chronic pain. The steroid injection may make the ankle feel better, short term, but it weakens the connective tissue resulting in greater ankle instability. I had a patient come to me with significant ankle swelling, pain, and instability. When he originally sprained his ankle, the attending doctor prescribed oral steroids to reduce the swelling and pain rather than elevate, immobilize and rest the ankle. This patient subsequently went back to work and thoroughly trashed the ankle legitimately requiring surgery to reattach the tendons and ligaments in his ankle.

Back to our original thought, as the patient continues to complain an orthopedic surgeon is usually consulted, frequently resulting in surgery to "correct" the instability. Usually it does not, scar tissue forms and the situation actually worsens. Sooner or later "arthritis" sets in and the patient who now may be in their twenties, thirties or forties is looking at possible fusion of the ankle/foot bones. Sometimes it doesn't take years for this process to play out. The surgery may occur within a couple years of the injury.

Further, just as the original injury is not corrected, nor is the reason the dancer was susceptible to this ankle injury. Consequently, pain and suffering progress from the ankle to include the lower leg, knee, and low back, perhaps even the upper back, shoulders, jaw and neck. Now the person develops chronic arthritis in multiple areas and "needs" to take anti-inflammatory and pain medications daily just to function. People think this is normal! It is commonplace but not normal.

The doctor must ask him/herself why is there pain. The answer lies with tissue or structure damage, neurovascular trauma and structural misalignment. All three of these areas must be addressed for complete healing to occur. Pain presents because of direct tissue injury, pressure in the injured area from swelling, misalignment of the joint triggering pain fibers, and ischemia of the tissue. Ischemia is frequently a post-inflammation phenomena experienced after anti-inflammatory medications or steroids have suppressed inflammation but nothing has been done to correct circulatory distress. Ice, steroids, and NSAIDS actually suppress the healing process, which includes the growth of new blood vessels at the site of injury. Consequently, scar tissue forms rather than healed normal tissue.

The appropriate treatment would be to apply ice only twelve to twenty-four hours, in rare cases up to seventy-two hours following the initial injury for the purpose of reducing the bleeding and pain control. Once the bleeding is stopped ice is contraindicated for healing. The standard practice of most doctors, trainers and physical therapists is to recommend icing after each manipulation treatment, after each athletic event, and anytime there is pain and/or swelling. Common sense goes a long way here contrary to the recommendations of orthopedists, sports medicine specialists, physical therapists, chiropractors, and athletic trainers. **Ice reduces circulation**. Healing tissue requires good circulation of blood and lymph. Anything that impinges this circulation arrests healing. Healing is our goal, quickly and completely.

One way of reducing edema and swelling in an injury is via the use of an Acuscope, a special instrument that helps stimulate increases in the tissue ATP (energy) level, tissue nutrient uptake, and angiogenesis. Consequently, blood and lymph circulation improves. Another is with hyperbaric oxygen treatment. A possible alternative way to reduce the swelling in injuries is with a vacuum boot on the feet regardless of the location of the injury. This is a reflexology technique that induces circulation.

Blood and lymph carry food to the tissue and waste products away. Therefore, I will recommend therapeutic doses of antioxidants and building nutrients such as glucosamine sulfate and MSM, vitamins and minerals, both oral and IV. I will then evaluate and isolate the functional patterns of the body correlated to the injury and the body's susceptibility to the injury followed by specific structural and soft tissue manipulation and mobilization. Ideally I would get the patient into a hyperbaric chamber for five to ten or more treatments to increase the oxygen concentration throughout the body and to stimulate angiogenesis (new blood vessel growth) at the site of injury.

Beginning ten days after HBOT, most patients will benefit from prolotherapy injections into the ligaments around the injured joint because most injuries tear, weaken or stretch the ligaments. Ligaments are the primary stabilizers of all joints and their integrity is critical to restabilization of the joint in question and elimination of pain. Finally, I will modify the diet if necessary to reduce inflammatory triggers and maximize nutritional inputs. Healing occurs rapidly, even regeneration of cartilage, ligaments, nerves.

A more comprehensive dissertation of this protocol is available from its author, Dr. Gary Emmerson in Santa Ana, California, whom I will mention again later. My point is simply that the treatment must match the patient, the illness/injury, and the goal of the patient and doctor. If mere cover-up of symptoms is desired then the conventional therapy is the treatment of choice. If complete correction of the problem is desired, then the "Emmerson" protocol is mandatory.

Injuries are an issue that most every family and most every person experiences sometime in their life. It is an issue, because of the complexity and the importance, warranting its own discussion section. My personal experience with injuries is that doctors, trainers, and physical therapists know little about the healing process. Yes, they know what they have been taught but that does not mean what they are taught is the best treatment for the patient.

In order for the body to heal there must first be blood flow to the injured area to both take away the waste products of the injury and also to deliver the nutrition/building blocks necessary for healing to occur.

Everything regarding injuries and healing are approached very mechanically and allopathically just like every other ailment conventional medicine addresses. It matters little whether one is talking about the average family doc or the sophisticated orthopedic surgeons and trainers treating the Olympic and professional sporting teams. Rarely is cause and effect addressed. Symptoms are suppressed with steroids, anti-inflammatory drugs, pain medications, ice, surgery (yes, surgery to suppress symptoms), psychology, taunting, intimidation, manipulation (yes, suppressive manipulation not corrective) or just avoidance.

Sometime the decision is made to put the replacement player in and forget about the injured one. I realize that I have probably ruffled some feathers here. The bottom line regarding injuries is the same as with chronic and "terminal" diseases; there is much more money in treating the ailments than curing them.

The best physician I have seen in this specialty is Dr. Gary Emmerson. He has a remarkable background in computers, physics, metal fabrication, hematology, electron microscopy and human health. I first met Dr. Emmerson at a seminar in 1996. I observed him working on an Olympic Greco wrestler, ranked fourth in the world, who two days earlier had suffered a grade III shoulder separation. It was two weeks before the Olympic trials. His orthopedic surgeon advised him emphatically that he needed surgery to correct this injury and he would need months to rehabilitate. Wrestling in the Olympic trial was out of the question. He got a second opinion from Dr. Emmerson.

Dr. Emmerson stopped the icing and worked on this young man daily for two weeks and emphatically warned this young man against any steroid injections or anti-inflammatory drugs. He complied and wrestled in the trials taking fourth place. Dr. Emmerson worked on him again daily for another two weeks and he wrestled in the final Olympic trials taking a second. He returned to his orthopedic surgeon for a follow up evaluation and was told that he no longer needed surgery; his shoulder was fine.

At this seminar I asked Dr. Emmerson for an evaluation on my own shoulder, which I originally separated as a junior in high school playing football. It never healed appropriately, continuing to bother me to this day. He found that I had a significant latissimus muscle tear as well as a latissimus impingement syndrome among other things. I about rocketed off the table in pain when he put his finger into the defect in the latissimus muscle in my armpit. I had never heard of such a thing and neither had the orthopedic surgeons I had been taken to see originally. They had simply given me a steroid shot into the joint area and said it would heal on its own. It did not. Further evaluation revealed a chronic supraspinous tendonitis which causes loading of my cervical spine, consequent hypertrophy of my SCM and scalene muscles resulting in symptoms of scalenus anticus (compression of the blood supply to the upper extremity).

Actually, I injured both shoulders in high school, the right twice and received steroid shots in both, so I speak about such injuries from a position of personal experience not just observation as a medical student or doctor in training.

The principle that Dr. Emmerson emphasized to me regarding the Olympic wrestler, my injuries and the majority of injuries everywhere is that there are basic principles of healing not to be confused with suppression of symptoms. In order for the body to heal there must first be blood flow to the injured area to both take away the waste products of the injury and also to deliver the nutrition/building blocks necessary for healing to occur. Trainers, doctors and, consequently, athletes and patients, typically view inflammation as a bad thing, which must be suppressed. Therefore ice, more ice, and more ice are recommended along with anti-inflammatory drugs and, if these don't work fast enough, subsequent steroid injections. What they fail to fathom is that inflammation is the first phase of healing. The more we suppress this the more we delay healing, the greater the occurrence of scar tissue. Scar tissue is weak and disallows normal movement of the surrounding tissue.

Ice

There is a time for ice; within twelve to twenty-four, maximum seventy-two hours of the injury to stop bleeding. Once the body's normal clotting mechanisms have done their job and stopped the hemorrhage ice is a NO-NO if the goal is tissue healing. Applying ice after this time, as is so commonly done, may block the pain sensation but it reduces circulation, which subsequently leads to ischemia, scar formation and incomplete healing. The common saying of PT's that, "ice is your friend," is simply false after seventy-two hours from time of injury.

Swelling is a result of a blocked transport system moving waste products away from the point of injury, consequently, part of the therapy for injury repair is to get drainage of the fluids away from the injury. This requires vascular flow, motion, proper alignment of the area (however we do not want motion of a fractured bone, we are talking about soft tissue injuries which include muscle, tendons, ligaments, cartilage) proper nutrition, and detoxification. Therefore, the next step in the healing protocol is to increase fluid exchange. This is done by the use of special instruments/techniques to increase the ATP production in the injured area and by realigning the joints and soft tissue so they function normally. Proper alignment and motion of the affected joint is critical to restoring appropriate autonomic nerve function and feedback for the joint as well as proper circulation. Many injuries, especially chronic or old injuries improperly treated, require autonomic nervous system retraining. This means that the healthy autonomic nervous system responses must be restored to replace the injury-triggered responses. This is often as simple as daily repetitive corrective range of motion exercises.

The next step in injury rehabilitation is to identify the actual physics and positioning in which the injury occurred and then shunt blood to that injured area. This provides critical nutrition (provided the patient's diet and supplementation possesses therapeutic nutritional levels) to the injured tissue and flow of waste products away from the injured area. This is a particularly critical process for rehabilitation of old injuries that have left scar tissue as the pseudo-repair mechanism for the injury. This scar tissue can be melted away and replaced with normal, healthy tissue using this complete protocol.

Further, we identify and correct what factors or weak links the body possessed prior to the injury that may have allowed the injury to occur at that specific location. This means looking at the entire body structure seeking areas that are misaligned and/or injured which put undue compensatory strain on the injured area being addressed making it more susceptible to injury. A classical pattern is the athlete with chronic knee injuries. Conventional medicine just ices the knee after each workout, shoots it with steroids and anesthetic periodically followed by occasional arthroscopic cleanup of the knee, taping and bracing, nonsteroidal anti-inflammatory drugs and eventually knee replacement. Never does the trainer or doctor look at the low back and pelvic area or foot for answers why the knee is susceptible to injury. They should. No joint in the human body is isolated unto itself.

Critical to the healing process, as mentioned many times, is getting the correct nutrition into the patient in *therapeutic dosages*. Therapeutic dosage means amounts above and beyond those necessary for survival and normal function. Those amounts that optimize healing of the injury. The more severe and extensive the injury, the greater the amounts of nutrition necessary to get complete healing. This is achieved with diet, supplementation and even IV's if necessary. When all these factors are addressed the injury heals completely without scar tissue or residual problems.

Arthritis

Arthritis in joints of middle-aged people, because of injuries experienced as youth, is completely due to inadequate injury care and healing at the time of injury. The TV ads are frequent with former professional athletes such as Joe Namath, Jimmy Conners and Joe Montana promoting the latest commercial remedy for arthritic pain. Unfortunately, it is a rare situation when patients actually heal completely after athletic injuries, motor vehicle accidents or work related injuries because the conventional approach to healing is founded in *symptom suppression rather than symptom resolution*. Once the injury acuteness is abated, the patient is usually left with complaints of nagging aches, pains, instabilities, and weaknesses in those injured areas.

Arthritis or degenerative joint disease (DJD) is said to be *normal* for anyone with a history of previous injury. For these complaints doctors prescribe chronic anti-inflammatory drugs, repeated steroid injections and eventually joint replacements. It need not be this way. Dr. Emmerson and myself are working to teach patients and doctors the previously outlined methods necessary to completely heal injuries and prevent the chronic DJD syndrome.

In a nutshell we are looking at restoring motion and alignment to the injured area, shunting blood to the area, establishing therapeutic levels of nutrition which includes hyperbaric oxygen therapy (oxygen is a critical nutrient) and finally strengthening the joint in balance with the rest of the body. For chronic problems that have significant scarring (scarring is caused by ischemia, lack of adequate blood flow/nutrition to the injured area) and impingement syndromes, we must detoxify the person by eliminating heavy metals (lead, arsenic, cadmium, aluminum, mercury), pesticides and chemicals and toxic foods (IgG foods test through ImmunoLabs) from the body. Once done, and the misalignments, tears, impingements, etc. are treated, the body can and will commence to heal. The following are additional case histories from my practice meant to give the reader a fuller understanding of this discussion.

Case Histories

Case #1 - A thirteen year old female came to see me with abdominal pain lasting several months. Like the twenty year old I previously discussed, her family doctor put her on birth control pills, which did not help. She was referred to a gynecologist who changed the birth control pills, which still did not relieve her pain. He subsequently suggested exploratory surgery to see if this thirteen year old girl had endometriosis, ovarian cysts, adhesions, or something, anything. She was placed on antidepressant medications and counseling because she was "depressed" and had home stressors. Finally, her mother, desperate for some help, drove her 2.5 hours to see me at the Born Clinic.

Getting a complete history I learned that she had been in a car accident at age seven suffering a "whip lash" injury to the neck, supposedly healed. Upon physical exam I found that she had significant positive trigger points in the abdomen with corresponding misalignments in the lumbar spine as well as misalignments in the thoracic spine and cervical spine. Her cervical x-ray showed straightening of the lordotic curve. Her neck injury from the auto accident had not healed. It simply accommodated and she admitted to frequent headaches and neck and back stiffness.

She was in obvious abdominal pain and was quite terrified of doctors having been poked and prodded repeatedly. She would not consent to receiving acupuncture nor sclerotherapy injections, but would allow me and Dr. Emmerson, who was visiting me that day, to adjust her. Her abdominal pain vanished with one treatment in the office. However, because her misalignments had become established over several years, that patterned memory remained. Consequently, the treatment only lasted a little over a day. I saw her twice a week for several weeks and then decreased to once weekly and then once every two weeks each time the treatment lasting longer. I took her off her reactive foods and put her on supplements as best I could with a teenager. Part of her challenges and lessons with healing are compliance as with any patient, myself included, but particularly teenagers. I also had her get custom made orthotics for her shoes.

Now 16 years old, I see her only periodically. Unfortunately, she has been able to get relief from adjustments only from myself, Dr. Baroody and Dr. Emmerson. She has specific structural challenges that need to be corrected. These include the external ear, cervical, thoracic, sometimes the clavicle, lumbar and occasionally the ankle. Nothing more, nothing less will do for her. Unfortunately, most doctors doing manipulation do not understand basic somatonethics. I was not taught it in medical school nor any postgraduate training or continuing medical education seminars.

Somatonethics is the patterning of the body where injury in one area affects other areas of the body in specific and predictable patterns. Trace down these patterns, correct them and the patient gets long-term relief and healing. I am gaining an understanding only because I have the same personal experience with my own structural challenges and have had the fortune to get treated and tutored by Drs. Baroody and Emmerson. Certain things need to be adjusted in certain ways to get the desired relief. Anything less does less. Please understand that this does not mean no one else knows how to adjust. It means that since every doctor has a unique personality, he or she will attract those patients who's ailment personality best fits the doctor's treatment personality. If and when the ailment personality changes, as it should with healing, then the doctor's treatment personality must change or the patient will need to change doctors.

Case #2 - A twenty year old woman was referred to me for a complaint of severe foot and ankle pain for over two years progressively getting worse to the point where she was having difficulty walking, sleeping, studying, and functioning in general. This pain was overshadowing her entire life. Her parents, particularly her father, were growing very short of patience with her condition.

Originally as a child, she injured her ankle in dance class. The injury was cared for conventionally with ice and rest. This left the ankle weak, consequently, she repeatedly reinjured the ankle followed each time with the same treatment of ice and rest. Each injury was progressively worse and finally she was taken to an orthopedic surgeon who determined that she had ligament damage necessitating surgery. Following surgery and rehabilitation (again a lot of icing) her pain and weakness remained so she was taken to surgery a second time and in fact a third time before the surgeon pronounced her ankle/foot structurally sound. He did mention that during the third surgery he observed her peroneal nerve appearing yellow in color (Nerves are supposed to be pearly white. Yellow means the nerve was suffering from ischemia and dying, but the surgeon did nothing and recommended nothing to address that problem. Yellow correlates to PAIN).

In his defense, I will say that the surgeon probably did not have a clue what to do about the ischemic nerve.

The pain persisted. She saw another specialist to no avail. As is typical with these cases the conclusion was made that since the "experts" did not recognize any problem on CT or MRI, the problem must be in the patient's head. (Few doctors can actually diagnose by physical exam anymore. In fact, unless most doctors have a CT or MRI film they are lost in finding a diagnosis. They fail to recognize that nearly 50% of the population having no symptoms will have abnormal CT or MRI findings and a large percentage of people with normal CT or MRI findings have significant disease.) This only made the situation worse for now her parents, particularly her father, were questioning her complaint.

At her first visit with me, she was hopeful but her parents were extremely skeptical. First, I was not an orthopedic surgeon nor podiatrist so how could I know something they did not. Second, I was at a clinic that was "alternative" and did weird, unproven things like nutrition, IV therapies, acupuncture, etc. I could appreciate her father's skepticism. My parents were also a bit skeptical of some medical therapies until I was just a couple years younger than this young lady. I listened to her history and was quite sure this case was beyond my medical youthfulness and I told them so. However, I knew enough to know that her problem was diagnosable and correctable and who could do it.

I had them call my friend and colleague Dr. Gary Emmerson in California. Though skeptical, they had no other options and they felt I had been honest and confident with them. Over the telephone Dr. Emmerson was able to describe to her the exact pain patterns, mechanism of injury, specific painful points and positions of posture. She was amazed and encouraged by his knowledge and understanding. Her father agreed to send her to California for two weeks treatment. Before she left we started the healing process with nutritional IV's and supplementation. Dr. Emmerson's initial two-week treatment found a chain of injuries and subsequent impingement syndrome of the peroneal nerve at several points along its course, significant misalignments of foot bones, leg, hip and spine. He put her in custom orthotics and taught me the manipulation techniques needed for her situation. Her pain was almost totally gone in two weeks. Enough so that she could go to Central America for Summer school. She was not healed, however. Much work and therapy lay ahead. She was unable to continue as much therapy as she needed and wanted due to school and student teaching.

Upon graduation from college she returned to California for another two weeks of therapy provided by both Dr. Emmerson and myself which included hyperbaric oxygen therapy, trigger point injections, diet modification, etc. Her foot and ankle had a tremendous amount of scar tissue from the surgeries that had to be dissolved. Blood flow had to be completely restored to the peroneal nerve. Her pain disappeared gradually. It takes time to heal nerves. As long as the foot bones remained aligned properly she was pain free. When they became misaligned she would come to me for manipulation and the pain would disappear as quickly as the bones realigned. Her treatment program now two years out from her initial visit to my office consists more of working on her low back than her foot and ankle. She now remains pain free the majority of time and continues on her diet and nutritional supplementation, enjoying her career as a gifted elementary teacher.

This case taught me much about injuries and the connection of everything in the body. Though her injury was to the ankle there were issues of stability in the neck, back, hips, legs and feet that related to her original injury and the subsequent expansion of her pain syndrome. She probably did not need the first surgery and would not have gotten it had her parents known then what they know now. The point to make here is that children and teenagers experience multiple injuries in various sports. They must be treated holistically to truly correct the injury and associative misalignments/weaknesses otherwise they lead to recurrent and/or more severe injuries and arthritis as adults.

Case #3 - This forty-five year old gentleman came to me with a diagnosis of RSD, reflex sympathetic dystrophy. This is a fancy term for severe nerve pain of unknown cause and unknown correction. He had the problem for ten years, was disabled as a result and, more devastating than that, he was unable to participate in activities with his children. He was simply in too much pain to function. The strongest of "narcotic" pain medications only took the edge off at best and left him feeling lethargic and dazed. This man was desperate and defeated.

After listening to his history and examining him, I explained to him that his condition was correctable and that I felt he could become totally pain free. He would need to change his diet first by eliminating those foods to which he had delayed sensitivity (ImmunoLabs IgG ELISA testing) to reduce general body inflammation and by therapeutic dosing of nutrients, which would include IV administration. He would need this program a minimum of two to four weeks before going to California to spend two to three weeks with Dr. Emmerson.

It took him a year to decide to do this program. There were a number of factors involved; finances, skepticism since the "experts" said there was nothing that could be done for RSD and patient procrastination. Finally he realized that he could not continue the rest of his life on high dose "narcotic" painkillers that were becoming less and less helpful. More importantly he wanted to regain his family life, participate with his children and earn a living. By the third day (keep in mind he had severe, debilitating pain daily for ten years) with Dr. Emmerson he was pain free the majority of the day and by the second week he was pain free and off all pain medication. I treated him with Dr. Emmerson in California and he cried when he explained that he had his life back, that he would be able to go hiking with his boys, relax without pain, and go back to work. As with the previous case we discovered nerve impingement in the foot and leg along with significantly misaligned foot and leg bones.

Case #4 - This forty year old lady came to me with a complaint of severe shoulder pain and debilitation for over eighteen months. She was unable to work, do house work, or even sleep in a bed. She was devastated, depressed, distraught, and without much hope. She had initially injured her shoulder handling large boxes at work. After initial therapy it was determined by an orthopedic surgeon that she had a SLAPP tear (meaning that the shoulder was too loose) necessitating surgical repair. (She did not have a SLAPP tear, she had hypermobility of all joints.) After surgery (first mistake) she had the shoulder immobilized (second mistake) for 8 weeks with ice compresses (third mistake). Upon physical exam I found her to have significant cervical and upper thoracic misalignments, medial clavical, anterior inferior humerus, acromial-clavicular misalignment and an externally rotated scapula. She had extensive inflammation in all muscle groups of the shoulder and was essentially unable to use her arm and shoulder due to pain, inflammation and weakness.

We started with dietary changes and eliminating her delayed sensitivity foods (ImmunoLabs IgG ELISA test), found she had sluggish liver detoxification and leaky gut. I put her on appropriate nutritional supplements to address these issues including digestive enzymes. I saw her weekly, starting with twice weekly adjustments and tender/trigger point injections. She also received prolotherapy injections to help stabilize the shoulder. Her shoulder was very unstable and muscle memory had to be changed. Over a several month period she lost 70 pounds, gradually improved her range of motion and strength, and significantly gained self-esteem and hope. Improvement was slow yet consistent. This caused problems with the insurance company and her employer/workman's compensation. They ordered several evaluations including finally another orthopedic consult. This doctor concluded that the original orthopedic surgeon had done an inadequate job in repairing the SLAPP tear and, combined with new surgical technique, he recommended another surgery on her shoulder. She refused the surgery per my recommendation and eventually had to settle the claim.

The entire case took almost two years and I found that our therapy plateaued at about 18 months. At that point she had regained about seventy-five percent normalcy of her shoulder yet we were unable to get beyond that and were challenged just to maintain the 75%. My experience and consult with Dr. Emmerson told me she would need to go to California for therapy with him, something I encouraged from day one. Within one week Dr. Emmerson was able to achieve nearly 100% use of her shoulder for very brief periods, however, unless he treated her several times per day she would quickly fall back to the 75%. He discovered that her instability of the shoulder was being caused by significant structural problems with her jaw and pallet, a problem he felt set up the original injury via inducing instability in the cervical and thoracic spine.

He found that all her joints were hyper mobile and, in fact, the surgeon's supposed repair of a possible SLAPP tear resulted in significant restriction in the one shoulder compared to the other. In other words, she did not need surgery; she had no tear requiring surgery. In fact, the shoulder tightening surgery significantly imbalanced her body dynamics.

Her actual problem resided in her jaw, a problem she had since childhood. Consult with an enlightened orthodontist concluded that jaw surgery and appliances would be necessary to correct the jaw problems. She is scheduled for this and follow through with the concluding therapy for her shoulder. In the mean time she is wearing a bite splint and as long as she follows her treatment plan she is pain free and has full function of her shoulder. If she chews something hard like steak her jaw misaligns and her shoulder pain returns. Fortunately, appropriate manipulation restores alignment and resolves her pain. It has been a very long road for this lady. There is still more progress to be had, but we have pieced the puzzle together, shown her that total recovery is achievable, and most importantly given her hope of a normal, pain-free life.

The key motto with all these injuries and conditions is "everything is connected to everything so find the underlying disturbance and fix it." The aforementioned case histories were not rare obscure problems. They were simply the result of a sequence of events compounded upon each other, which eventually resulted in the pain and disability experienced by the patient. In none of these cases was their original surgery necessary. In none of these cases was physical therapy appropriately applied nor helpful. In none of these cases was there a "narcotic" or any other drug deficiency. Certainly these people were depressed. They were in pain, debilitated and defeated by the mechanical indifference of the doctors that ineptly treated them. None of these patients had accurate diagnoses or treatments. Is this because of incompetent doctors. I think not. I believe "the standard of care" is inappropriate.

The paradigm, the belief system of conventional medicine is at fault. It is the medical education system and additionally the socialized/managed care medical system that has created this belief system. The standard protocols imposed upon all these patients were the protocols I was taught in medical school and postgraduate training. I was not taught the corrective principles of appropriate diet, nutrition, manipulation, mobilization, blood shunting and somatonethics in medical school nor postgraduate training. I was taught the party line, staying within the "box" per a given protocol.

This protocol teaches doctors to get the patient in and out of the office efficiently and expeditiously in fifteen minutes or less. There is no way that an appropriate understanding of these patients and their conditions can be obtained in less than forty to sixty minutes, not to mention the daily therapy including manipulation for another thirty to sixty minutes. These problems and patients do not respond to "wham, bam, thank you ma'am" approaches. Healing the human body cannot be stuffed into some arbitrary "box" or expeditious protocol.

The human body must be nurtured, given the time to adjust and heal in its own time, one appropriate step at a time. This means the doctor must practice quality medicine over quantity medicine. It is putting the patient first rather than patronizing the drug and appliance companies, the procedure quotas, and social payment allotments.

There is one last issue to discuss before moving on. Many patients will ask why they need to get adjustments from a chiropractor, osteopath, or medical doctor weekly or more over a period of time for injuries. The key term is injury. If one is pain free except for rare times of indiscretion when a muscle is pulled or a vertebrae or joint gets misaligned, then a one or two time treatment plan will usually suffice. However, if a person experiences a trauma or injury of some type that causes significant damage to the body, the healing process will take some time. The longer the patient waits for appropriate therapy, the more suppressive (scar causing) therapies received, the longer will be the healing process. Frequent adjustments plus complementary care are needed to both encourage proper healing and to retrain the proprioceptive function of the body so that correct body mechanics and motion will be restored. If the repeat treatments are only temporarily relieving patient distress and not resulting in overall improved health then these treatments are missing the mark. Find a doctor whose treatment program promotes correction and healing if that is what you really want, not just immediate symptom relief.

When the treatment plan is designed to correct structural problems, frequent treatment is appropriate and necessary to retrain muscles and achieve bone remodeling. These changes will be seen by patient postural changes, in flexibility and range of motion improvements, in x-rays and by symptom resolution. It is important to realize that drugs can cover symptoms; therefore, symptom resolution without the other observations noted is purely symptom suppression and not an indication of healing.

There are a number of doctors, DC's, MD's, DO's, who will prescribe ice after each manipulative treatment. Ice causes vasoconstriction resulting in tissue ischemia. Ischemia inhibits healing, so if the goal is correction of a problem requiring tissue healing, DO NOT ICE. If the goal is mere suppression of symptoms and repeat treatment of the same problem over and over again, ICE it every time.

Massage

Massage is a wonderful therapy, potentially. Massage can also be injurious and further perpetuate a person's problem if done incorrectly. There are a number of different methods or techniques of massage ranging from Swedish to Ralphing. Massage, like every other treatment modality, should have a purpose and end point to determine success. If the massage is simply to relax the person then a soft, flowing, light touch is most appropriate. On the other had for some people a very aggressive, pressure point oriented massage is needed to relax them. If the massage is intended to enhance healing and fluid drainage of an injured area, the technique utilized must accomplish this task without inflicting further injury.

Some massage therapists have the theory that lack of motion in a joint and tight, ropy muscles simply need more pressure. The belief is that if enough force or pressure is applied the tightness and lack of motion will resolve. This is not always the case and in some cases there will be further injury with more pressure.

Tight muscles most often restrict joint motion because there is instability in the ligaments that hold the joint together; therefore, the muscles will splint in order to attempt stabilization of the joint. Pressure on a muscle eventually exhausts the muscle and it relaxes. If the joint is unstable, being stabilized by splinting muscles, exhausting the muscles around that joint will circumvent the body's secondary joint stabilizers and increase the susceptibility of the joint to further injury.

One must always ask the question, "Why is the range of motion limited and why is the muscle tight?" Too often people believe that restricted range of motion is corrected solely by applying more force through the therapy. This is the theory behind Ralphing and most people that have received this therapy will admit that it was excruciatingly painful. Perhaps that type of therapy and painful experience is appropriate for some people, but it is not for my patients.

I enjoy massage and I feel better if I receive weekly full-body massages. They are good for increasing circulation, lymphatic drainage, and moving fluids around the body. I recommend massages routinely to patients. If massage is going to be used in a comprehensive therapy program for an orthopedic problem or injury, it must be gentle and focused on lymphatic drainage, not on forcing joint motion and muscle relaxation. Those issues will be addressed with the Acuscope, trigger point injection, prolotherapy and osteopathic/chiropractic manipulation.

Pain Syndromes: Fibromyalgia, Post-polio Syndrome, Rheumatoid Arthritis, etc.

Before leaving the neuromusculoskeletal system, I will briefly discuss one last topic, chronic pain from other than physical injury. This is the pain associated with Fibromyalgia, Post-polio Syndrome, Rheumatoid Arthritis, and other named with uncertain cause pain conditions. Most people with these illnesses suffer life long pain despite taking numerous pain medications, steroids, methotrexate and a long list of other drugs. Few find satisfactory relief from their pain from conventional medical therapies and many find little relief from alternative medical therapies.

These pain conditions are complex in their biochemistry/biophysics but have commonalities. These patients seem to have problems with dysbiosis, chronic or subclinical infections, perhaps parasites, heavy metals and problems with detoxification pathways in the liver. They all seem to respond to auricular therapy combined with correction of the above named problems. There is a formal auricular (ear) protocol applying the acuscope to the acupressure points of the ear for post-polio syndrome. I have seen this protocol significantly reduce pain and increase mobility in these patients.

This brings me to my last case example, a very good friend that was injured from gun shot wounds in the back and legs. His spine was damaged paralyzing him on the left side from the waist down so he did not have bowel or bladder control either. He was in significant pain that was not controlled with drugs. The neurologist, neurosurgeon and rehabilitation doctors told him he would just have to learn to live with the disability and pain, recommending only increased doses of the medication. The greatest problem was that due to their belief that he would always be paralyzed, they neglected to have therapy on his left leg to maintain the muscle tone and mass. About two months after the injury the pain was so bad and the new neurologist made him so mad telling him he would always be paralyzed that he consented to follow our, mine and Dr. Emmerson's, program. Now 4 months into the therapy he is walking on crutches, has feeling in the left leg, can lift the leg almost a foot off the table, swims daily, has lost the pins and needles feeling, has nearly regained bowel and bladder control and is fully confident and determined to walk normally again. We estimate it will take about a year of therapy to get to that point. We have simply applied the principles already mentioned, nutrition, HBOT, acuscope, IV therapy, hgh, physical therapy, kindness and encouragement. Our greatest hurdle is regaining the muscle mass the "experts" allowed to atrophy because they did not believe he would recover the use of his left side. Miracles happen every day!

A unique group of people requiring multiple modalities and

awareness are professional athletes, farmers, construction workers, firemen and oil rig roughnecks. These people have frequent new injuries including micro-trauma of repetitive motion on top of old injuries with developing degeneration. They require extra nutrition, directed preventive medical care, and assertive healing therapy. They truly should receive therapy for performance enhancement rather than therapy only for gross injury treatment. They should receive therapy rather than drugs for performance enhancement. Proper patient care actually prevents injury, identifies hidden or occult weaknesses, and optimizes body function. This is comparable to any medical practice that espouses the prevention of cancer, heart disease, diabetes or any other chronic condition by detection of stressed biological parameters.

Prolotherapy is the infection of products such as procaine or lidocaine, glucose and other substances that stimulate a regenerative inflammatory response. These injections are directed into the areas where ligaments and tendons attach to the bone. These attachment points are the most common sites of injury and subsequent cause of acute and chronic musculoskeletal pain. These injections, supported by appropriate nutrition and rehabilitation, stimulate the regeneration and tightening of ligaments and tendons, thus stabilizing joints and correcting the cause of pain. This therapy is over eighty percent successful and has helped such dignitaries as former US Surgeon General C. Everett Coop get relief of chronic, refractory back pain.

Neuromusculoskeletal Medicine Summary

Issues:

- Pain
- Lack of Motion
- Instability

- Performance

Treatment Considerations:
- Auricular Therapy
- Find the underlying problem(s)
- Remove Inflammatory Triggers
  - Reactive Foods
  - Molds and Environmental Factors
  - Infections and Parasites
- Diet and Nutritional Modification
  - Supplementation
  - Nutritional IV
- Hyperbaric Oxygen
  - Increase tissue oxygen
  - Stimulate Angiogenesis (blood vessel growth)
- Corrective, rather than Paliative, Manipulation
- Prolotherapeutic Injection Therapy
- Proprioceptive, Postural, and Motion Retraining
- Appropriate Strength and Performance Retraining

Chronic Fatigue/Fibromyalgia

Chronic Fatigue Syndrome is an ailment often referred to as CFIDS, chronic fatigue immunodeficiency syndrome. It is an elusive ailment. Because it is a syndrome there is no single diagnostic pearl that defines *Chronic Fatigue*, rather it requires a constellation of symptoms and "rule outs" to get to the diagnosis of *chronic fatigue*. There are some groups of doctors that don't believe there is such an ailment, medically, that it is purely a psychological problem/diagnosis. I think it is futile to have such an argument with such drones of medicine because one must still holistically ask the question, "what is causing the fatigue?" whether medically, psychologically, or both.

I find that chronic fatigue is fairly common in women diagnosed with fibromyalgia. In all these cases there seems to be a malfunction in the metabolism, detoxification, and elimination systems of the body. Dr. Jeffery Bland has some very intriguing information regarding the biochemical peculiarities found in these people. He believes that these people have a disruption if their energy metabolism mechanism within each cell of their body, particularly in the mitochondria (the energy engine/factory of the cell). These people have a problem with aerobic metabolism thus have difficulty with aerobic exercise. If they exercise they must do anaerobic exercise such as weight lifting.

I have found that all these people have excessive inflammation throughout their bodies, digestive system problems, sluggish livers, poor sweat mechanisms, and of course depression and anxiety. The brain is connected to the body so anything that is happening in the body will affect the brain. Once we clean up the body the brain with also clear. An excellent book along this line is *Nutrition and Your Mind* by Dr. George Watson, 1972.

From our combined work Dr. Emmerson and I feel that chronic fatigue and fibromyalgia are also ischemia related ailments meaning that there is inadequate oxygenation (which correlates with Jeffrey Blands findings) of the body tissue further exacerbating or causing the pain and fatigue. Therefore, part of our therapy includes HBOT (hyperbaric oxygen therapy). We start our therapy with the IgG ELISA food test from ImmunoLabs and change the patient's diet, get them on the appropriate supplements, which at times may require IV administration, increase their oxygenation and ATP production, have them take special baths, daily sweating if they can tolerate it, daily sunshine, water, and whatever other modality deemed appropriate for that particular patient.

Many of these patients need counseling to help them overcome the long-term effects of being debilitated, to help them regain their hope, self-esteem, and courage. Certainly improvement in their physical body goes a long way in this area.

I feel that environmental toxins, e.g. agricultural poisons, industrial chemicals, plastics, along with electromagnetic pollution and ultimately denutritionalized food are the key triggering factors for chronic fatigue. Nutrition is the most important for the body cannot deal with all the toxins and stressors of life without the proper and adequate fuel to do so. Again, we must correct the ills of agriculture to get at the root of chronic fatigue.

There is a group of doctors working in association with Hemex Labs that have found that people with chronic fatigue frequently have problems in their blood clotting mechanism. These patients seem to have hypercoagulopathies meaning their blood is thicker than it should be which decreases the oxygen and other nutrient flow to the tissue, thus, fatigue. This group of doctors recommends a treatment course of low molecular weight Heparin, perhaps 6 to 12 months to correct this problem. I mention this because it is interesting and available. However, it is still treating a symptom, which of course may be very appropriate. I am not totally convinced in this method but I mention it because it may be appropriate for a certain group of chronic fatigue patients.

Cancer: The Big "C"

The United States Constitution and Bill of Rights guarantee U.S. citizens many freedoms, but apparently not the freedom of choice in health-related matters. The production, sale, and distribution of "officially" approved proprietary cancer drugs contributes to the $12 billion-a-year cancer industry, which constitutes a legalized monopoly. This, of course, is immediately threatened by the introduction of any "unapproved," low-cost, nontoxic cancer therapy."

~ From A *Curious Man: The Life and Works of Dr. Hans Nieper*
Hans A. Nieper, MD (1928-1998)

Cancer is a very devastating and complex illness. The medical industry states that it is winning the war on cancer because its statistics say that fewer people are dying from cancer. Perhaps. It depends upon how one reports and interprets statistics. However, the statistics also say that the incidence of cancer in younger and younger people is actually increasing so not only are we losing that war, the war is expanding into a greater segment of the population. Cancer is, perhaps, the most profitable of all illnesses for the medical industry. Cures are only allowed to the degree that the industry is perpetuated and the "right" people/companies make windfall profits.

Think for a moment what would happen to the millions of people involved in the current cancer treatment industry, from doctors and nurses to drug reps, chemo and radiation equipment manufacturers, charity organizations, home health providers, etc. if tomorrow evening all three major networks plus CNN and Fox reported on their evening prime time news that "a cure" for cancer had been found that was simple, near 100% effective, and was relatively inexpensive, developed by an unknown doctor or scientist who actually wanted the therapy **donated** to humankind? Cancer patients and their immediate loved ones would be joyous. The conventional cancer industry would be panicked, angry, and plotting to rebuff the claim of cure. The stock market would be anticipating a crash in the stocks of cancer treatment research companies.

Tens of thousands of people would be devastated because their jobs would be no longer needed. The money flow would stop. Even more devastating, the egos of those occupying the prominent research institutions would be deflated. Something would have to be invented to discredit this therapy so the status quo could continue.

It would be the same as if it were announced that an inexpensive and clean replacement for gasoline was now available. The millions of people making a living in the gasoline fuel industry would be devastated in the short term. Where would they find work, how would they support their families and pay their bills?

The obstacles to such breakthroughs as a cure for cancer or a clean and efficient replacement for gasoline are not scientific in character. Rather, the obstacles to such breakthroughs are purely political.

So with politics and economics aside, I wish to reiterate that cancer is a very complex problem. There seems to be a number of factors involved in the evolution of cancer. Rarely does a patient contract cancer acutely, meaning suddenly as if they were contracting an infection. Generally it is acknowledged that cancer may be kindling in a person for years and even decades before it is detected or before it causes symptoms. Keep in mind that everyone produces cancer cells daily that our immune system scavenges and destroys. It is only when the cancer cells or proliferation of cancer cells overwhelms the immune system that "cancer" actually appears in one's body.

Because there appears to be a constellation of causes of cancer, no single cause has, nor do I believe, will be identified. That doesn't mean there aren't already in existence, successful treatment programs for curing people with cancer. Emotion and psychology seem to play an important part in the manifestation and treatment of this disease. Some people suffering from cancer are more afraid of and resistant to the treatment program necessary to actually get them well, than they are of the cancer. I have found that Dr. Bernie Siegel's book "Love, Medicine, and Miracles" to be an excellent introduction to this concept. Some people have religious disagreements with what they perceive in some of his statements. This is fine. I find it to be more of a semantics argument on terminology than actual problems with his concepts spiritually. There are numerous studies linking diet and lifestyle to cancer. There are numerous studies linking pesticides and industrial chemicals to cancer. There are many studies also linking genetics to cancer. I feel they all play a part, thus, the complexity of the problem. Therefore, I believe that all or as many as possible of these factors must be considered and included in the treatment plan for the patient.

Important point here is that I treat patients, not diseases, lab tests, MRI's, or protocols. I believe that as long as I treat people miracles will happen. They happen everyday, some are instantaneous healings as my friend, an evangelist experiences in his evangelical tours while others are gradual healings over the course of a lifetime. Some are healings of the soul and spirit while others are healings also of the body. It is not for me to judge.

> *Much of what is done in the treatment of cancer…is directed at the existence of already established cancer cells, but not at the mechanisms by which cells become neoplastic (cancerous).*
> ~ From *The Lives of a Cell*, Dr. Lewis Thomas (1913-)

More than any other illness I feel cancer is the great humbler. I find that we must be very comprehensive in our treatment plan for these people. We alter the person's diet and eliminate the stressful foods identified via IgG ELISA testing with ImmunoLabs, supplement the digestive system particularly with digestive enzymes and often extra proteolytic enzymes, evaluate the liver via a stimulated detox panel and supplement specifically to nurture the liver's ability to detoxify chemicals and toxins. The patient must keep the colon clear and in good working order (daily BMs), get the heavy metals out of the body via IV chelation if possible, and achieve therapeutic levels of antioxidants meaning as much C as the body can tolerate, E over 1000, A 25,000 to 200,000, etc.

I recommend the Pantox test from Pantox Labs in California to evaluate the levels of antioxidants in your body then supplement to achieve the highest levels of balance possible. Get at least half your body's weight in ounces of water daily. A 200-pound person would drink 100 ounces of water by this calculation. Get daily exercise if only a 30 to 60 minute walk. Get a massage a month or more if available and affordable. Watch at least one comedy or read something funny daily. Laughter is vital. Take time to do the tasks Dr. Siegel recommends in his book. Live every day.

There are a number of alternative therapies for cancer patients. There are many clinics in Mexico to attend, a few in Germany and other parts of the world. These may be the key choices for some patients. My parents went out of country 20 years ago for 4 weeks to a clinic and were very pleased. I have read about and, in some cases experienced, a number of alternative therapies in my practice.

One therapy that has gained considerable notoriety is that of Gaston Naessens from Canada. Gaston Naessens discovered many years ago that cancer cells seem to have a track record so to speak of preliminary occurrences seen in the blood before the actually cancer cell develops. Out of this research he developed what he calls "somatid therapy" or 714-X which is the injection of a special serum into the lymphatic vessels daily however long is necessary to return the body to health. This therapy has been thoroughly scrutinized by the Canadian Governments and, thus, allowed to be marketed and available to anyone. A book about his work by Christopher Bird *The Persecution and Trial of Gaston Naessens* and *The Life and Trials of Gaston Naessens, The Galileo of the Microscope* are a good place to start. There is a wealth of information regarding 714-X and Naessens on the web under Gaston Naessens. Here also one can get the information on how and where to obtain the 714-X.

Another very promising therapy is dendritic cell therapy whereby special immune cells of the patient's blood are grown out in association with the cancer cells so that the immune cells develop specific recognition of the cancer cells. This is then refined into a serum that the patient injects him/herself daily. The result is that the immune system is stimulated to target the specific tumor present in the person. Specifically, actual pieces of a tumor are taken and specially handled to keep the tumor alive. Blood is also taken from the patient and the lymphocyte/dendritic cells are separated and placed in a special nutrient solution (lactin – PHA in very small dosage). This stimulates the dendritic cell activity. These stimulated dendritic cells are then mixed with the tumor for several days to "teach" them what specific target they are to engage. The mixture is then separated and purified so that the only materials remaining in the serum are proteins, glycoproteins and polysaccharides (cytokines). This serum is then given to the patient for up to 90 days.

The serum is essentially a collection of messengers to teach the body's immune system more specifically what to target, the cancer. Pre-, mid-, and post-treatment immune markers are taken from the patient's blood to both monitor immune response and specifically customize the nutritional support of the immune system. I have observed wonderful results with this therapy in my own practice. It is available at The Dove Clinic for Integrated Medicine in Hampshire, England. This therapy was available in this country through Dr. George Kindness at AmScot Laboratories, Cincinnati, Ohio. Dr. Kindness perfected the safe and effective manufacture of dendritic cell therapy per FDA protocol, approval, and oversight.

So successful was his work in the human trials with dendritic cell therapy for treating cancer that he felt confident any person with prostate cancer, breast cancer or melanoma could be successfully treated provided their immune system was still able to be stimulated. Dr. Kindness fulfilled every criterion down to the last detail required by the FDA for this therapy. Unfortunately, he and AmScot Laboratories are very "small fish" and the cancer treatment industry is a "huge ocean."

Dr. Kindness's work apparently threatened the profitability of this huge industry and stepped on the toes of certain politically correct researchers. Subsequently, a couple years ago, on a normal Southern Ohio morning at the office, AmScot Laboratories, Dr. Kindness and a couple secretaries were raided by an FDA SWAT team of more than a dozen, fully armed brazen solders. Dr. Kindness and his staff were held at gunpoint for two days while his computers, patient files, laboratory supplies and 6 months billing records were stolen without the benefit of justification or inventory. He was informed not to discuss his research with anyone and later given a gag order regarding such discussion. I was subsequently called to active duty with the Air Force and am not privy to the current status of the case. He has continued operation of his excellent medical testing laboratory. I have heard, however, that some doctors, using his services, have been contacted by government agents warning the doctors that if they continued to use AmScot Laboratories for testing, FDA, Medicare and perhaps IRS would audit them. It appears that the goal is to put Dr. Kindness "quietly" out of business. See U.S. patent application number 20020187130. Also see patent number 6,534,540 for his prostate cancer therapy.

The very same day that Dr. Kindness was assaulted by FDA, Dr. Roy Page, oncology surgeon in Memphis, Tennessee was similarly assaulted by an FDA SWAT team, his computers, patient and billing records were likewise stolen and he was told to cease and desist his involvement in the dendritic cell therapy. He as well had followed FDA protocol to the letter for this study.

The reality of this situation is that two truly humanitarian doctors, following their medical oath to help people with illness, following our government's imposed guidelines for study and development of new treatment therapies, perfected a cancer treatment therapy that would potentially dry up billions of dollars in cancer research money being funneled to the politically correct organizations. These men have broken no laws, have done nothing wrong; yet, like all the pioneers in medicine before them who were "small time" private doctors, they have been assaulted, defamed and harassed by unchecked government agencies.

Two years later, an article appeared in the November 2002 issue of *Scientific American*, pp. 52 – 59, "The Long Arm of the Immune System" by Jacques Banchereau telling of the promising new cancer therapy, dendritic cell vaccine, being researched at four "politically correct" institutions in the US, one in Paris, France, one in Oxford, England and one in Warrington, England. No mention is made of Dr. George Kindness who holds the U.S. patent application on this therapy.

As civil rulers, not having their duty to the people duly before them, may attempt to Tyrannize, and as the military forces which must be occasionally raised to defend our Country, might pervert their power to the injury of their fellow citizens,...

~ Tench Coxe (1755-1824) U.S. Founding Father

Another cancer therapy which I have heard about but with which I have no personal experience is that offered by a physician in Houston, Texas, Dr. Bruzynski. Dr. Bruzynski developed his injection therapy years ago and brought it to the US. He has had great success with patients that had been given up upon by conventional oncology. After several years of battling with the FDA, he finally received approval to give his therapy to patients that have no other options; their oncologist feels there is nothing that can be done for them. He has had excellent success. *The Bruzynski Breakthrough*, by Thomas D. Elias, is a book about this wonderful therapy.

Another cancer treatment program available in Germany is that developed by Dr. Hans Nieper. This program includes a number of specific supplemental agents including, but not limited to, laetrile or its derivatives and Venus fly trap plant extract, valerian plant extract, iridodials, shark liver oil and DHEA. Despite this therapy program being accepted in Germany, proven safe, and even much of it proven safe and effective by the Sloan-Kettering Cancer Institute in New York, the U.S. F.D.A. and the National Cancer Institute have done everything in their power to discourage and prevent the employment of this program in the U.S. Despite this, thousands of Americans have traveled to Germany for this successful cancer treatment.

When the government fear the people there is liberty. When the people fear The government, there is tyranny.
~ Thomas Jefferson

There are a number of other approaches to treating cancer or more importantly treating patients with cancer. Some treatment programs appear to have merit, some do not. There are a number of treatment clinics in Mexico that provide wonderful treatment programs with many patient successes. The Donsbach clinic is one of these such clinics. As with any venture is this nature, I feel it is important to obtain and contact references for these establishments.

There are also a number of organizations, businesses and individuals purporting to have "Rife Machines" or employing "Rife Technology." Royal Rife was a brilliant researcher who developed a unique microscope capable of great magnifications and subsequently developed a broadcasting instrument for treating microbial infections based upon isolating their resonant frequencies and broadcasting the appropriate frequencies to destroy the specific microbe. It was and is a legitimate technology.

The problem is that the physics and the potential collateral ramifications of using such technology in an unprofessional manner or setting can be serious. Since few people really understand the physics adequately, particularly consumers, there are untold numbers of bogus "Rife Machines" in consumers' homes. Many of them are benign because they do nothing. Some, however, are dangerous because they are uncontrolled and unshielded, consequently, can and do cause collateral damage, potentially serious collateral damage. To know whether an instrument is legitimate and safe, it must be evaluated by a knowledgeable technician and tested on an oscilloscope.

Once determined to be safe and effective, the instrument must still be used with caution and care. If one uses such an instrument targeting a specific infective microorganism without considering all the physiological consequences of that treatment and subsequently allowing for said consequences, there could be a dead patient.

Resonance technology devices (Rife Machines) kill infective agents by driving a frequency into the organism that causes that organism, literally, to explode. This is the same phenomena which occurs when one shatters a glass on the table by broadcasting a specific musical note. The question to ask is, "Does the shattered glass disappear into thin air?" No, of course it does not, which means one is left with all the shattered glass fragments to clean up.

Picture shattering billions of infective microbial cells in the body of the patient all at the same time. There will be billions of cells worth of debris spread throughout the person's body. This debris must be collected, detoxified, and eliminated from the person's body. For some people this quantity of debris, toxic or not, would totally overwhelm the elimination organs particularly the liver and kidneys. The consequence would be kidney failure and subsequently liver failure and finally patient death.

The "Rife Technology" is profound technology. It is neither a toy nor a benign slice of panacea that can be applied randomly without consequence. As with all technology it should be used in a holistic treatment process rather than in the conventional, allopathic, reductionistic, warring treatment program.

Speaking of electromagnetic devices, there has been a great proliferation of "instruments" in the open market over the past decade. One in particular causes some concern. It is called the "zapper." This device was coined and described by Hulga Clark in her several books including *A Cure For All Diseases*. This device is a simple transmitter costing less than $50 for parts that is supposed to be used to successfully rid one's body of parasites.

Parasites is what Ms. Clark claims is *the* cause of all disease. I agree that parasites are a problem with which one must reckon. However, one must ask why the parasites are present and able to thrive. As is the case in the soil and plants, there is a reason that takes one back to nutrition

I will acknowledge that parasites can, as all living organisms, be influenced by electromagnetic energy. The assumption that all species of parasitic organisms, while not affecting the benevolent organisms, will be either killed or dislodged from a person's body by the "zapper" is very unrealistic to anyone who understands a little physics. The resonant signature necessary to do such a feat would be extremely complex and difficult to stabilize. Can there be some parasitic organisms that will mobilize and exit the body as a result of such a device, sure this can happen. Most of these devices do very little regarding parasites, but some of the more "commercial" versions are quite hazardous to some individuals. The broadcast spectrum of these units potentially causes significant disruption of the patient's bioelectrical system, which in turn, may possibly contribute to headaches, psychosis, sleep disturbances and cardiac arrhythmias.

I certainly wish not to appear as a stick in the mud regarding the latter two topics. I am excited about electromagnetic technologies. Aside from their potential financial misgivings, they have a potential dark side with very undesirable biological consequences for the uninformed and the misguided.

Summarizing my approach to treating patients with cancer I feel, as with all illnesses, that a holistic approach is best. I feel that a consult with Cancer Treatment Centers of America is the best place to get a perspective on what conventional therapy has to offer. They are very caring and compassionate and very aggressive with the therapies. As an example, I had a patient with Chronic Lymphocytic Leukemia, which I discovered on a routine annual physical exam. He had no symptoms, yet it was the policy of our clinic to run a complete blood profile on annual physical exams. His white blood count was 20,000. I ordered further evaluation on the blood and confirmed the diagnosis. I sent him to the local oncologist, who is a very good doctor, but conventional. He started on a nutritional and dietary program and he felt well. After several months he began to develop enlarged lymph nodes and his white blood count gradually increased. His oncologist was undaunted explaining that no treatment was warranted until the white count reached 100,000 (standard protocol).

This situation was simply not acceptable to my patient or me, considering the significant discomfort he was experiencing with the lymph nodes in the neck, underarms, and groin. I referred him to *Cancer Treatment Centers of America*. The oncologist there told my patient that they treated anytime the white blood count doubled and there were symptoms. His white count was over 50,000 so my patient received the chemotherapy and within a couple months all his nodes were again normal size and his white count back below 20,000. He was back to work and happy.

I have sent several patients to Cancer Treatment Centers of America all with great satisfaction. I am not promoting conventional cancer therapy. I am simply saying that when it is appropriate and when we need a comprehensive conventional consult with people open to alternative approaches I recommend Cancer Treatment Centers of America. If the patient desires a certified medical oncologist with alternative therapies, I refer them to Dr. Victor Vega in Miami, Florida. Dr. Vega has consulted me a number of times and is one of the most gracious men with whom I have had the privilege of speaking.

When a patient comes to me with the possibility of needing surgery as a part of their cancer therapy, I refer them to Dr. Roy Page in Memphis, Tennessee. Dr. Page is Sloan-Kettering trained in surgical oncology with over 35 years of experience and extremely open to alternative approaches. The key is that he is perhaps the most gifted surgeon available. He also does thermal ablation of some tumors so that they are destroyed without having to do open surgical removal. In some cases, such as liver tumors, thermal ablation is the only option for destroying the tumors. I have sent many patients to see him. Every patient has experienced healing by the experience itself and many fewer postsurgical complaints than with any other surgery experience.

Anytime I have a patient who is dealing with cancer, I get specialty consultation with both the medical oncology side of the problem and the surgical oncology side of the problem. Then the patient can, hopefully, better choose the course of action suited to them whether standard conventional, alternative or a combination of both.

Should a patient decide to have chemotherapy, I recommend that he/she find a doctor that gives insulin potentiation therapy, IPT. This therapy utilizes a reduced dose of chemotherapy drug combined with an IV infusion of insulin. Cancer cells have 6 times the number of insulin receptors as normal cells making them much more receptive and reactive to insulin than normal cells. Insulin triggers the uptake of chemicals and nutrients by the cells. When chemotherapy drugs are given with insulin they are much more readily taken up by the cancer cells so a much lower dose of drug can be given yet still get as good or frequently better results than with the chemo drug alone at high doses. This is great for the rest of the body because a lower dose of poison causes less collateral damage. Thus, the cancer is more effectively killed with fewer side effects. Additional information is available on the Internet at IPTQ.org.

As mentioned earlier in this book, a device called the Priori Device invented by Antoine Priori, a French scientist during the early 1960's was successful in treating cancer. This device was extensively tested by the U.S. Navy and found to be safe and effective in the treatment of cancer. Also in 1922, Albert Abrams, MD, a world-renowned pathologist at Cooper Medical Clinic (now Stanford Medical Center) invented the *oscilloclast*, a device for analyzing and treating human maladies including successfully treating cancer. That system today is labeled *radionics*.

Radionics is an accepted and reimbursed medical treatment modality in England but illegal for human treatment in the U.S. since the F.D.A. ruled that radionics instruments are unapproved medical devices.

There are many more valid, proven, scientific, and inexpensive devices and therapies that have been deliberately suppressed by government and industry in the U.S. over the past Century. As a result people with means are forced to go to other countries for their medical care.

It is my feeling that the more the patient knows the easier my job will be in helping that person decide upon a treatment program. The bottom line is that we must detoxify and de-stress the body as much as possible. We must, at the same time, feed the body therapeutic levels of nutrition so healing can occur. We must also help the person alter their lifestyle to reduce or prevent what brought on the illness. And most importantly we must help the person live life to the fullest, whatever that means for that particular person.

Man discovers his own wealth when God comes to ask gifts of him.

~ Rabindranath Tagore (1861-1941), Nobel Prize for Literature 1913

The first big lesson for me as a new doctor, wet behind the ears, in private practice came just a couple months after beginning practice. A man came into our office with very advanced and aggressive muscle cancer in the legs and groin. He had surgery, chemotherapy and radiation over the previous eighteen months and was told, essentially, to go home to die, nothing more could be done for him. This man did not come in to see me, however, I asked to sit in on his consultation as a learning experience. After about forty-five minutes of discussion the doctor he came to see told him that he did not think there was anything we could do for him.

This visit was the family's last hope and they were obviously devastated by this news. I quizzed the other doctor afterwards and asked why he had handled the consult this way. He explained to me that he had seen such cancers before. Being eighteen months into the illness after chemo, surgery and radiation there was nothing he felt could be done for the patient so why waste time and resources or get the patient's or his family's hopes up to the contrary. Without much thought, I asked him if it would be OK that I take the case. He iterated that I was a bit naive but I had permission to pursue it.

I called the family back and told them that I would like to give them a second consultation. They consented and I saw first hand how important it was to just have a ray of hope, not a promise or guarantee, but just a ray of hope. This man had just retired at age 62 from the auto industry. He and his wife had planned a long retirement with family, travels, and winters in Florida. Testing over the next several months revealed that he was loaded with heavy metals, probably from the paint and metal dust of the auto industry from which he had retired.

My experience is that most patients with cancer also have some level of heavy metal burden. (Heavy metals are very hard on the immune system.) We changed his diet and gave him IV and oral nutritional support. He passed away on Christmas Eve, over six months later than had been predicted. Most importantly, as explained to me by his wife and family at the funeral, was that this man was able to live life every day right up to his passing. He was able to play with his grandchildren, visit friends, live at home. They were so grateful that he had been able to enjoy his last months and weeks and days. Had it not been for the IV's to keep up his strength he would not have been able to do so. I cried and thinking about him still brings tears to my eyes.

He was a wonderful man with a wonderful family. At least I was able to help him maintain his quality of life to the end. The other doctor was correct in that there was nothing I could do about the cancer, but he was wrong that I could do nothing for the patient. I was able to help this man's quality of life for the time he had left. It was a great lesson that God provided me. Miracles happen every day and all healing comes from God. My job as a physician is to facilitate the opportunities, help maximize quality of life, provide the patient with treatment options and monitoring, listen, be a friend and confidant, and pray.

I can say today that my recommendation for a cancer treatment hospital would be the Oasis of Hope in Tijuana, Mexico directed by Dr. Francisco Contreras. Dr. Contreras is a surgical oncologist, originally conventionally trained and converted to holistic therapy after observing the excellent results achieved at the Oasis of Hope by its founder, his late father Dr. Ernesto Contreras. It is a wonderful healing center and hospital, equipped as well as any modern, medium sized hospital in the US. The therapies are comprehensive and centered on fresh organic foods as the foundation of detoxification and healing. Contact Daniel Kennedy or Luis Miguel Barajas at health@oasisofhope.com, 1-888-500-HOPE or go to their website at oasisofhope.com.

Cancer Summary

Issues:
- Correct Diagnosis
- Holistic Perspective of All Options
- Goal of the Patient
- Costs
- Lifestyle
- Fears
- Patient Overall State of Health

Treatment Considerations:
- Cancer Treatment Centers of America
- Surgery – Dr. Roy Page
- 714X

- Dendritic Cell Therapy
- Bruzynski Therapy
- Hyperthermia
- Nieper Protocol
- Noordenstrom Therapy
- Foreign Clinics
    - Oasis of Hope, Tijuana, Mexico
- Pantox Blood Test
- Nutritional IV's
- Antioxidants
- IV EDTA Chelation
- *Love, Medicine & Miracles*
- Laughter

Idiopathic Illness: No One Knows The Cause!

Several times in my career as a doctor I have heard patients tell me that they have an illness that no one can name, much less figure out what is causing the illness. Medicine gives this a fancy term of idiopathic illness. It is extremely frustrating for patients to have such a diagnosis because their doctor cannot reel off the latest statistics on the patient's prospects for recovery or the statistical probability of the latest miracle drug or surgical procedure "curing" this dastardly illness.

Frequently, when doctors do not find laboratory data to clinch a diagnosis on a patient, the patient is told to go home only to return when they are "really" sick. This is classic of the situation all too common in today's socialized medical care world where doctors' primary focus in patient care is to treat laboratory test results or symptoms rather than treating patients and causes of ill health.

These cases are not that much different than any other case. The doctor must take a thorough history and do an appropriate physical exam. The patient will reveal the problem.

I look at the diet, food sensitivities, environmental exposures, injuries, and nutrition. Some of these people have contracted parasites, which must be purged. Some have genetic disorders that must be addressed. All these cases of unknown conditions with unknown causes are solvable with a little patience, common sense, good medicine, intuition and prayer.

Healing Crisis

Healing crisis is a term commonly expressed in alternative medical therapy circles referring to the onset of symptoms of malaise, fatigue, nausea, perhaps diarrhea and vomiting, fever, rashes, and headache supposedly associated with the body's detoxification process as it moves to a state of improved health. I have heard this term used for years, accepting it at first as fact when described by more "informed" people than I. However, after years of observing people, animals, plants, and microorganisms moving from a state of illness to a state of improved health, I question the healing crisis concept as a mandatory process required in achieving improved health.

Certainly, it is possible that our body will experience these symptoms attributed to a healing crisis as it attempts to purge and detoxify itself of undesirable and life suppressing materials/ chemicals. I have observed that this "healing crisis" is experienced in direct proportion to the ready reserve of nutrients critical to the detoxification process. If there is a continuous, uninterrupted supply of key nutrients to the detoxification processes throughout the body, the "healing crisis" symptoms are rarely, if at all, experienced; yet detoxification successfully proceeds.

The symptoms of a "healing crisis" occur because the body runs out of nutrients necessary to complete the detoxification process, thus, toxic intermediate compounds are left in the system. The body then resorts to its secondary detoxification mechanisms of sweating (fever), vomiting, diarrhea, urination and respiration to purge the body of unwanted and toxic materials. It is when this secondary detoxification system is engaged that the symptoms of a "healing crisis" are encountered.

This is where I differ with mainstream alternative medicine in that I feel we must aggressively support the body with nutrition including intravenous nutrition to minimize the experience of any "healing crisis."

Fasting

Many people would naturally think that a person with multiple chemical sensitivities should respond very well to fasting. Fasting is generally a very effective way to cleanse the body. However, in the case of cleansing the body of many of the toxic chemicals found in today's environment, fasting could actually make some people worse. Detoxification, the conversion of toxic chemicals to less toxic and eventually harmless excretions of the body, requires a significant amount of energy and nutrients.

The liver is the major organ of detoxification in our bodies and it requires many nutrients to do its job. A fast triggers the body to rapidly move unwanted materials and toxins to the liver for detoxification and elimination. This is turn consumes large quantities of nutrients. Since most people do not take any supplements during a fast they rapidly exhaust the storehouses of liver nutrients. Once this happens the toxins, now mobilized, freely accumulate in the liver and spill over to other parts of the body causing further intoxification of the body. The person may actually become more ill than if he/she had not fasted. What needs to be said here is that nutritional supplementation should be a part of any fasting program for people with chronic or serious illnesses.

These include antioxidants, glutathione, NAC, MSM, water, oxygen and others. Colonics may also be appropriate to accompany the fast. Rest is also a must with a fast. Exercise can rob nutrients and antioxidants needed by the liver.

Dr. Carey Reams was notorious for using fasts at the onset of an aggressive treatment program. He made a point, though, to closely monitor the patient frequently during the entire fast and had them drinking fresh lemon juice water sweetened according to the individual's glycemic status. He was an adamant advocate of fresh vegetable juices, medical foods and vitamin and mineral supplementation according to an individual's body chemistry. If I were going to fast a patient with multiple chemical sensitivity I would only do so in a monitored clinical situation incorporating all appropriate supplementary and supportive care.

People forget that the environment, food sources and human stressors are much different today than thirty or fifty years ago when Dr. Reams was actively working. His principles are as valid today as they were then; the methodology with which these principles are executed today must take into account today's biochemistry. What most Reams students today fail to understand is that there are many toxic chemicals, viruses, resistant bacterial infections, and mycotoxins today with which to deal that Dr. Reams did not have. Further, the nutritional density of the food has declined from Dr. Reams' nutritional therapy days and even more challenging are the genetically modified "franken-foods" of today with which Dr. Reams would have never dealt. As I mentioned, the Reams principles are still very applicable today as they were decades ago. The logistics with which one applies these principles, however, must be modernized to get the results desired.

Hyperbaric Oxygen Therapy (HBOT)

HBOT is a therapy whereby the person/patient breathes 100% oxygen in a chamber under pressure. Hyperbaric oxygen therapy was originally developed to treat divers who surfaced from a dive too rapidly and got the "bends." The "bends" is a situation where the tissue is saturated with dissolved nitrogen from being under the pressure of the water. As the person rises to the surface the pressure decreases and the nitrogen converts from its dissolved "liquid" form into a gas in the blood vessels. If done slowly the person gets rid of the gas through the lungs with each exhale. If done too fast too many gas bubbles form in the blood and tissue causing blood flow obstruction and pain. A person in this condition must get back under pressure to shrink the bubbles. In an HBO chamber, the person will also breathe 100% oxygen to replace the nitrogen. Pressure is gradually reduced back to normal atmospheric pressure.

Over the years it has been found that there are a number of additional therapeutic benefits from hyperbaric oxygen therapy. There has also been considerable controversy because there are individuals that have made extravagant claims for the benefits of HBOT, thus undermining the acceptance of the true benefits of this therapy. Also, as with any inexpensive, natural therapy there are those who wish to discredit the therapy outright regardless of scientific proof because it cuts into the profits of competitive therapies.

HBOT has been used for Jehovah Witness patients getting "blood-less" surgery. These people will not accept blood transfusions during surgery so they are given HBOT treatments to keep their actual tissue oxygen levels normal for healing. Also there are operating rooms built completely inside hyperbaric chambers so the patient can receive hyperbaric oxygen therapy during the entire course of the surgery. Though this is a wonderful process for surgery for the patient, pressure issues must be considered for the staff and the duration of their pressurization particularly if they are scheduled to do so multiple times and over several hours per day. The same cautions must be taken as those with scuba divers. The benefits to the patient are tremendous including lower infection rates, faster healing, less swelling, and faster recovery after anesthesia.

It has been my experience that HBOT has a place in all *regenerative* therapy programs, not necessarily all therapy programs. I have found that when we need to detoxify a person, reduce inflammation, stimulate tissue regeneration, assist the immune system against pathogens, oxygenate nerve and brain tissue, thus reduce ischemia, HBOT is the treatment of choice. I fully understand that there are many other therapies available including ozone, hydrogen peroxide, vitamin O, etc. All these are still alternative choices to HBOT when HBOT is not available. The best way to oxygenate is via hyperbaric oxygen therapy.

I attended the physician-training course at Richmond Medical Center, USC, Columbia, SC several years ago. I was also briefed on hyperbaric oxygen therapy while attending aerospace medicine school at Brooks Air Force Base in San Antonio, Texas. Research at Richmond Medical Center in the mid 1990's demonstrated that HBOT was an excellent therapy for stroke and heart attack patients. The sooner the patient received HBOT treatments the better. If the patient received HBOT within hours of the event there frequently would be zero damage to the brain or heart from the stroke or heart attack. Do you think that other institutions around the country were interested in this information? NO! Actually a resounding NO! HBOT could possibly replace more profitable drug and surgical therapies. That was, still is not acceptable. Patient be damned, finance rules the decision-making process.

I don't really care what the medical politicians think. I have seen patient benefit with great safety and low risk. Common sense tells me to use HBOT and recommend it, which I do regularly. My patients come to me for help not the political party line. The following are a couple examples when I have treated patients with HBOT.

I had a young girl come to me with chronic recurring gangrene of the breasts. She had breast reduction surgery and gotten infection. The plastic surgeon and infectious disease doctors had treated her repeatedly without success. I immediately called the hospital requesting this young lady be admitted for HBOT. Fortunately the HBOT clinic in Grand Rapids agreed to this and within a couple weeks she was completely healed. Simple! It was covered by insurance and actually the treatment of choice, the "standard of care" for this condition. The surgeon and infectious disease doctors couldn't think outside of the box. Had this young lady not been treated with HBOT, she would probably have been looking at bilateral mastectomies or even death from the spreading gangrene.

I had a gentleman come to me scheduled for amputation of both hands and one leg. He had already lost the one leg due to poor circulation. His fingers and toes were rotting off, literally. In addition to chelation (he also had a transplanted kidney), nutritional and dietary therapy I sent him for HBOT. Fortunately again the hospital agreed to treat him and we saved his leg and hands. I make the comment about the hospital agreeing to treat my patients with HBOT because at this HBOT clinic they are very conventional and usually only treat near drowning, carbon monoxide poisoning, and advanced diabetic ulcer patients. It is a real chore getting them to accept patients outside this conventional box. I have had many turned down and had to send them out of state to get HBOT therapy.

Hyperbaric oxygen therapy is not a panacea. It is, however, a wonderfully beneficial therapy to augment many other therapies for restoring health to patients. It is a critical therapy for healing injuries and treating deep-seated infections such as osteomyelitis, infection in the bone. It has shown great promise in treating many neurological illnesses such as multiple sclerosis. Certainly more research needs to be done as with all therapies. It doesn't take a rocket scientist to figure out that since oxygen is the key element in keeping living tissue alive, it just might be beneficial for tissue regeneration/healing.

Labs And Numbers

I will end this section with a brief overview of lab test values and environmental data. The general public is often misguided because it is unaware of the terms and/or numbers being used when discussing, in particular, pesticides in our environment.

Frequently, chemical company representatives will speak down to farmers and consumers regarding public concern about the quantities of pesticides found in the environment. Pesticides are commonly detected in soil, water and foods at concentrations of parts per million and parts per billion. Especially regarding the parts per billion (ppb), parts per trillion (ppt) concentrations or less, the speakers mock the danger as such "minute" quantities of pesticides. Unfortunately, the general public does not realize that these minute quantities are the equivalent minute quantities that hormones in the human body are found.

Consider the following hormone levels in blood or blood serum of men and women.

Progesterone in nanograms per milliliter (ppb)
Female: 0.1 to 0.6 / post menopausal
4.5 to 25.2 / midcycle
11.2 to 422 / pregnancy
Male: 0.3 to 1.0
Estradiol (estrogen) in picograms per milliliter (ppt)
Female: 42 to 289
Male: 3 to 70
Testosterone in nanograms per deciliter (pp100b)
Female: 14 to 76
Male: 241 to 827

Think for a moment the potential effect that an estrogen-like pesticide contaminating the drinking water, food, or air might have on a person when the EPA allowed level is in the parts per billion range and the normal estrogen level in human blood is in the parts per trillion range? The upper range for estrogen in men is 70 parts per trillion. To put that in perspective, this would be equivalent to 70 milliliters (2.4 ounces) in the amount of water necessary to cover 100 hectares (250 acres) one meter (39 inches) deep. This is also equal to 812.5 acre-feet of water or 264,753,937.5 gallons (one billion liters). Small quantities of pesticides do make a difference to human health.

Looking at other labs that are commonly seen by patients:

- Thyroid tests of TSH - thyroid-stimulating hormone which will read high with hypothyroid and low with hyperthyroid; free T4 thyroxin which is the inactive form commonly given as Synthroid; free T3 which is the active form converted from T4.

- Cholesterol is given as total cholesterol divided into "bad" cholesterol LDL and "good" cholesterol HDL; triglycerides which are independent of cholesterol and affected by carbohydrates in the diet.

- Liver enzymes/tests include AST, ALT, Alkaline Phospatase and total bilirubin.

- Kidney function is evaluated by BUN (blood urea nitrogen) and Cr (creatinine).

- Complete blood count particularly looking at WBC (white blood cells reflecting potential immune response), RBC (red blood cells reflecting bone marrow production), HGB (hemoglobin reflecting anemia).

Summary

Idiopathic illnesses need holistic perspective/approach, patient symptoms tell the story. Healing crisis is most often due to inadequate supportive nutrition for the detoxification. Fasting can be valuable but must be supported nutritionally so body has nutrients necessary for detoxification and elimination of toxic body metabolites.

Hyperbaric oxygen therapy is a valuable adjunct to the detoxification and healing processes and a critical treatment for deep-seated and antibiotic resistant infections. It has been shown to be beneficial in the treatment of neurological and cardiac diseases.

Laboratory values and numbers are helpful in confirming patient health status. The patient must become familiar with these numbers to properly converse about their own illness and discussion regarding environmental risk factors such as pesticides.

Part 3: Health and the Holistic View

The responsibility for the well being of an individual's own body must be returned to the individual.
~ Hans A. Nieper, MD (1928-1998)

Soil-Crop-Food-Human Health Connection

Every person interested in their health, at some point in time, considers the quality of the food they put into their mouths. I never met a person that accidentally ate anything. Unfortunately, the general public is quite uninformed and greatly misinformed about the food they consume and the industry that produces it. To be healthy in this day of superstores, multinational produce brokers and the ever invasive drug and chemical industry, consumers must become informed, they must become discerning in their purchasing habits and they must become proactive regarding their food handling and preparation.

Bringing out the realization that human health is intimately linked to soil fertility and subsequently effecting positive change in that regard is the area of my greatest passion. I have spent nearly a lifetime studying and correlating the two. Dr. Carey Reams was my first mentor in this quest. It is an area of immense complexity and extension, yet quite simple in concept and application once one understands the direct link between soil and human health, their interdependence, and the science encompassing the concept.

It is amazing that one need not look far to encounter a heated argument between liberal environmentalists and staunch industrialists regarding everything from the importance of endangered animal species to fish spawning grounds, from wetlands and rain forest preservation to human economics, jobs, and common sense. These arguments often follow political party lines and frequently boil down to one side saying that we must preserve some identified natural resource and the other side saying we must preserve economic and industrial solvency.

Inevitably, all these arguments revolve around some aspect of agriculture and human health (physical, mental, spiritual, economic). The truth of the matter is that neither side really wants to solve the problem. Each only wants to perpetuate *their view* of the issue. If the solution were actually enacted, both arguments would be moot and both participants would need to find other employment. Here both the Democrats and the Republicans sit, continuing the argument to stir public frenzy in order to solicit votes for election/reelection. Both quote their own science and sources. Both are subsidized by the same industries. So while the arguments blaze away in the media forum stirring public polarity, the chemical/drug industries continue their trade virtually unchecked, perpetuating the con game.

Nature is designed to survive, to perpetuate and procreate, to harmonize. The laws of nature have not changed since the beginning of time. Cause and effect are the rule for every life form on this planet. For any organism to survive, procreate, and perpetuate, it must be healthy in the long term. Nature is very swift in its elimination of sick, defective, or deformed organisms and does so without hesitancy.

Every biological scientist worth their salt understands that all organisms on this planet exist in some type of interactive, interdependent saga. From the smallest of nano-bacteria to the largest of trees, from the smallest of amoeba to the largest of mammals, all exist dependently. Though most scientists, in concept, acknowledge this dependence it is not really understood nor applied in their daily work developing new products, solving problems, or growing businesses. Unfortunately, as a consequence, the majority of the consuming public also does not really believe in this dependence between all living organisms. Sadly, belief of the public overrides fact and belief is what the industry preys upon to perpetuate its profits and its monopoly.

> *...the soil environment farmers create with the fertilizers and tillage processes they use determines what microorganisms flourish in that particular soil.*

As mentioned before, all organisms are environment dependent. This means that the environment will determine what organisms survive and proliferate in any given system. Environment, relative to living organisms, must account for food, water, air, and comfort. Whatever the status of these four conditions there will be organisms that will thrive and organisms that will falter.

Humans are no different. We need appropriate status of food, water, air and comfort for us to survive. This is fundamental biology. If these four conditions are compromised in an area, we cannot live in that given area. Prime examples of such would be life in the ocean, at the top of Mt. McKinley, in the middle of Death Valley. Though we cannot live in these places without the aid of artificial life support there are many organisms that are adapted to these environments and thrive there.

With this knowledge we can manage the area environments so that humans and organisms we depend upon can live, actually thrive. The expression and evolution of this management is agriculture.

Disease enters through the mouth
~ Old Chinese Saying

The schematic of this interdependence begins with the soil. The soil is the foundation upon which most of our food is grown.

Seafood is, of course, the exception to soil being the foundation. Still the basic principles of interdependence exist in the oceans as well. The characteristics of the soil determine the organisms that thrive in the soil, and, consequently the plants that flourish in and on that particular soil. These characteristics can be summed to four components: water, oxygen, food, and comfort. The status of these four components, completely manageable by human intervention, determines whether disease or beneficial organisms thrive underground, and, consequently, whether healthy crops or weeds thrive above ground. The nutrient mix/complexity/smorgasbord present in the soil determines what microorganisms survive and flourish and which ones fade and die. This is a key, perhaps profound, concept to grasp. *Environment determines inhabitant.*

This means that the soil environment farmers create with the fertilizers and tillage processes they use determines what microorganisms flourish in that particular soil. A priori, **the rampant disease problems plaguing commercial agriculture worldwide are created by the farmers themselves.** These problems are the logical consequence of the farming methods used, as are the solutions, if they are employed. Unfortunately, most farmers and agronomists fail completely to understand the basics of microbiology outside of the chemical warfare model, which requires the farmer to identify "culprit" disease critters and subsequently purchase and apply the "right killer" chemical to the crop.

Agriculturalists, most everyone for that matter, like to differentiate microorganisms into two categories, "good guys" and "bad guys." We generally think of the "good guys" as inconsequential, having no significant economic contribution to soil fertility, growing healthy crops, protecting valuable natural resources. The "good guys" are simply viewed in the context of an absence of the "bad guys" i.e. problems/disease.

This simplistic perception arises out of a lack of understanding and appreciation of microbiology. Reality is much more complex and "good microorganisms" **mean much more** than just the absence of disease. The "good guys" are actually *necessary* for the survival of the organisms seen as desirable, e.g. food crops, animals, people. The reality is that if it were not for the "good guy microbes" *all life, as we know it, including human would cease to exist.*

Humans, animals and plants are dependent upon the beneficial microorganisms for survival. Consider for a moment that 10% of the weight of a person is microorganisms. If it were not for these microorganisms, humans would be quickly invaded by infective microorganisms through every square inch of their skin surface and digestive system and killed.

People associate the "bad guys" with disease, spoilage, and undesirable outcomes. Both categories of organisms, "good guys" and "bad guys," are simply fulfilling their appropriate and designed status in the recycling of resources whether it be plant debris, chemicals, nutrients, oils, acids, alcohols, toxins, etc. Our differentiation, regarding soil, of these organisms as "good guys" or "bad guys" is different than in an artificial environment where we want to produce ethanol for fuel, for example. Alcohol producing microorganisms confined in a commercial ethanol operation converting corn, sugar cane, or sugar beets to ethanol would be desirable but that same conversion in the soil of a forest or food crop would be disastrous.

The soil characteristics determine which organisms dominate and which subordinate. I will say this again; soil characteristics determine which organisms dominate and which organisms subordinate. Think about that. Let it sink deep into your mind. Consequently, if we want to have the "good guys" dominate our soil; we must manage the soil characteristics in such a way that creates the environment most conducive to the "good guys" survival and proliferation, which will naturally be antagonistic to the "bad guys." The "good guys" and "bad guys" cannot and do not flourish in the same environment. Read these sentences again and again until you really grasp the concept, until you really understand the *ramifications* of the concept.

Soil nutritional management practices determine what types of soil microbial populations thrive, "good" or "bad." If the farmer manages for disease organisms because he believes these disease organisms are simply due to a deficiency of poisonous chemicals, then his fields will be infested with disease microorganisms requiring repeated applications of these poisons to grow his crops.

Conversely, if the farmer understands basic botany and microbiology and manages his/her soil to promote beneficial microorganisms, his/her soil will be naturally free of diseases as will be the crops growing on that soil without the need for toxic rescue chemicals. It is no accident which microorganisms dominate any soil on every farm the world over. It is neither the "wrath of God," nor an automatic occurrence. Human intervention determines which population dominates, "good" or "bad."

Soil becomes dominated by the "bad guys" because the farmer's soil management created a soil environment most conducive for "bad guys" to dominate. It is not due to a deficiency of poisonous soil fumigants, nematocides, fungicides, insecticides, or herbicides. Those "bad guys" dominate a given soil solely because the farmer's soil management practices created the environment hostile to the "good guys" and cozy for the "bad guys." It is that simple and straightforward.

I suggest you review the writings of Dr. Elaine Ingham at Oregon State University and many other microbiologists who have spent their entire professional careers documenting, proving and explaining this very basic, yet profound principle; **living organisms are environment dependent.**

If one looks at the current commercial production of most of our fruits and vegetables one will find that the "bad guys" dominate these soils. Consequently, the farmers insist they need the extensive arsenal of poisonous chemicals to kill these "bad guys" or else their crops will be wiped out and we will all starve to death. It is an ingenious scam from a business perspective.

The chemical manufacturers have done extremely well to perpetuate the latter belief that the "bad guys" are there simply because we are growing food commercially and that we would all starve to death if farmers did not spray these poisons on our foods. That is one reason the industry stopped calling these poisons "pesticides," "insecticides," "fungicides," etc. and now calls them "crop protection products." "Why enlighten the public to the true nature of these products; be politically correct and soft pedal them to the public. They will never question it."

Perhaps the best example of the end result of this "kill or be killed" mentality in agriculture is the situation in which many strawberry farmers in California find themselves. In the San Joaquin and Salinas valleys of California strawberry farmers over the past couple decades have been faced with greater and greater pressures from nematodes and fungal diseases destroying their strawberry crops. Their response began with poisonous fumigation of the soil every five years. That gradually degraded to fumigation every year and over the past decade to fumigation after every crop and finally to the inability to economically grow strawberries in some fields due to the enormous populations and vigor of infective nematodes and fungal diseases. With the deadline approaching for removal of methyl bromide from the allowable pesticide list, farmers are faced with the possibility of not being able to grow any high-value food crops on these soils; conventional chemical farmers that is.

One very large farming operation that had encountered this problem, growing several thousand acres of strawberries, decided to look for other options. They connected with Dr. Elaine Ingham, started a large scale composting operation and discovered that by implementing sound biological practices on the farm, not only were they able to subsequently grow strawberries without poisonous soil fumigation, they were able to grow greater yields of strawberries at less cost per acre with these biological practices than they were with fumigation.

It is important to understand that the mere addition of beneficial organisms to the soil guarantees nothing. An appropriate management program must include extensive mineral balancing to provide the "dinner table" necessary for the beneficial organisms to survive after their application to the soil.

The chemical companies have, thus far, been more correct about the public apathy regarding chemical farming than not. I find it very interesting how one can actually believe that adding a poison to one's food improves the quality and value of that food. Gee, we should all have bottles of these wonderful poisons on our kitchen tables right next to the salt and pepper shakers so we can add these poisons to our food along with the salt and pepper. The chemical companies and university agricultural professors tell the public these poisons improve the quality of the food. I am sure it makes everyone's mouth water with joyful anticipation just thinking about it. "Pass the organophosphates please."

Farmers will reap the consequence of whatever the soil character their management creates. A soil dominated by "good guys" will grow crops that are fully mineralized, healthy, healthful to eat, naturally good tasting, that do not spoil (spoilage is a result of "bad guy" domination precipitated by toxic soil management). These wonderful crops, full of nutrition, when consumed by animals and people supply them with the nutrition necessary to build strong, healthy bodies AND the nutrition necessary to nurture the "good guys" in our digestive system and those encompassing our bodies all of which protect us from illness, disease and infections.

Further, full nutrition from foods also helps protect the consumer from the ravages of environmental pollution and heavy metals. As the saying goes, "The best defense is a good offense." Full nutrition is necessary for our bodies to resist the effects of polluting chemicals and heavy metals and equally necessary for our body to detoxify and expel these contaminants.

Unfortunately, the reality of current society is that farmers/gardeners, via the encouragement of the chemical manufacturers and their financially obliged university professors, manage soils in a deliberate fashion that maximizes the "bad guys" "forcing" farmers/gardeners to purchase "crop protection products" to rescue their defective crops.

> Note: not all University professors have prostituted themselves to the chemical companies. Sadly, most of the department heads in the Colleges of Agriculture at every Land Grant University have done so in order to keep the money flowing to the various college departments. This makes it very difficult for real scientists to do legitimate research independently at these universities. These people must be quiet and low key going about their business largely unnoticed within the agricultural community. They usually have to get research money from private philanthropists or like Phil Callahan did, from the Department of Defense and have their research efforts *classified*. The system exudes the old adage, "follow the money."

The truth in biology is that insects, disease organisms and weeds are only manifestations of unbalanced nutrition. They are **not** "deficiencies" of agricultural chemicals. These "problems" are nature's way of eliminating defective "food" sources from the food chain that are not fit to maintain health of the consumer. These are Nature's messengers. Nature is not self-destructive. But, humans in their fictitious wisdom (and greed) spray poisons on their (our) food to kill the messengers and then consume the "food" and poisons. The result is that people manifest in their own bodies the very diseases supposedly "cured" by the poison applications of the growing crops. Consequently, people must buy "medicines" for the resultant diseases from the same companies that manufacture the "crop protection products."

> It is an ingenious business plan. Create the disease prob-
> lem in the soil, sell a product to cover up the disease
> while convincing the public the food, thus covered with
> poison, is safe and healthful; then sell to the consumer
> a drug to treat/cover up the disease he/she develops
> because of the defective and contaminated food. It is a
> self-fulfilling, never-ending business opportunity.

The logical next step in the business plan is to convince the
public that the new problems in food production of pesticide
resistant weeds, diseases and insects created by years of poison
applications, are rooted in genetic flaws in the crops themselves.
Next, develop an entire line of genetically modified crops that
"require" your specific "crop protection product" (Monsanto's
RoundUp for Monsanto's RoundUp Ready Soybeans). Once
done the companies like Monsanto can completely monopolize
agricultural production. These companies sell the fertilizer, which
creates the original soil and crop imbalance; they sell the crop
seed and all the chemicals that the farmer applies to the soil
and crop.

The final piece of the pie is to sell the consumer the "magic bullet"
drug he/she needs to combat the symptoms caused by the defective
"food" the chemical companies had a hand in producing at the
beginning. Sound like a conspiracy or sci-fi story? Well, I think it
is simply a very effective business plan. The desire to monopolize
any industry is what the antitrust laws are about. The chemical
companies are public companies, traded publicly with the sole
intent of producing great returns on stockholder investment plus
lucrative company executive bonuses and "golden parachutes."
As such there is a tremendous amount of public financial and
economic inertia perpetuating this cycle.

This monopolization leverage will be automatically changed as
the understanding of basic biological science, health, nutrition,

and common sense begin to prevail. The roadblock to this change occurs, more often than not, because discussion regarding agricultural management becomes purely a political debate between seemingly opposed philosophies with nothing more than mere political objectives lying in the balance. Neither of these political camps actually understands the basic science NOR really wants to understand because it would, as said earlier, solve the problem and put both out of a job.

The prime example of this lies with the genetically modified crops issue. Take the Bt corn as an example. This corn, whose patent is owned by a chemical company, has been impregnated with the gene of the Bacillus thuringensis bacteria that produces the toxin/poison to kill corn borer. This means that every cell of this corn plant produces this toxin including the pollen that can travel for miles in the wind. This toxin is also in every cell of the roots. The toxin has been shown by Dr. Elaine Ingham to kill mycorrhizal fungi, the vital beneficial fungi that completely envelops the roots of most domesticated crops, including corn. This fungi is responsible for transporting many vital nutrients including phosphate and iron from the soil to the plant AND it is responsible for protecting the plant roots from invasion by pathogenic fungi and other microorganisms.

It does not take a rocket scientist to figure out that if the farmer puts a mycorrhizal poison into the soil, via the roots and incorporated fodder from the Bt corn, that the vitality of the beneficial mycorrhizal fungi in that soil will be greatly compromised thus leaving subsequent crops more susceptible to pathogenic organisms. The chemical companies conveniently have a solution to the death of the beneficial fungi, which they caused; more soil fungicides, nematicides and fumigants.

The saga continues. Already, farmers are seeing resistance by the corn borer insect to the Bt toxic corn so the panacea has not manifested nor will it ever. The corn borer insect attacks the corn because there is a nutritional deficiency in the corn, pure and simple, which will never be corrected with an insecticide nor toxin producing gene implant. Yet the financial cycle continues with the chemical company selling the patented corn, the follow up insecticides and the subsequent soil poisons.

A great example of insect behavior correlated to crop nutrition is that of silk beetles in corn. This example was researched and proven in the field by the late David Larson, founder of AgriEnergy Resources, Princeton, Illinois. This insect eats the silk at the end of the corn ear and, in doing so, prevents pollination of the ear, and subsequent corn kernel development. If the brix (sugar level to be explained later) in the corn stalk, opposite the ear shank is eight or above, regardless of their numbers in the field, the silk beetles will NOT eat the ear silk. No insecticide is needed. Whenever, the brix drops below 8, beetles will eat the silk and prevent pollination. This occurs regardless of corn variety.

The real point to get here is that the current system of farming, the great "green revolution" is an absolute failure for the farmer, the consumer and the environment. In 2001, the British government commissioned a study by the Policy Commission on the Future of Farming and Food made up of some of the most prominent scientists in the UK,

> "To advise the Government on how we can create a sustainable, competitive and diverse farming and food sector which contributes to a thriving and sustainable rural economy, advances environmental, economic, health and animal welfare goals, and is consistent with the Government's aims for CAP reform, enlargement of the EU and increased trade liberalization."

Why would the British Government need to find a way to create a *sustainable* agriculture, an agriculture that advances *health* goals? Because as the British report states, "After half a century of production-driven farming and food policy, the old model has outlived its usefulness." Worse than outliving its usefulness, the current system of chemical warfare agriculture is killing us. The medical, not agricultural, literature is full of research findings linking agricultural poisons to our most dastardly illnesses.

> The journal *Cancer*, 85:1353 stated the confirmed link between cancer and fungicides and herbicides and ALS/Parkinson's as did Dr. Perlmutter in his book, *BrainRecovery.com*. Research at the University of Texas linking Gulf War Illness associated neuronal damage/dopamine abnormality to organophosphate and pyridostigmiine bromide was presented in the *Archives of Neurology*, 9/2000)

Dr. Warren Porter, Univ. of Wisconsin, Toxicologist, wrote in the Mid-March 1999 issue of *Toxicology and Industrial Health:*

> "...Combinations of chemicals can alter thyroid hormones, suppress immune systems and affect nervous system functions..." These effects were strongest when a single pesticide or herbicide was combined with nitrate (nitrogen). Dr. Porter further reported that, "Minnesota study found that birth defects in children of pesticide applicators occurred at higher rates than in the general population.

Sandra Steingraber, wrote in her book, *Living Downstream*, based upon her Ph.D. work at Harvard:

> "Additive effects of low levels of pesticides significantly increase cancer risk."

Children living in pesticide treated homes had nearly 4 times greater risk of developing leukemia (cancer of the blood). If children lived in homes where pesticides were used in the garden as well, the risk was 6.5 times greater. All of the children in the study were 10 years of age or younger. Reported from "Home Pesticides Increase Risk of Leukemia in Children," Dr. John Peters,

University of Southern California, Journal of the National Cancer Institute, July 1987 - on www.chem-tox.com - 2002.

> The pesticide DBCP is conclusively proven to cause reproductive problems, particularly sterility in males (Moses, "Designer Poisons"). Breast milk, as well as semen, appears to store toxic substances (Rachel's, April 20, 1995). Some females have more pesticide in their breast milk than is allowed in cow's milk. A female needs only one exposure to a pesticide at a critical stage during her pregnancy for her offspring to be severely affected (Moses, "Designer Poisons"), and male sperm can be genetically altered for ninety days from one pesticide exposure (from the book, "Is This Your Child's World?" by Dr. Doris Rapp, 1996. Dr. Rapp is a well-known physician specializing in Environmental Medicine, Pediatrics, and Pediatric Allergies. She is Clinical Assistant Professor of Pediatrics at the State University of New York at Buffalo).

In a study of Canadian farmers, a significant dose-response relationship was found between risk of non-Hodgkin's lymphoma and acres sprayed with herbicides (J. Natl. Cancer Inst, 1990). Another study found that dogs whose owners used the herbicide 2,4-D on their lawns had a greater risk of developing malignant lymphoma (J. Natl. Cancer Inst. 1991) http://www.jrussellshealth. com/pestschild.html

> "There is a lot of evidence linking RoundUp to human illness, a recent paper that's come out showing for example that RoundUp can interfere with steroid hormone production.

There are data in the literature now showing that at least in some circumstances RoundUp can be around for as much as three years in the forest, for example, where it's been applied. The decay rate on it is much longer in some circumstances than originally had been expected. Also we're finding, not we, but the scientific literature is showing, things like the impacts of RoundUp on the ability to maintain defensive enzymes in the body against other toxins." *Warren Porter, Environmental Toxicologist & Zoologist,* Warren Porter Interviewed, Wisconsin Public Television 13 Nov 01 www.mindfully.org/Pesticide/pesticide.htm

British Commission on Food and Farming

Dr. Jules Pretty, University of Sussex, one of the members of the British Commission stated, "…the costs of industrialized farming have simultaneously been very severe. Modern agriculture has caused significant pollution from **pesticide and nitrate leakage**. This costs **£135 million each year to remove from drinking water** - costs paid for by water consumers, not by the polluters. (Indeed, the farming sector effectively receives a hidden subsidy by not having to pay to clean up the mess.) It has brought a severe loss of rural biodiversity, from practices such as the removal of hedgerows, monocultural planting patterns and use of pesticides. … And industrialized farming has led to harm to human health through BSE, pathogens and antibiotic overuse. **Overall, the total costs of environmental and health damage from agriculture are estimated to be £1-2 billion a year** (in the UK alone).

For these reasons it is entirely wrong to think – as we have for so long been told – that we have a "cheap food" policy. **Food only appears to be cheap when we focus on the price in the shop. In fact, each of us pays … to clean up the environmental and health problems of modern agriculture.** In truth, food is expensive, and the sooner we appreciate this fact the better.

The UK Commission summarized its report to the Government by stating that, "…health is the central consideration of the nation's farming and food system." It went on to recommend to the Government: "Farming and food strategy should put health for all as a central tenet. Farming and food should give equal weight to both human and environmental health."

The British Government and the UK's top scientists are not the only ones suggesting that the current system needs a significant overhaul. In the United States a University of Louisiana study using **best management practices** of conventional agriculture showed no benefit/inadequate benefit in decreasing farm nutrient runoff (nitrogens, phosphates, pesticides, fungicides, herbicides, etc. that end up in our lakes, rivers and aquifers). The study concluded that agricultural management must change basic farm management practices and philosophy in order to solve the problems created by chemical agriculture. Simply altering current practices fails to solve the problems. (Dr. Charles Reith, Tulane University, Full Circle LLC)

When the consumer then looks at the nutritional density of the foods produced today by the chemical farming system, there is absolutely not doubt left that the system is a complete failure. Despite all the marvelous hybridization of plant varieties, "improvement" in fertilizer manufacturing and delivery, the nutrient content of the foods today compared to a half century ago range from 15 percent to 75 percent less. So I guess we could say it is like the light beer commercials where you can consume more volume because it is less filling. See table at the end of this section.

The most common political counter argument to chemical farming is the conversion of farming to *organic farming;* the avoidance of all *synthetic* fertilizers and pesticides. Sadly "organic farming" has become more a political philosophy than "standard of quality/integrity." Yes, there are some legitimate "organic" farmers employing sound biological science doing exactly what they should be doing; raising highly nutritious foods.

Growing highly nutritious foods requires extensive mineralization and beneficial microbial colonization of the soil. Most "organic" farmers, however are producing crops, nutritionally no better than their chemical farmer counterparts with the exception that *organic farmers* use "natural poisons" rather than manufactured poisons. Woopie!! The nutrient density of the crops is what is really important and if the farmer, whether "organic" or "conventional" has weeds, diseases, and insect pests, the nutrient density (quantity of calcium, magnesium, selenium, vitamins, etc.) is lacking. Organic certification alone guarantees nothing about the food quality. Proof of this fact comes from the major store chains that claim only 20 percent of organic produce is superior to conventional produce while the other 80 percent of organic produce is worse quality than conventionally grown produce. It is junk! There lies their quandary in large-scale promotion of organic produce, its quality.

Further, just because a pesticide is approved for *organic farming* does not mean that it is safe and nontoxic for human and animal consumption nor does it mean that agricultural pests will not develop resistance to the products. Pyrethroids are a classic example of both the potential toxicity to humans and animals and the development of resistance by the target pests.

What this discussion means to the consumer is that regardless of whether one is evaluating a food commodity grown under conventional farming methods or under organic farming methods, if the food commodity is so minerally deficient that the farmer needed to apply pesticides, synthetic or organically approved, in order to get the food commodity to market, that commodity is inferior, period. When these minerally deficient foods are consumed, whether conventionally grown or organically grown, the consumer will not be getting the necessary calcium, magnesium, selenium, vitamins, enzymes, etc. they need to be healthy.

More and more medical literature is linking low selenium intake to increased cancer risk. Low calcium intake has long been associated with increased risk of osteoporosis and bone fractures. Low magnesium intake is associated with some cardiac arrhythmias, elevated blood pressure, and muscle cramps. Inadequate vitamin intake has been associated with increased risk of heart disease, eye disorders, skin afflictions and nerve problems. Enzyme deficiencies are associated with digestive problems and sluggish detoxification.

The point is, and I hope I have conveyed this point adequately, that *the reason there are* "problems" (*weeds, diseases and insect pests*) in the crop which the farmer needs to "kill" is *because the farmer has not properly managed the soil and crop nutrition*. It really matters not whether the farmer is using a synthetic or "natural" pesticide. Weeds, diseases and insects pests are NOT due to pesticide deficiencies, natural or synthetic. They are due to lack of balanced nutrition. *The issue comes back to nutritional management of the soil, NOT what poison source (synthetic or "natural") the farmer selects to kill the "bad guys" because the "bad guys" would not be there if the soil nutritional management were appropriate in the first place.*

Certainly there is a difference in the impact upon the environment between the synthetic poisons applied by conventional farmers and the organically approved chemicals applied by organic farmers. Certainly, while farmers are working on improving the nutrition of their soils and crops, it is much better if they can use organically approved chemicals or materials than the synthetic poisons. The point must be clear, however, that the need for and use of these materials should only be a passing experience during the farm's transition to balanced health and nutrition.

The farmer will get whatever result for which he manages. If he manages for pests, he will have pests. Soil management as prescribed by our land grant agricultural universities, funded by the chemical industry, will yield a bounty of reasons to "need" "crop protection products," (natural or synthetic) and genetically modified seeds. On the other hand, managing the soil as prescribed by actual natural science, well documented in University research particularly at the University of Missouri by Dr. William Albrecht in soil science and at Oregon State University by Dr. Elaine Ingham in microbiology, will yield the farmer bountiful, healthy crops naturally free of pests without having to use poisonous chemicals.

The kind of farm management I am describing that is needed is termed "biological" farm management. This produces "biologically" grown crops, not necessarily "organically" grown crops. This means that we take the best of conventional technology and the best of "organic" technology and marry the two together for the best management system. If the reader is interested in early University research proving these concepts, read *The Albrecht Papers*. Dr. William Albrecht, while department head of soil science at the University of Missouri in the late 1940's, proved that crop and animal diseases were caused and cured by the state of soil nutrition. He was forced into early retirement when his integrity would not allow him to retract his findings and skew soil and crop research in favor of a chemical company's wishes in return for a $1 million dollar research grant to the University. (Private Conversations with Charles Walters)

This latter approach to farm management is taught collectively by many people including Dan Skow, Phil Wheeler, Elaine Ingham, Fred Wood, Edwin Blosser, Phil Callahan, William Albrecht, Carey Reams, Gary Zimmer, myself, and others. For those wondering about crop yield and economics, conventional management cannot match the potential yield and economics of biological management. Unfortunately it takes time to convert our sick and abused soils to biological powerhouses. This conversion requires applying the good management techniques of chemical farming with the sound scientific principles of biological soil and crop management in a three to five year transitional management program. This management program must always keep at the top of its goal list, "high crop nutrient density without disease and chemical residue while maintaining maximized farm profit." Without profit farmers will cease to exist.

An excellent example of the nutrition-farm profit link is from a client of mine in Mexico. This farmer is an excellent farmer in all ways from his crop management to his worker relations. He had a crop of cantaloupe melons, which he managed with a combination of biological fertilizers and conventional fertilizers. He had an excellent crop but the market price at harvest time was terrible. The price would not cover even the cost of production. One must understand that melons have a very narrow window for harvesting and marketing. They "spoil" rapidly. Typically, the farmer must get the melons to market immediately from the field or they will spoil. This farmer harvested his entire crop and put the melons into cold storage for ten days, an unheard of practice for melons. Typically they just don't keep in cold storage. After ten days the market price rebounded and he was able to sell the melons at a profit. "Remarkably" the melons looked as fresh after ten days in storage as they did the day of harvest, truly remarkable for commercial melons. This experience had nothing to do with variety or cultivar being grown. It was solely an issue of nutrition.

I feel it is very important that the consumer really understand the soil-food-human health connection. It is the consumer that votes everyday with his/her dollars at the grocery stores where the real ground work begins. We live in a consumer driven world. As consumers intelligently and informedly demand better quality foods, the market will rise up to supply it. As the market supplies it, more and more people will reap the health benefits of more nutritious food, the result being a greater quality of life and a better environment.

For more than a decade the medical literature has been flooded with study after study showing the direct connections between nutrition/diet/pesticides (food quality) and human health. The only question remaining is whether or not society will act upon this information and demand that agriculture clean up its act.

*Men stumble over the truth from time to time, but most pick
themselves up and hurry off as if nothing happened.*
~ Sir Winston Churchill

Every consumer can take charge by voting with their dollars for
better health, better environment, and better economics. As the
biological management of our soils and foods gains momentum,
less and less poison is dumped into the environment because it
is not needed, less and less soil is eroded into our rivers and gulfs
because the soil is less erodible, less and less dependence on oil
is needed because we need less oil-based pesticides and less fuel
because the soil takes less horsepower to till. Biological farm
management is THE solution to our agricultural, environmental,
public health and economic woes. It is not a panacea rather basic
natural science. Everything is connected to everything else.

For lack of a better place to put the following information, I will
put it here and that is in regards to food preparation. Regardless
of the preparation method, the real quality of food is determined
by it nutrient density, determined by the nutritional program
used to grow it on the farm. The lower the nutritional integrity
of any food the more it will degenerate with processing and/or
cooking. Much debate has been afforded various methods of food
preparation and particularly assurance by "father government"
that such methods of processing/cooking to include irradiation
and microwaving are not only safe but do not adversely affect
the food. I completely disagree. Ionizing radiation adversely affect the enzymes, nutrient metals and usable energy of the food.
Granted much of the study on this are anecdotal, but I have to
make decisions based upon clinical observation and judgment.
One recent study done in Denmark on the effects of microwave
cooking was published in the Journal of the Science of Food and
Agriculture demonstrated that microwaving vegetables causes
the loss of up to 97 percent of the valuable cancer-fighting
compounds such as flavonoids, sinapics and caffeoyl-quinic
derivatives. ("Microwave zaps body boosting antioxidants,"
foodnavigator.com/news/news-NG.asp?id=47623) The full article

is published in the *Journal of the Science of Food and Agriculture*. 2003 Volume 83(14) by Vallejo, et al. I have also had patients that have adverse effects from microwaved food. My father will have significant cardiac arrhythmia after eating anything, including butter, that has been microwaved. Please keep in mind that some people have sensitive bodies and seemingly insignificant things can be major issues to them.

Clinical Nutrition

Albrecht, Sept. 1, 1945 stated, "...we are what we eat... people might eat three square meals a day and still suffer from it (hunger)"

Did You Know? Mineral Depletion in Food 1940-1991

Vegetables: Lost 76% of their copper content
Lost 49% of their sodium content
Lost 46% of their calcium content
Lost 27% of their iron content
Lost 24% of their magnesium content
Lost 16% of their potassium content

Fruits: Lost 19% of their copper content
Lost 29% of their sodium content
Lost 16% of their calcium content
Lost 24% of their iron content
Lost 15% of their magnesium content
Lost 22% of their potassium content

The Composition of Foods, Ministry of Agriculture, Fisheries and Foods and the Royal Society of Chemistry, UK

Nutritional Values of Foods

This brings up a very important issue, that is, the use of vitamin and mineral supplements. There are many people, both lay people and professionals that contend "synthetic vitamins" are of no value to human health. They contend that only "food-derived" vitamins and minerals are of value. That is a very nice principle that works in an ideal world. The reality is that there is very little food today, including that which is grown for supplement manufacture, that has a high refractometer reading and a high nutrient density.

Consider the grading scale used in school, A, B, C, D, E, where A is excellent, near perfect, and E is failing. This same scale can be applied to food quality and human heath status. Much of the food grown today is between a D- and an E. It rots quickly and must be covered with chemicals to get it to store long enough to get to the consumer. What the store chains consider "excellent"-quality produce because it "looks" good and "stores" well, compared to the mass majority of produce, in reality grades about a D to D+ relative to actual food value.

Consequently, the health grade for most people, that don't have obvious disease, is around a D, with those that have disease between a D- and an E. Because this is common, people think this is "normal." It is normal for a D or E grade. When we have such a poor standard of health and food quality, any nutrition that improves the "grade" is beneficial.

It is true, in my opinion, that we will only achieve nutritional quality with a grade of A or B via nutrient-dense food. This quality of food is currently very rare, if available at all. However, to get the health from a grade of D or E up to a C, we can use "C"-grade nutrition, and should, when that is the best we have available. I feel the manufactured vitamins and minerals range in quality between a C and an E. Without question, many doctors and patients have experienced improvement in their health and well-being, taking good-quality manufactured supplements. I find this particularly regarding intravenous vitamins and minerals.

Without exception, people that are fighting an infection of some type, virus, bacteria, fungus, or combating a wasting illness such as cancer, administering intravenous vitamins and minerals frequently helps these people more than any other therapy.

Administering IV vitamins and minerals for people suffering from viral infections such as hepatitis, CMV/EBV (mononucleosis/glandular fever), flu, common cold, SARS, etc., is the single most effective means of stimulating the person's immune system to overcome the virus. (In fact, there is no excuse for anyone dying from SARS or flu as long as we have IV nutrients, to include 10 grams or more vitamin C, and HBOT). This is key because there are very few, and with most viruses, no drugs to combat viral infections. They must be overcome by the person's immune system and IV nutrition is the most effective means of doing this. I have not seen any oral supplement come close to IV nutrition in this situation.

I will acknowledge that we may only be raising the person's health grade from a D or E up to a maximum of a C, but that is an improvement greatly appreciated by the patient and the doctor.

There is one caveat regarding manufactured vitamins and minerals that must be considered. When vitamins are manufactured, the manufacturing process usually results in two products. One product is the vitamin that animals and people can use. It is functional in the living body. Unfortunately, there is also a mirror image of this functional product that has the exact same chemical formula, but has the opposite structural rotation of the functional product. This product should be discarded.

The feed manufacturing and vet industries today have figured out that it is very profitable to manufacture and sell the nonfunctional vitamin products. The problem is that, though the feed ration has the "correct" numbers for the various nutrients, since some or many of the vitamins are of the nonfunctional type, the animals will still experience vitamin deficiencies as if the vitamin supplements were not present in the feed and will get sick accordingly. This, in turn, provides additional market for more drug sales and lends itself to the contention, by the pro-drug lobby, that vitamin therapy is useless for the treatment of illness.

This deceptive practice can occur in human vitamin manufacturing also. These nonfunctional vitamins would have a grade of E, and be available at bargain basement prices. Consequently, taking these supplements will not give the consumer any benefit in their health and play perfectly into the hands of the pro-drug lobby contending that vitamin therapy is useless.

The point that I desire to convey, is that manufactured functional vitamins and minerals, though they are not as good as what would be available from nutrient-dense food (if that were available today), they do assist in the improvement of body chemistry and health of anyone and everyone whose health grade is below the quality grade of the supplement. And "natural" in today's market does not guarantee that the product is any better than manufactured or even as good as manufactured.

A concept greatly missed by the manufacturing industry, particularly related to the herbal market, however, is the fact that many "natural" supplements are beneficial because of the complex interaction of associative compounds found in the natural supplement. In other words, there is an interactive additive effect between the "key" compound and the many other compounds found associated with it in the natural product. Pharmaceutical companies seek to isolate the single active ingredient, patent it for monopolization, and manufacture it in its isolated state. Their impetus is said to be because there is no standardization in the herb industry. Frequently, the manufactured product does not give the same benefit as it did in its natural "parent" product. It is simple biochemistry. Nature is all about systems and interactive relationships. Every chemical effects every other chemical and system. What we really need to do is get better nutrition into commercial herb production, not look to manufacture the isolated chemical "magic bullet."

Genetically Modified/Engineered Organisms (GMO's)

Genetically modified organisms are the "fad" or "craze" of the 21st Century. Americans have a love affair with technology and "religiously" and blindly assume and accept that technology must be good just because it is technology. Even more dogmatic is the assumption that since the genetically modified food crops are genetically modified to thwart disease, kill insect pests, improve shelf presentation and shipping tolerance, speed growth or allow for more herbicide to be applied to kill weeds, these crops must be benevolent. If one asks about safety regarding GMO's, he/she is mocked and looked upon with reproach at how absurd to even broach the subject of safety. Prove that they are not safe is the response of the industry manufacturing and selling these "franken-foods."

When one investigates, he finds that these products have not been tested for long-term health effects nor have they been tested extensively for their ramifications to the environment. There have, however, been several short-term health studies by independent researchers, particularly outside of the US and several covert studies done by US University researchers. Every one of these studies demonstrates that GMO foods are harmful to our immune systems and quite probably directly hazardous to our health.

The British government funded GMO potato studies are noteworthy. The British government initially commissioned a study by Professor Arpad Pusztai, at the Rowett Research Institute, Aberdeen finding that GMO potatoes caused damage to rat immune systems and major organs resulting in increased incidences of cancer. The British government was terribly upset by Professor Pusztai's findings because they discredited the governments' position of promoting GMO foods as being safe for human consumption and publicly stating that there were no scientific studies to the contrary. Consequently, the British government commissioned a follow-up study with 20 handpicked researchers to dispel Pusztai's findings. All 20 researchers independently confirmed every aspect of Pusztai's findings placing the British government in a very precarious situation. Their public rhetoric contended GMO foods to be safe for human consumption but their own replicated studies proved otherwise.

Unfortunately, these British studies have been quickly suppressed by the GMO industry and ignored by the US mainstream media. The only reports the public hears are from the skewed studies managed by the GMO manufacturers themselves.

When these studies are investigated, their absurdity is glaring. An example is the study done on genetically modified corn to show the FDA that its pollen does not pose a threat of getting loose into the environment and contaminating other corn. The researchers said there is no chance of the pollen escaping because, as they reported to Congress, the corn pollen falls within three feet of the mother plant. I guess, for the typical city kid or politician whose concept of farming was formed by the TV show "Green Acres" with Eddie Albert, this report might seem feasible. The reality of the situation is that the study was done in a greenhouse with no wind so of course the pollen dropped within three feet of the mother plant. Take the corn plant out-of-doors to a field where there is wind and rain and it is obvious how GMO corn pollen has now spread all around the world. It now potentially taints all varieties of corn. The 2000/2001 nationwide recall ordered by USDA of corn chips and tortillas because of GMO corn contamination is a prime example. The German rejection of a shipment of "organic" corn chips found to have GMO contamination is another.

Early in the development of genetically modified organisms, companies used organisms from one environment, genetically altered them and transplanted them to foreign environments. Most of these organisms died without consequence as would be expected. However, one company took a common soil organism, Klebsiella planticularus, genetically modified it to produce large quantities of alcohol and put it back into the soil. Since this organism came from the soil, as expected, it thrived in the soil.

Fortunately, before the manufacturer released this product to the public it contracted Dr. Elaine Ingham at Oregon State University to test this new organism in the greenhouse. Within 24 hours after introducing this organism into pots, the growing crops in these pots were dead and dissolving, being converted to alcohol. Woops! Engineering K. planticularus to convert organic material to alcohol seemed like a great idea at the time.

All urban green/organic waste could be placed into containers with the organism and converted to alcohol. This alcohol could be sold as a fuel and the left over mash could be sold as organic fertilizer. It seemed like a win-win opportunity for the cities and the environment. The only problem was that the mash was loaded with this GM organism, which, when released into the environment would convert most all types of crop roots and tree roots to alcohol. Had this organism spread into the landscape it would have completely wiped out ALL forests and most of our domesticated crops. Only a few crops like rice would have been immune. Fortunately the manufacturer of this genetically modified Klebsiella bacterium canceled its plans to release this organism to the public even though FDA had approved it for public release.

The Klebsiella planticularus example is only one of many such potential disasters. It is an example of an obvious potential problem. Unfortunately, most other genetically modified organisms do not present their danger quite so obviously. Most are subtle and require deliberate observation and time to reveal their dirty work. As can be seen by this example the FDA seems quite inept at consumer and environmental protection.

The literature, contrary to the claims of the chemical industry that owns the seed companies and the university professors that depend upon these monopolies for funding, is full of indicting evidence against genetically modified organisms/plants. Consider the following:

GE Pseudomonoas putida, engineered to digest 2,4-D (a common herbicide), was found to kill beneficial fungi in the soil which are key to protecting the plants from disease organisms. (This technology guarantees the farmer will need more chemicals to combat the additional diseases precipitated by the technology itself.) Further, GE Bt endotoxins (the toxins produced in every cell of the genetically engineered plant) are ubiquitous and indiscriminate causing resistant pests meaning that the farmer will need yet more poisons in the future to combat these resistant pests. And further consider that GE Bt recombinant DNA persist in the soil for minimum of 24 weeks, available for other organisms to ingest and alter their genetic structures, which leads to antibiotic/Bt resistance in many organisms. This is excellent work from Dr. Ann Clark, University of Guelph, Canada. Additional information on the University of Guelph website includes research that the post-harvest effects of proteinase inhibitor I, insecticidal protein in GE tobacco residues alters soil biota and subsequently organic matter digestion meaning that the crop residue from the previous crop will not be properly recycled back into usable soil humus, thus further degrading the soil and increasing the risk of disease. Donegan et al. (1997). There is more; Ladybugs eating aphids from GE potatoes had 30% fewer progeny and lived half the life-span.

Birch et al. (1997) in Scotland. The Swiss Federal Research Station for Agroecology and Agriculture found that GE corn

Bt endotoxin killed green lacewings feeding on corn borers. In fact, 50% more lacewings died eating Bt fed caterpillars than if fed Bt directly. www.plant.uoguelph.ca/research/homepages/eclark/assumptions.htm

This means that the beneficial predator insects, ladybugs and lacewings, will be reduced, further increasing the proliferation of the pest insects, which soon become resistant to the Bt toxin. This guarantees yet more sales for the chemical companies for new and more toxic chemical weapons. Of even greater concern, is the fact that the pollen from genetically engineered crops spreads around the world via birds, bees and other insects, the wind and the water contaminating non-genetically engineered crops. This means that we are at risk for killing our beneficial predator insects everywhere. Why aren't the FDA, USDA, Agricultural Universities, and the news media telling the public about these legitimate scientific studies involving genetically modified crops? Why aren't they telling the public about the food safety risks that these "franken-foods" pose to us? It is the risk to our food sources that is the real issue here and the consumer is not being told the truth. Again, just follow the money.

Consumers, even "scientists" who do not understand biophysics and biochemistry have difficulty grasping why GMO foods are a risk to human health. The GMO industry's spin doctors have done a very effective job hoodwinking the public by keeping the debate in the philosophical arena and avoiding the science, specifically physics and biology. The human body functions as a result of energy, energy from the foods we eat. That energy is used to fuel our bodies while the "physical" components of the food are used as building blocks for our cells, tissues, and organs to regenerate. When foreign genes are spliced into a food, that food no longer contains the appropriate energy signature recognized by our body to digest properly nor the physical signature recognized by our body necessary to build a healthy cell. Our bodies gradually expend more energy trying to deal with the "franken-food" than it gets from the "food."

It is the same concept of getting an organ transplant. Sure the implanted kidney functions in another person's body but only if the receiving person is given immune suppressing drugs to prevent the body from rejecting it. Eventually rejection can no longer be suppressed and the organ system fails. The body still sees a transplanted kidney, for example, as a foreign invader to the body as it does GMO foods, which, in fact, are foreign. We could continue this debate forever and the companies selling these products will just spend millions more dollars to "sell" you, the public on the virtues of their products, on their humanitarian endeavors to "fight disease," "stamp our pesky insects," and "tantalize your taste buds" with the latest in "genetically improved" foods.

The real scam, however, is the assumption and the campaign, to get the public to believe that the reason we have crop diseases, pesky insects, weeds, and flavor/hardiness problems in food and fiber crops is because there is a problem with their genes. A problem that man can "correct" by splicing a foreign gene into the plant.

It is a scam because there is no genetic defect or inferiority in these plants. There is only an imbalance in the nutritional integrity of the plant caused by inappropriate soil/crop nutritional management, period. Conventional soil fertility management has caused these nutrient deficiencies in the soils and in the crops because the managers refuse to acknowledge the connection between nutrition and health/disease. The belief that crop disease, insect pests and weeds are due simply to the lack of a big enough "gun" to kill these "invaders" is a belief strongly ingrained in the farmer, consultant, professor, and consumer mind/psyche. This is because that belief concept is what the public has been taught and sold from the beginning of grade school through college. This skewed belief has fostered the most profitable business industry in the history of the world: manufacturing and marketing agricultural poisons and medicinal drugs.

When one studies the history of plant breeding and selection, it becomes apparent how society arrived at its present predicament. During World War II the chemical industry tooled up its manufacturing of chemical warfare agents, anhydrous ammonia, and mineral acids to support the war effort. After the war, huge stockpiles of these materials existed along with the huge manufacturing facilities. Rather than properly dispose of these poisonous and hazardous chemicals and dismantle the manufacturing behemoths, the industry figured out that it could dump these materials into the food chain via agriculture, appear to stimulate production and save farmers from the ravages of insect pests, diseases and weeds. Not only did this solve the immediate industry disposal problems, it launched a whole new industry, the agricultural chemical and fertilizer industry.

Over time, farmers added these chemical fertilizers to their soils and crops initially observing *supposed* crop yield increases. Over the decades, these same crops responded less and less to greater and greater quantities of chemical fertilizers. The initial yield increases did not come from better nutritional balance; rather they came from synthetic chemical stimulation as evidenced by the parallel increase in weeds, diseases, and insect pests. Nutrition actually has become increasingly unbalanced and skewed toward high levels of free nitrogen, particularly correlated to nonfunctional protein. Nature's pressure to eliminate these nutritionally bankrupt crops has consequently intensified to the point that we now face an ever increasing proliferation of pesticide-resistant weeds, diseases and insect pests.

> The experience of getting "fictitious" gains in production/ output using synthetic products is very familiar to the general public. For decades, amateur and professional athletes have illegally used anabolic steroids and even street drugs such as cocaine to enhance their athletic performances. Though these athletes are able to present a muscular physique and a facade of greater performance, the consequences to the individuals' personal health have been devastating. While the athlete gets enhanced

muscular physique and strength due to anabolic steroids, their tendons and ligaments cannot tolerate the resulting increased strains. Consequently, the tendons and ligaments frequently fail and the athlete suffers injury much more readily than he/she would ordinarily. Further, the drugs accelerate the aging process of the body and lead to premature hardening of the arteries, sexual dysfunction, and illnesses. Former Oakland Raiders defenseman, Lyle Alzado is a prime example, dying in his mid-forties of brain cancer. When the athlete discontinues the steroids, he/she looses muscle mass and strength rapidly despite continued exercising.

Athletes that take stimulants, such as cocaine, do receive surges in energy and, thus, short-term performance as well as a dulled reality of pain. Athletic performance may be seen as superior, but, because the body is not conditioned for the increased strain of such performance, injuries are more frequent. Since the cocaine constricts small blood vessels and leads to accelerated small vessel atherosclerosis, healing of injuries is impaired and the incidence of sudden cardiac death is significantly increased.

Summarizing, even though the drugs appear to increase short-term performance, they do so at the expense of shortening performance longevity while at the same time shortening the person's overall life-span and inhibiting their body's ability to heal.

Plant breeders have selected for plants and varieties that responded best to these synthetic stimulants deliberately ignoring Nature's desire to remove these crops from the food chain via insect pests, diseases and weeds. In fact, part of their crop management plans calls for more and more increasingly toxic pesticides to kill off Nature's garbage crew, the insects that are becoming increasingly resistant to the present toxic pesticides.

Breeders simply select for those plants that perform best *using the prescribed chemical fertilizer programs, which include the application of pesticides and herbicides to keep the crops from being eliminated by Nature.* Since these breeders did not and still do not understand that insect pests, diseases and weeds prevail because of improper crop nutritional management, they perceived and continue to perceive the application of these poisonous chemicals as *normal, necessary, and legitimate science*.

Over time they cross bred these plants eventually developing sophisticated hybrids with a range of different "desired" traits. The desired traits were simply the ability of the selected varieties to survive and flourish in synthetic, unnatural environments kept alive by ever more toxic pesticides. Eventually, it became commonplace to use hybrid seeds and actually disastrous, in many cases, to use the old open- pollinated or native crop varieties because the native varieties could not tolerate the synthetic environments.

Plant breeders, like medical specialists refusing the holistic perspective of looking outside their specialty, assumed that the agronomists knew what they were doing and, consequently, assumed that the fertilization programs used in the test plots and, subsequently the seed fields, were balanced and appropriate for healthy crop production. The problem was and still is that the fertilization programs were not/are not balanced and did not/do not provide for healthy crop production.

These crops would not survive without the addition of the poisonous chemicals to kill nature's garbage collectors. Consequently, today's world is left with a food production system seriously lacking in nutritional integrity; very expensive in terms of environmental cost units of input per crop production unit of output; a system that is becoming ever more fragile with each passing crop season; and a system blindly addicted to ever more toxic poisons. A good place to start with one's verification of this evolution, if one so desires, is with the *Albrecht Papers* by William Albrecht available from Acres, USA, Austin, Texas.

These new varieties, including the GMO's, have the nutritional deficiencies akin to the soils they are grown upon. Nature would normally eliminate these plants from the food chain, but human-kind wages a daily poison battle in the attempt to prevent that from happening by spraying pesticides to kill nature's garbage collectors/recyclers. This practice dumps nutritionally deficient foods into the marketplace and allows the perpetuation of less and less healthful food production, environmental destruction, and further solidifies the chemical industry's monopolization.

One need not look far to confirm the shortsightedness of commercial chemical agriculture. Simply consider that over time, the agricultural "pests" have become resistant to the chemical poisons and the soils have become more degraded. Soil erosion today is worse than it was 50 years ago. (Science In Ag)

Over time, companies have developed more toxic chemicals only to more quickly be thwarted by farm "pests." By the 1980's, though the application of agricultural poisons had increased by 13 times since WWII, crop loss due to farm "pests" had doubled. Fertilizer applications increased many fold over the decades yet crop yields peaked and actually declined by the end of the 20th Century. "Conventional U.S. farms used nine hundred eleven million pounds of synthetic pesticides last year (2001), nearly one-third of which are suspected in playing some role in causing cancer, according to author Dr. John Wargo, director of the Center for Children's Environmental Health at Yale University." (www.yale.edu) Aware that it was and is loosing the "war" on agricultural pests, the chemical industry looked(s) to outsmart Nature. Out of this quest evolved genetic manipulation of crops. Unfortunately the stupidity of this quest lies with humankind.

The reasoning for genetically modifying crops follows conventional logic rather than common sense. It is still reasoned that if the genes can be changed then the pests will be outsmarted and the crops will grow unmolested. No consideration is given toward correcting the *cause* of farm "pests," which is nutritional imbalance. Mind you, correcting the nutritional imbalances in the soils would eliminate the need for most of the agricultural chemicals and the genetically modified crops resulting in the significant downsizing of the chemical industry. The latter is simply not an option the bean counters or stockholders want to hear.

As with every attempt humankind makes to bypass the laws of nature, reality sooner or later comes back to haunt. In every case of genetically modified crops, "pest" resistance has developed requiring repeated genetic modification for the geneticists to stay one step ahead of the garbage crew.

A study done at the University of Missouri, published in *Farm Industry News* by Primedia Business Magazine & Media Inc, April 24, 2001 by Gil Gullikson showed that Monsanto's RoundUp (glyphosate) stimulates the growth of the disease causing fungus fusarium. Consequently, farmers growing GMO crops engineered to tolerate glyphosate can subsequently purchase more fungicide to combat the fusarium stimulated by the herbicide glyphosate.

It is obvious that the chemical industry is not going to change its focus on producing poisonous chemicals and GMOs. It is up to the consumer to demand clean, healthy/nutritious, and unadulterated food commodities from the grocery stores voting daily with "dollars." This demand will change the production on the farm and begin to clean up the world environment.

When farmers change their soil/crop nutritional management to a nutritional and biological centered strategy, the diseases, pesky insects and weeds disappear without the use of pesticides. It matters not whether these pesticides are synthetic chemicals or "natural chemicals."

They are not needed. Further, with biologically centered farm management, crop yields improve, the crop quality (nutrient content) improves and farmer profit improves. Particularly, biologically minded management maximizes yield per unit of input (efficiency).

For those that wish to observe these contentions first hand, I suggest contacting either AgriEnergy Resources in Princeton, Illinois or International Ag Labs in Fairmont, Minnesota, BioAgrology, BioAg or Australian BioLife, Optima Agriculture, TNN or Advanced Nutrients in Australia, and attend one of their annual farm field days.

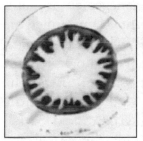  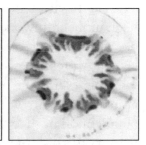

| Soy chunk from a certified organic quality mark. | Soy chunk also from an organic quality mark, but different trade mark. Presumably this product is partly contaminated with genetically modified soy beans. | Soy chunk reportedly containing 100% genetically modified soy beans. |

The quality images above are chromatograms of meat substitutes made of soy beans, respectively from organic and biotechnological sources. The left chromatogram, from the soy of the certified organic trade mark, shows the normal imager of a chromatogram. The chromatogram image in the center and on the right were first obtained last year, in 2001. Before that we had not encountered such images in our investigations nor in the literature on radial chromatography. The chromatograms of the biotechnical soy are virtually exploding. They show a very inharmonious image. The DNA is no longer organized according to the phi-ratio, resulting in severe protein digestion problems. First the shape is not recognized by the body, thus the wrong enzymes are made available and next there is a severe imbalance in the proteins. Due to the imbalance in proteins the body requires three to four times as much food to arrive at a satisfied feeling and will still remain imbalanced with respect to essential amino acids, such as lysine. Moreover the body will inject lysine into the intestines to provide for the impaired amino acids composition of the food, leading to an increased deficiency of amino acids in the body. This results in a fatigued body, without knowing resulting in excessive touchiness/ill-temperedness (ADHD?).

A Dutch high school student in Hilversum did his thesis in 2000 on feeding gmo corn and soybeans to laboratory rats. The rats did not eat the soy beans. However, feeding the corn/maize he observed either depressiveness or increased levels of aggressiveness and ADHD symptoms. Refer to www.i-sis.org.uk the website of Dr. Mae-Wan Ho, for the unbiased information about biotechnology.

Literature: **Pfeiffer, E.E., 1984**, Chromatography applied to Quality testing, Bio Dynamic literature, Wyoming, RI, USA AcresUSA #6374, USA

Pfeiffer, E.E., 1948-1959, Ehrenfried Pfeiffer himself: eight audio tapes in a shelf binder. Acres USA, Austin, TX, USA.

Above are three chromographs of soy products done by my friend Roelf Havinga in The Netherlands. Chromographs are very simple tools to evaluate protein integrity of materials. Compare the chromograph on the left of certified organic soy with the chromograph on the right of genetically modified soy. Now tell me that there is absolutely no difference between genetically engineered soy and the real thing?

The catch with biologically minded farm management is that it takes more brainwork and better management. Many farmers are not willing to put forth that effort particularly when the chemical company prescribes such a "simple" program of automatic spray schedules, "franken" seeds, and convenient salt fertilizers. The farmer need only write the check and drive the tractor. Little brainwork is needed. No conscience is needed or wanted for that matter. With conventional chemical farming the farmer and his suppliers can have no concern for the environment, one's neighbors, one's children or pets; and certainly they cannot have any conscience regarding nor concern for the consumers of the "junk" being produced, labeled and sold as food.

Mr. and Mrs. Consumer *we have the technology* **to grow more nutritious, better tasting, more bountiful food crops without toxic poisons polluting our foods and environment, at a better profit per acre than do conventional agricultural systems.** It is being done and is expanding as farmers learn of the technology and consumers demand the better food and fiber products.

We the consumer are the key to the change. We must be informed and we must demand better food, more nutritious food. We must reject the GMO "franken-foods" and know why. Life starts in the soil and as farmers learn real soil science they will find solutions to their disease, insect, weed production and economic problems. They will find independence from the chemical industry. We the consumers will find better food and better health along with a cleaner environment. It all works together. It all either dies together or lives together. Consumers must vote with their dollars at the grocery store. They must vote with their dollars at the yard and garden store by NOT buying the pesticides and chlorinated fertilizers that promote further decline in the soil resulting in more weeds, pesky insects, and diseases requiring the consumer to buy more toxic chemicals year after year. Consumers must read product labels and be aware of what they are buying. www.nitron.com is an excellent place to obtain appropriate lawn and garden products. I have no financial ties to this company.

The most political decision you make as a consumer is not how you vote, but how and where you buy food.

> ~ Jules Pretty, professor and director of the Centre for Environment and Society at the University of Essex in England. Acres U.S.A., December 2003, p. 25.

Health, Diet and the Religious Experience

Do you not know that you are the temple of God and that the Spirit of God dwells in you? If anyone defiles the temple of God, God will destroy him. For the temple of God is holy, which temple you are. (1 Cor. 3:16-17)

I will be very clear at the beginning of this section to state that I am a Christian man and have been a Christian all my life. I was raised in a Christian family, appreciated and was fascinated by the life of Christ and the teachings of the Bible particularly with the additional enlightenments gained from reading about the discovery and translations of many ancient works in recent times such as the Dead Sea Scrolls. I also studied other religions briefly so I could be an informed Christian about the beliefs of my fellow humans. I believe that Christ taught about every aspect of daily life to include morality, diet, lifestyle, business ethics, family, medicine, agriculture, natural science, and miracles. I believe that miracles happen every day. I believe that every person is entitled to freedom, happiness, and health regardless of religious belief. I believe that Spirituality, not religious dogma, is the key to understanding God and his Creation.

Tradition is honorable as long as it does not infringe upon the freedom of another, place judgment upon another, or prevent the expression of life from anyone. Religious dogma has done more to promote the profitable use of chemotherapy and radiation, surgery and drug treatment, the horrible suffering of thousands of people, especially women, the harassment of gifted professionals, and the suppression of legitimate natural healing modalities than any other force on earth.

The diet one follows sustains our temple and the Bible in 1 Corinthians is quite clear about how we ought care for that temple. Disease in the body is simply a manifestation of being out of harmony with God's law. That disharmony starts in the soil. In Genesis, God told how after the fall the earth would be infested with thorns and thistles. If read and understood in the context of Genesis and the entire Bible one realizes that these thorns and thistles are manifestations of being out of harmony with God's law. Manage the soil, according to God's law, and the thorns and thistles do not grow!

Too many religious traditions have been and are mere means to control, wield power over, judge, or figuratively assassinate other human beings. Christian traditions imposing such beliefs that the earth was flat, the sun revolved around the earth, diseases were purely demonic possession, herbal medicine was witchcraft, and adepts were sorcerers/witches, prevailed for centuries and caused the untimely deaths of millions of people at the hand of the Church. Unfortunately, many of these same traditions, in some form, prevail to this day with similar human consequences.

The thought of hearing voices from a mechanical device with no physical attachment (cell phones, computers) is still looked upon as demonic by some Christian groups in the 21st Century. The use of acupuncture, healing touch, and homeopathy are yet today seen as demonic expressions by some charismatic "Christian" churches leading to public chastisement and character assassination of many practitioners.

> *Do not be afraid of being free thinkers! If you think strongly enough you will be forced by science to the belief in God, which is the foundation of all religion. You will find science not antagonistic but helpful to religion.*
> ~ From *The Words of The Lord Kelvin*
> Sir William Thomson (Lord Kelvin,1824-1907)

It is an extremely rare time that a minister, Christian teacher or evangelist speaks about diet, nutrition, natural medicine, biological agriculture or environmental common sense except in a derogatory manner. Yet The Bible is specific about caring for the temple of God, our body. These people will talk about doing good deeds, international missions, morality, "Christian lifestyle," how it is bad to do illicit drugs, beat the wife and kids, have promiscuous sexual habits, etc. all of which directly affect one's health. Yet they will say little or nothing positive about cleaning up our environment, improving the nutrition of our soils and crops, cleaning up our diets, providing our bodies with appropriate nutrition and clean water, using natural medicines and foods, and healing our bodies.

Oddly, if some medical modality includes a high tech device or procedure or toxic chemical these people are 100% in favor of it, in fact encourage their members to embrace it, but mention a natural or holistic product or process and they scorn it, frequently labeling it as the work of the devil. I find this amazing how people can construe in their mind that natural things are of the devil, while toxic things invented by man are benevolent, even Godly.

Healing, from my study of medicine, agriculture and the Bible is a natural process, a state of harmony with God/Nature. It fails to occur when people stray outside of the laws of Nature.

For some, the healing process requires more work than for others to come back into harmony with Nature. Either way, God helps those who help themselves. Waiting around for God to heal a cancer while the patient continues to smoke, refuse diet change and supplements, deny psycho-emotional introspection, and avoid lifestyle change is a bit unrealistic and out of touch. Miracles still happen even in these situations. All healing is a miracle. It is just more likely to occur when the patient participates in the process.

People, who truly live with the Holy Spirit in their hearts, exemplify that faith and conviction through their daily lives and their personal health habits. The others simply spew rhetoric to that effect while their actions demonstrate primitive, even barbarian spirituality. It was not long ago that anyone interested in healing, natural medicines, herbs, foods, etc. was tortured and/or burned at the stake as a witch while bloodletting a patient to death and barbaric surgery said to release demons were sanctioned and promoted by the Christian Church.

Still in the 21ˢᵗ Century people who are engaged in natural medicine and healing are frequently scorned, ridiculed, tormented, persecuted and often prosecuted by Christian fanatics. Their view is that eating at McDonald's is good Christian activity while eating at the health food store is demonic; drinking herbal tea and using a homeopathic remedy is working with the devil while slugging down cases of diet Coke with their daily dose of Prozac is chic.

It amazes me that in spite of the Bible being full of medical, dietary, and lifestyle directives most professed Christians know nothing about them much less practice the directives in their daily lives. If it were not for the Christian Crusades destroying the universities, doctors and masses of information during the 16ᵗʰ and 17ᵗʰ Centuries in Europe, what we call alternative medicine today would have been mainstream medicine several hundred years ago. It was mainstream at that time in Spain, SE Europe and the Middle East until the invading Christian armies destroyed it by burning its books, slaughtering its teachers and practitioners and threatening its students.

One noble cleric of this period, Pope Sylvester II, went to Spain and studied natural medicine. This was medicine that included nutrition, hygiene, herbal medicines, etc. It was considered demonism in Christian Europe, at this time, to suggest that washing one's hands prevented disease let alone to pursue nutritional and herbal therapies. As a result Pope Sylvester II was accused of sorcery and forced to flee for his life.

It is hoped that the reader will understand that health is a natural outcome and to maintain health one must provide the body with those things it needs, most notably nutrition. Disease occurs when the supply of nutrition is compromised and not because God decided this person needed to pay some cosmic debt. Yes, there is a lesson in illness. The lesson is that straying outside of the laws of nature has its consequences. The straying and the consequences start with the soil and track all the way through to the consumer.

God has created a wonderfully complex universe, the most profound of which is life itself. Every living organism in the universe has its purpose. Discerning that purpose is our greatest challenge, our greatest lesson, our greatest achievement, that of enlightenment.

I suggest one read a delightful book by Don Colbert, M.D. titled *What Would Jesus Eat?* It is a good place to start understanding that, as the Ten Commandments are God's laws to be honored, so are the Biblical teachings of diet, exercise, and health laws of God to be equally honored.

Nutritional IV's, Chelation, Homeopathics, Colonics, Massage, Manipulation, Nutritional Supplements, Diet, Exercise, Sex, Rest, Play, Prayer, Relationships, Work, Giving. I believe all these activities are necessary to live a healthy, happy, and fulfilling life whether that life on earth is 20 years or 120 years makes no difference. I have met many people that did not become happy, really happy until they were in their 40's, 50's, 60's or even 70's. In the big scheme of life that is all that matters. One year of fulfillment and happiness is more valuable than 100 years of misery.

A lifetime is only a day at a time, a year at a time. Unfortunately, many people have one year of life experience repeated for the rest of their lives, perhaps 50 years. At the end of their life they look back and wish there had been 50 years of fulfillment rather than just one year repeated 50 times. Other people can look back and marvel at an entire life of bliss. It matters not for there is only today to live on this earth. So in whatever situation we find ourselves we must find some joy, some fulfillment, some happiness, some health, some life in today.

I find it sad that some of the most vocal religionists are also some of the most ardent and prolific applicators of chemical poisons on their fellow human beings' food. These people have totally missed the magnitude of their profession; the impact their crop has on every person that consumes it. Doctors are given significant social status in Western society because they care for the ill and dispense remedies and medicines. What must be realized is the fact that it is the farmer who grows the remedies and medicines.

Let your food be your medicine and let your medicine be your food.
~ Hippocrates (460-377 BC)

My intention here is to get you to reflect upon yourself and your place in this wonderful world. Happiness comes from within and, once found, we can then exude it in our daily and lifetime actions, work ethic, play ethic, spiritual ethic, body condition and language, and dietary habits. Through these expressions of life, doing what is right, doing what is true, we may challenge some people and we may terrify others by triggering their insecurities.

Consequently, there are times when we must stand up for what we believe, for what we are, not for conquest, rather for freedom, for life. Too often, people elect to deny the truth, deny what they know in their heart is correct because it is the easy way out. They are afraid to "rock the boat." They pass through life never knowing their real potential, never really feeling alive. Their life is a maze of tainted compromises made out of fear rather than confidence.

I believe that we must stand up for biological agriculture, for the detoxification and nutrification of our soils and foods. I believe that we must stand up for good medicine, for the detoxification and nutrification of our bodies, minds, and spirits. The earth was not created with a deficiency of or a need for DDT, Parathione, RoundUp or any other agricultural poison. Nor were our crops created with genetic defects that *mistakenly* allow insect pests, diseases and weeds to overwhelm them.

Life on this planet did not evolve nor was it created with the intent that Monsanto and the other agricultural chemical companies would come along and save the day with poisonous chemicals and genetically modified "franken-foods."

People were not created nor did they evolve with deficiencies of toxic drugs, antibiotics, vitamin "P" (for Prozac), Valium or any other suppressant drug. These are man-made conditions with man-made prescriptions designed to maximize man-made profit. There is, with some exception, no consideration for the short or long-term destruction and harm these things impose upon human health because side effects create more opportunity for additional drug sales.

> ...(*disease, insect pests, weeds, production, profitability*) *are* **more easily corrected** *and* **actually prevented** *with less cost to society by straightforward, sound nutritional management on the farm.*

There are times when agricultural chemicals and human drugs are appropriate to use. These are as temporary measures to get one over the hump on the journey to restoring health to the biological systems. They are not replacements for nutrition.

I believe that as a good citizen of any "free" country, it is our obligation to become informed, to know what is happening in our world, to our food, to our air and water and to be responsible for the sustainable stewardship of it all, including our own bodies.

Most sad and frustrating to me working in agriculture is that the problems that the chemical manufacturers/users are trying to solve (disease, insect pests, weeds, production, profitability) are **more easily corrected** and **actually prevented** with less cost to society by straightforward, sound nutritional management on the farm. But nutritional management on the farm is neither *chic* nor profitable for the chemical industry. It does not get the public all starry-eyed and awe struck about high tech bio-tech. It doesn't convince them to invest in tech stocks.

The chemical industry has perpetuated a belief in the public that the weed problems, disease and insect infestations that wipe out farmer's crops are *only* solved by applying poisonous pesticides (herbicides, insecticides, fungicides, nematacides, mitacides), now termed *crop protection products*, which they develop, manufacture and sell at very nice profits to solidify solid, attractive stock portfolios.

The truth is, we do **not** actually need the toxic products from the chemical industry in order to farm and grow **all the food and fiber the world needs**. I will rephrase that statement to drive it home. These chemicals are not manufactured and sold to fill a *need* in Nature or farming. They are simply manufactured to create and perpetuate the most profitable industry in the history of the modern world.

Poor crop production, insect pests, weeds and plant diseases are due to poor crop nutritional management, period, not deficiencies of toxic agrochemicals now so cleverly disguised as "crop protection agents." Tell me how a lethal poison sprayed on your food for you to consume protects you. The agricultural extension services and their funding agents, the chemical companies, want you to believe this lie. The truth is, **when farmers/gardeners correct the nutritional management on the farm, in the garden, these problems disappear just as surely as they appeared**. Correcting soil nutritional problems would not be politically correct. Money would not continue to flow away from the farmer and the consumer to the corporate monopolies

The point of this entire book, ladies and gentlemen, is that we already have the knowledge and understanding to solve the ills of agriculture, the environment and human health. We have had this technology for decades. It is in the public domain. It is a gift from God. It is not patentable (its greatest downfall). The ravages of soil erosion, pesky insects, weeds, and finally plant, animal, and human disease are not present because God calculated that Monsanto, Navartus, Shell or any other company would find the magic bullets and "save" the world.

The issue is NOT a deficiency of poisonous chemicals or gene splicing. The issue is nutritional management of the soil, crops, animals and human. God created everything this way. For those that feel evolution is the generator of life on this planet the answer is still the same, nutritional management.

We have many problems around the world. These include dying plankton and coral reefs; diminishing fish populations; disappearing rain forests; chemical poisoning of the oceans; ground waters and food sources; altered weather patterns, air pollution and tainted soils. The destruction, abuse and contamination of our environment over the past two centuries, particularly the 20th century, potentially threaten the survival of planet earth including humankind.

Conventional scientific thought (inherently ignoring that conventional technology, being petrochemical in nature, is itself THE cause of these problems) seeks only to perpetuate itself and further the sale of petrochemical products. This system follows good standard business objectives unfortunately cloaked in "scientific" clothing. Since the "scientists" (who have families to support, bills to pay, life dreams for which to pay) are all funded by this industry, is there any surprise that they invent only solutions that perpetuate their industry? Expecting anything different would be like expecting the fox to invent a solution to protect the chickens from the fox.

Nature has the capability to clean itself of the toxicity and death that humankind has perpetuated, if only given the chance to do so. The cleansing simply requires appropriate nutritional management on all fronts. Along this theme, I have overviewed several therapeutic approaches to various human aliments. They are not theoretical possibilities. They are approaches, which I have actually applied both to my own healing and to the healing of my patients.

The American diet of fast foods, diet soft drinks, processed snacks and antacids has engulfed Americans in a serious health crisis. American's health status is one of the worst in the world. As of 1981, America was ranked 95th in the world regarding the health of its citizens after having been 1st at the turn of the 20th Century. (*What Would Jesus Eat?*, Dr. Don Colbert) The icon of the American diet is the McDonald's Big Mac, said to fulfill all the requirements of the USDA's food pyramid for a balanced diet. The bun constitutes the grain, the meat constitutes the protein, the lettuce, tomato and pickle constitute the vegetable, the mayo and cheese constitute the dairy. Voila, the Big Mac is a complete, healthful meal... NOT!

The white flour bun is virtually void of everything except starch. The meat is loaded with saturated fat from "grain fed" beef animals. The lettuce is iceberg, the tomato usually hothouse both with minimal vitamin and mineral content; the pickle is processed. The cheese and mayo are processed and inundated with additives and colorings. Not only is there a lack of complete nutrition, there is a problem with additives that burden the body. Then add to this "meal" another "vegetable" in the form of french fries (gosh those fries are delicious) for a hydrogenated-oil, starch-to-sugar hyperglycemic rush. Top off this "gourmet splendor" with a diet soda to stimulate an even greater sugar craving not to mention the added "benefit" of neurotoxicity. Is there any wonder that one in three Americans are medically classified as obese and that the number one killer of Americans is cardiovascular disease? Is there any wonder why 33-year-old professional pitchers drop dead of heart attacks? Is there any wonder why diabetes is increasing by nearly 760,000 persons per year and only 30% of these new cases are in the elderly, meaning 70% of the cases occur in young people? (Centers for Disease Control and Prevention, Diabetes Surveillance, 1999) Is there any wonder why the US now has the highest incident rate of kidney failure in the world and 40% of new cases are diabetics? (*Am Soc. of Nephrology*, June 1, 1999)

It would be wise for every American to review the work of Dr. Westin Price done in the 1930's and 1940's. Dr. Price researched the correlation between "primitive" diets and the American diet finding that as food became more chemically grown, more processed and less diverse, human health, including dental health declined proportionately. His writings are available through the Price-Pottenger Foundation at www.price-pottenger.org.

I have written about concepts and principles regarding soil-food-human health correlations, philosophy regarding the industry and research. As mentioned several times throughout this book, one must bring human health full circle back to soil fertility and health. Agriculture already possesses the management practices necessary to achieve the desired results of nutritional control of those pesky insects, diseases and weeds. Managed appropriately, these principles are actually more profitable than conventional practices without the detrimental environmental impact. Most importantly they achieve or exceed the crop yields of conventional chemical farm management. Biological farming, unlike "organic farming" is more efficient than conventional chemical farming, matches or exceeds the yields of conventional farming and is more profitable per unit of input.

Contrary to what the chemical industry spin doctors want the public to believe, farmers employing biological farming practices do not have to accept lower yields and increased input costs, greater insect and disease damage and compromised commodity aesthetics. Yes, with biological farming, one can completely control pathogenic nematodes like root knot, pathogenic fungi diseases like fusarium, verticillium, phytophthera, and rhizoctonia, insect pests like aphids, red spotted mites and Colorado Potato Beetles, weeds like Quackgrass and Nut Grass. These achievements are not accomplished over night. It will take a good manager three to five years to achieve these milestones without the use of pesticides, whether synthetic or organic. What difference does it make if it took ten years if in ten years that farmer no longer had the insect, disease and weed problems, was producing more crop than before, at less cost per unit of input, with greater nutritional value? It is still a win-win proposition for everyone, except of course the companies selling the chemical weapons.

Biological farming is the combination of the best practices of conventional farming with the best practices of organic farming plus the understanding that nutrition is the cornerstone around which all other practices are exercised. Biological farming does require more thought, better crop management, and extensive record keeping and analyses as does any successful business enterprise. If one desires a more thorough discussion on this topic I suggest reading my book *Science In Agriculture* or obtaining my audio and videotape series from Acres U.S.A. at www.acresusa.com. Also, my follow-up book to this, *Real Food*, is the consumers guide to gardening and real food production.

I sincerely hope that this book has given the reader a glimmer of hope for those illnesses or conditions that have been unresponsive to conventional therapies. There really are no magic potions or quick fixes so often promised by conventional medicine. But there are real solutions to the many problems for which conventional medicine readily contends nothing can be done for the patient. Fundamentally, these real solutions go back to the basics of science and common sense, back to that of which we are made, nutrition. Here resides Real Medicine.

Disease enters through the mouth
> ~ Ancient Chinese Saying

Summary for Diet-Health-GMO's and Religion

Health and disease are determined by nutrition

Nutrition is determined by diet and supplementation

Food quality is determined by soil/plant nutrition

We do not have a problem with plant genes, we have a problem with soil/crop nutritional management

Genetically modified foods are hazardous to our health

Spiritual values apply to all parts of our life including diet, lifestyle, farm management, environmental care

Resources

Advanced Nutrients	www.advancednutrients.com.au
AgriEnergy Resources	www.agrienergy.net
ACOPMS (Sclero/Prolotherapy)	www.acopms.com
American Academy of Osteopathy	www.academyofosteopathy.org
American Academy for Advancement in Medicine	www.acam.org
AmScot Medical Laboratories	800-851-1708
Acres USA	www.acresusa.com
American College of Orgonomy	www.orgonomy.org
Australian BioLife	www.aussiebiolife.com.au
Chek Institute	www.chekinstitute.com
Defeat Autism Now!	www.defeatautismnow.com
Dr. Gary Emmerson	951-699-0104
Holographic Health	www.holographichealth.com
International Ag Labs	www.aglabs.com
MidWestBioSystems	800-689-0714
Nitron Industries	www.nitron.com
Optima Agriculture	www.optimaagriculture.com.au
Oasis of Hope	www.oasisofhope.com
SoilFoodWeb	www.soilfoodweb.com

References

Baroody, Theodore A. Jr., *Holographic Health Book One*, Eclectic Press, Waynesville, N.C.

Antidepressants..., Newsweek, July 15, 2002

Banchereau, Jacques, "The Long Arm of the Immune System" *Scientific American*, November 2002, pp. 52 – 59.

"Emerging links between chronic disease and environmental exposure." Archives of Neurology 9/2000.

Frustaci, Andrea, et.al. "Marked elevation myocardial trace elements in IDC compared with secondary cardiac dysfunction." American College of Cardiology, May 1999, 33(6) p. 1578-83.

Gullikson, Gil, *Farm Industry News* by Primedia Business Magazine & Media Inc, April 24, 2001. Monsanto's RoundUp (glyphosate) stimulates the growth of the disease causing fungus fusarium.

Hardell, L. & M. Eriksson, "A Case-control Study of Non-Hodgkin's Lymphoma and Exposure to Pesticides." *Cancer*, 85: 1353.

Johnson, Alison, "Gulf War Syndrome: Legacy of a Perfect War." Alison Johnson speech, Gulf War Syndrome, C-SPAN, June 3/02

"Matrix and Matrix Regulation: Basis for a Holistic Theory in Medicine," Haug 1991, Alfred Pischinger, MD

Matsukura, T., H. Tanaka. "Applicability of Zinc Complex of L-Carnosine for Medical Use." *Biochemistry (Moscow)*, Vol. 65, No. 7, 2000, pp. 817-823.

Nieper, Hans A. *Revolution in Medicine, Technology and Society*, Druchhaus Neue Stalling: Oldenburg, F.R.G.; 1983.

Raloff, Janet, "Drugged Waters," Science News, March 21, 1998.

Palumbi, Stephen R., "Humans as the World's Greatest Evolutionary Force." *Science*, September 7, 2001, Vol. 293, pp. 1786-1790.

Peters, John, "Home Pesticides Increase Risk of Leukemia in Children,", University of Southern California, Journal of the National Cancer Institute, July 1987 - on www.chem-tox.com - 2002.

Reaven, MD, Gerald, *Syndrome X: Overcoming The Silent Killer That Can Give You A Heart Attack*, Simon & Schuster, New York, 2000.

Smirz, MD, Linda, "Hormone Therapy," Indiana Osteopathic Association Winter Update, December 5, 2003, Indianapolis.

Strandberg et al, JAMA 1991 Prostaglandins....., www.foodnavigator.com/news/news-NG.asp?id=39079

Wollschlaeger, Bernd, MD, FAAFP. "Zinc-Carnosine for the Management of Gastric Ulcers: Clinical Application and Literature Review." *J. Am. Nutr. Assoc.* Vol. 6, No. 2, Spring 2003.

"Where are environmental estrogens found?" *Environmental Estrogens and Other Hormones*, CBR, Tulane & Xavier University, New Orleans, La.

Centers for Disease Control & Prevention, Diabetes Surveillance, 1999

"US incidence of kidney failure is highest in the world," *Am*

Soc. of Nephrology, June 1, 1999. http://medicalreporter.health. org/tmr0799/kidney.html www.asn-online.org.

Warren Porter, Environmental Toxicologist & Zoologist, Warren Porter Interviewed, Wisconsin Public Television 13 Nov 01 www. mindfully.org/Pesticide/pesticide.htm

"Microwave zaps body boosting antioxidants," www.foodnaviga-tor.com/news/news-NG.asp?id=47623. The full article is published in the *Journal of the Science of Food and Agriculture*. 2003 Volume 83(14) by Vallejo, et al.

www.plant.uoguelph.ca/research/homepages/eclark/assumptions. htm

Clinical Pearls, www.clinicalpearls.com

J. Natl. Cancer Inst. 1991 http://www.jrussellshealth.com/pest-schild.html

Recommended Reading

Dr. Atkins' New Diet Revolution by Robert Atkins

The Blues by Albert Abrams

Biomedical Assessment Options for Children with Autism and Related Problems: A Consensus Report of the Defeat Autism Now! (DAN!) Scientific Effort by Jon B. Pangborn and Sidney Baker.

Detoxification and Healing by Sidney Baker

Alkalize or Die by Ted Baroody

The Body Electric and *Cross Currents* both by Robert Becker

Excitotoxins: The Taste That Kills by Russell Blaylock

The Persecution and Trial of Gaston Naessens and *The Life and Trials of Gaston Naessens, The Galileo of the Microscope* both by Christopher Bird

Nutritional Management of Inflammatory Disorders by Jeff Bland's Institute for Functional Medicine

Dr. Braly's Food Allergy and Nutrition Revolution by James Braly

Tuning Into Nature by Phil Callahan

Silent Spring by Rachel Carson

Genetic Engineering: The Hazards by John Fagan

Breaking the Vicious Cycle by Elaine Gottschall

Enzyme Nutrition by Edward Howell

Nutritional Herbology by Mark Pedersen

Dr. Jensen's Guide to Better Bowel Care: A Complete Program for Tissue Cleansing Through Bowel Management by Bernard Jensen

The Cancer Cure That Worked by Barry Lynes

Chemical Children by Peter Mansfield and Jean Monroe

Pesticide Alert by Lawrie Mott and Karen Snyder

Delayed Posttraumatic Stress Disorders From Infancy: The Two Trauma Mechanism by Dr. Clancy McKenzie co-authored with Dr. Lance Wright

Light, Radiation and You by John Ott

The Curious Man: The Life and Works of Dr. Hans Nieper and *Dr. Nieper's Revolution in Technology, Medicine and Society* both by Hans Nieper

Metal and Elemental Nutrients: A Physicians Guide to Nutrition and Healthcare and *Nutrition and Mental Illness: An Orthomolecular Approach to Balancing Body Chemistry* both by Carl Pfeiffer

Adjuvant Nutrition In Cancer Treatment by Patrick Quillin

Childhood Ear Infections by Michael Schmidt

Sugar Busters by Steward, Andrews, Bethea, and Balart

Diabetes Solutions by Richard K. Bernastein, MD

Living Downstream by Sandra Steingraber

The Secret Life of Your Cells by Robert Stone

Nutrition and Your Mind by George Watson

Soil, Grass and Cancer by Andre Voisin

Discoveries of a Dowser by Kathe Bachler

Is This Your Child's World? by Dr. Doris Rapp, 1996

Love, Medicine, and Miracles by Bernie Siegel, MD

What Would Jesus Eat? by Don Colbert, MD

Breaking The Vicious Cycle by Elaine Gotchaw

Closing Thoughts

It is with great excitement that I write these closing thoughts to inform the reader, the consumer, the patient, that a system of testing to determine the true health effects of our food is available in North America at AML Agricultural. This testing protocol developed by AmScot Medical Laboratories, an FDA certified medical lab, tests not only for heavy metals and toxic chemical residues (pesticides, herbicides, fungicides) but also tests for antioxidant levels, key amino acids, major and minor minerals and fungal toxins. In order for food to truly be our medicine, it must be free of toxic materials AND provide the necessary nutrients, which our bodies need to detoxify, repair tissue, fight/prevent disease, and function at the level we desire to enjoy life.

I am involved in the development of a noninvasive testing instrument for fruit and vegetables that will enable farmers and consumers to evaluate fruits and vegetables for nutrient density and real quality. Regardless of the label or sales presentation, consumers will be able to get the real value of the food they are purchasing.

The premise of this entire process is that we are producing **food for people**, not widgets/gadgets for industry. Therefore, we must evaluate the food as described and make corrections accordingly, where these corrections count, on the farm. There are more and more farmers around the world converting their operations to biologically sustainable operations. By doing so, they are getting greater yields than their conventional counterparts, getting better nutritional value in the crops, needing less and in some cases zero chemicals to grow these better crops and, consequently, making better profits. There is hope Mr. and Ms. Consumer. The road is still rocky and hilly, but we are making headway on the journey to growing better food, cleaning up the environment and ultimately improving the health of us all. We must be ever diligent to pursue truth, happiness and health freedom.

If ye love wealth better than liberty, the tranquility of servitude better than the animating contest of freedom, go home...

We ask not your counsel.... Crouch down and lick the hands that feed you. May your chains set lightly upon you and may posterity forget that you were our countrymen.

~ Sam Adams, Signing Father, Declaration of Independence
United States of America

About the Author

Dr. Arden Andersen is a very diversified and unique professional. As early as age 10, Arden was reading about chelation therapy, laetrile and alternative cancer therapies, medical and political history, revolutionary war history and particularly the works of the founding fathers of the U.S. He established himself as an accomplished athlete, musician and academic. After growing up on a dairy farm in Michigan, he earned his bachelor's degree in agriculture, majoring in agricultural education, from the University of Arizona. He subsequently worked in The Netherlands as a work exchange student on a dairy, sugar beet and potato farm. He has taught high school vocational agriculture and coached a league champion track team.

During a 10-year, full-time consulting practice that took him all over the world, he earned his Ph.D. in agricultural biophysics and decided to enter the medical profession. He subsequently completed medical school in California at Western University of Health Sciences, post-graduate training at Muskegon-General Hospital and established his initial medical practice at the Born Preventative Health Care Clinic in Grand Rapids, Michigan.

He adds to this already full career a dedication to his country by serving as a flight surgeon in the United States Air Force Reserves at Grissom Air Reserve Base, Indiana, receiving the Air Force Commendation Medal and the Warrior's Creed Award while serving on active duty during Operation Enduring Freedom, after the 9/11 terrorist attacks.

His professional agricultural courses have qualified for the Australian Government's FarmBiz tuition reimbursement program and have also qualified for college credit. He has an open invitation to lecture at the University of Western Australia in Perth and is regularly interviewed by the Australian Broadcasting Company. At every opportunity, Dr. Andersen connects farm and human health epitomizing the statement, "Let food be your medicine," and literally has patients from around the world traveling to see him. He has developed a reputation as a loving, compassionate, and skilled doctor who finds solutions.

Also by Dr. Arden B. Andersen

Science in Agriculture

The Anatomy of Life and Energy in Agriculture

Soils & Agronomy Video School for the Biological Farmer

Radionics in Agriculture Video School

Body Electronics